D1572289

11/2/17

CIVILIZATIONS BEYOND EARTH

Extraterrestrial Life and Society

Edited by
Douglas A. Vakoch and Albert A. Harrison

berghahn
NEW YORK · OXFORD
www.berghahnbooks.com

Published in 2011 by
Berghahn Books
www.berghahnbooks.com

Library of Congress Cataloging-in-Publication Data

Civilizations beyond earth : extraterrestrial life and society / edited by Douglas A. Vakoch
and Albert A. Harrison.
    p. cm.
  Includes bibliographical references and index.
  ISBN 978-0-85745-211-5 (hardback : alk. paper) — ISBN 978-0-85745-212-2
(institutional ebook) — ISBN 978-1-78238-315-4 (paperback) —
ISBN 978-1-78238-316-1 (retail ebook)
  1. Extraterrestrial beings. I. Vakoch, Douglas A. II. Harrison, Albert A.
QB54.C562 2011
999—dc22

                2011014736

British Library Cataloguing in Publication Data

A catalogue record for this book is available from the British Library

Printed in the United States on acid-free paper.

ISBN 978-1-78238-315-4 paperback
ISBN 978-1-78238-316-1 retail ebook

To Jill Tarter,
for a career of leadership in the
Search for Extraterrestrial Intelligence.

CONTENTS

Tables and Figures

Tables

Figures

ACKNOWLEDGMENTS

We thank our many colleagues from the SETI Institute who have provided us with insights over the past decade into the search for life beyond Earth—especially Anu Bhagat, John Billingham, Edna DeVore, Frank Drake, Andy Fraknoi, John Gertz, Gerry Harp, Jane Jordan, Chris Munson, Chris Neller, Tom Pierson, Karen Randall, Jon Richards, Pierre Schwob, Seth Shostak, and Jill Tarter.

More recently, we warmly acknowledge the administration, faculty, and staff of the California Institute of Integral Studies, where the work of editing this volume was made possible through a research leave supported by Joseph Subbiondo, Judie Wexler, and Tanya Wilkinson.

Early stages of this work were supported through generous funding from the John Templeton Foundation, whose leadership has encouraged scholarship that does not always fit within traditional philanthropic programs. Paul Wason, Pamela Thompson, Charles Harper, Jr., and Arthur Schwartz have been especially gracious about providing feedback on this and related projects.

Among the many organizations that have fostered discussions on the topics in this volume, we especially recognize the American Anthropological Association, the International Academy of Astronautics, the International Association for Semiotic Studies, the International Astronomical Union, the International Institute of Space Law, the Society for Cross-Cultural Research, and the Society for Psychological Anthropology. We particularly thank Harry and Joyce Letaw, as well as Jamie Baswell, for their intellectual and financial contributions to these and other discussions.

For her willingness to add a nontraditional area to her book list, we are especially grateful to Marion Berghahn. We appreciate the insight, care, and thoroughness of the entire Berghahn team throughout the development, production, and marketing of this volume, with special thanks to Ann Przyzycki DeVita, Melissa Spinelli, and Caitlin Mahon for seeing the book through to publication, to Mike Dempsey for his careful copyediting, and to Abigail Major and Geoff Colquitt for publicizing the book. Elizabeth Berg has our gratitude for overseeing production of the paperback edition.

For creating compelling cover art inspired by his reading of this book, we thank Paul Duffield.

Finally, for guidance and support in more ways than we can begin to list, we gratefully thank Julie Bayless and Mary Ann Harrison.

Introduction
The Search for Extraterrestrial Intelligence as an Interdisciplinary Effort

Albert A. Harrison and Douglas A. Vakoch

During the last half of the twentieth century, rapid advancements in science and technology prompted many people to begin rethinking our place in the universe. These developments included ideas about cosmic evolution (which claims that the universe is evolving in the direction of greater complexity, consciousness, and culture), space exploration, recognition that asteroids and comets pose a threat to the survival of our species, and growing circumstantial evidence that we may share the universe with extraterrestrial civilizations (Harrison 2007).

Astrobiology and SETI are scientific efforts to find evidence of life beyond Earth (Tarter 2011). Astrobiology is the National Aeronautics and Space Administration's (NASA) approach to the study of the origin, distribution, and future of life throughout the universe (Darling 2001). Within our solar system, astrobiologists study the Earth as well as other planets and moons, with NASA's most recent biennial Astrobiology Science Conference including an examination of "evidence of past and perhaps present liquid water on Mars as well as an ice-covered liquid water ocean on Europa, the discovery of hundreds of extrasolar planets, observations of plumes of water-ice particles erupting from Saturn's moon Enceladus, the possibility of prebiotic chemistry on and liquid water beneath the surface of Titan, and identification of new forms of microbial life in an ever-widening range of extreme Earth environments" (Billings, Conrad, and Siefert 2011).

SETI is an acronym for the Search for Extraterrestrial Intelligence. Approximately fifty years ago, scientists realized that interstellar communication was theoretically possible, and they began searches for extraterrestrial microwave transmissions using radio telescopes. More recently, radio astronomers have been joined by optical astronomers, who are searching for brief but powerful laser pulses (e.g., Mead and Horowitz 2011; Siemion et al. 2011).

Astrobiology and SETI are interdisciplinary efforts that draw upon the physical, biological, and social sciences. The chapters in this book examine three major questions from multiple disciplinary perspectives: Does extraterrestrial life exist? How would we react to the discovery of life beyond Earth? And, can we communicate with extraterrestrial intelligence? To help pave the way for these discussions, this introduction reviews the role of the behavioral and social sciences—anthropology, history, political science, psychology, and sociology—in the search for extraterrestrial life.

An Early Beginning

In 1960, while Frank Drake was undertaking *Project Ozma*, the first microwave radio search for extraterrestrial intelligence, a committee under the leadership of psychologist Donald N. Michael was completing a report on the peaceful uses of space to be presented to the United States Congress (Committee on Science and Astronautics 1961). The resulting report, generally known as the "Brookings Report" after the contracting institution, presented extended discussions of communications satellites, space exploration by humans, and other then-futuristic (but now-common) ideas. It also mentioned the potential discovery of life beyond Earth, which the committee felt was most likely to come about as the result of microwave observation. The committee expressed concern about how the discovery might affect people, pointing to its potentially devastating effects on religion and noting that contact between more and less technologically advanced civilizations typically works to the latter's disadvantage. If, as astronomer Ray Norris estimates, the average extraterrestrial civilization is two billion years older than our own, this could be a cause for concern (Norris 2000).

Early on, the physical and biological scientists involved in the search understood that their efforts could have profound effects for humanity, and by the 1970s they actively sought to involve social scientists in SETI (Finney 2000; Dick 2006). A conference on contacting extraterrestrial intelligence that was held in 1971 included participants from anthropology, archaeology, linguistics, history, and sociology (Sagan 1978). Workshops conducted at NASA's Ames Research Center during that decade underscored the need to prepare with comparative studies:

> The investigation of the nature and origins of behavioral diversity among the intelligent and semi-intelligent higher animals is [an important effort parallel to SETI]. Our goals should be: (1) to catalog and classify all behavioral patterns and cultural differences; (2) to determine how these are related to the environment, physiology, and evolutionary history of each species studied; (3) to determine what traits, if any, appear common to all intelligent animals; (4) to gain experience in communication with other terrestrial species; and (5) to develop powerful theoretical models that will allow extrapolation to extraterrestrial cultures, and allow us to evaluate at least semi-quantitatively the uncertainties in such an extrapolation. To the extent this approach might enable us to better understand human behavior it could result in one of the most important benefits of the SETI program. (Black and Stull 1977: 100)

In the mid 1970s, Mary M. Connors of NASA Ames Research Center wrote two unpublished papers that outlined some of the psychological, social, and cultural implications of the discovery of extraterrestrial life (1976, 1977). After hypothesizing that people's pre-existing beliefs would be the most powerful determinant of their reactions to contact, she went on to distinguish between short-term effects of contact—which would be measured in days, weeks, and months—and long-term effects measured in years, decades, and centuries. She also explored the role of the media in shaping public reactions. Connors organized social scientific issues in terms of (1) the organization and implementation of the search; (2) contact with extraterrestrial civilizations; (3) the impact of the search on humankind; and (4) terrestrial/extraterrestrial relations (1977). Her papers were a resource for later work (Harrison and Elms 1990), and many of the ideas that she presented have carried forward to the present day (e.g., Harrison et al. 2000). In fact, our interest in the social psychological aspects of SETI was sparked by a serendipitous discussion of this work with Connors and Michael when working with Connors on a separate project (Connors, Harrison, and Akins 1985).

Also in the 1970s, Magorah Maruyama and Arthur Harkins published *Cultures beyond Earth: The Role of Anthropology in Outer Space* (1977). Acknowledging that someday we may have to communicate with non-human forms of intelligence, they suggested that anthropological methods could be extended to extraterrestrial cultures. At the time, the Apollo program remained vivid in memory, and *Cultures beyond Earth* mentioned astronauts and cosmonauts encountering alien astronauts in their voyages.

Anthropologist Ben Finney and astrophysicist Eric M. Jones strengthened the link between anthropology and SETI by including material on SETI in their book *Interstellar Migration and the Human Experience* (1984). Discussions of human migration to the high frontier are pertinent to the search, because they give us some ideas about the nature of technologically advanced civilizations. Since that time, Finney—long distinguished for his work on the migration of Polynesian islanders—has sustained his interest in both SETI and interstellar migration, and he has carefully explicated the relationship between the two (Finney 2000).

Psychologist John Baird's *The Inner Limits of Outer Space* draws heavily on cognitive and developmental psychology and shows high sensitivity to inter-species and cross-cultural differences (1987). He suggests that our limited information-processing abilities may make it difficult to perceive, never mind understand, super-intelligent organisms. Baird noted that anthropocentric biases will limit our ability to detect extraterrestrial intelligence, and he added that the success of our searches will depend not only on their technology, but also on their values (not every civilization will be willing to proclaim its place in the universe). Management consultant Frank White also took a psychological approach, and his book *The SETI Factor* systematizes the likely consequences of the confirmation of detection of extraterrestrial life (1990).

Other early work by psychologists includes Albert Harrison and Alan Elms's review of a broad range of psychological issues (1990) and Harrison's attempt to apply Living Systems Theory (LST) to biosocial systems (1993, 1997). Using exobiology as a model, Harrison and Elms proposed the term "exopsychology" for their endeavors. Today, the field of astrobiology would be a better model—except, perhaps, for the New Age connotations of "astropsychology"! Despite this, following the transition of exotheology to astrotheology (Peters 2009), Harrison recently opted for the name change to astropsychology (2010).

An outgrowth of Open Systems Theory—with its well-known concepts of inputs, throughputs, outputs, feedback, homeostasis, and entropy—LST seeks principles that cut across all species, historical periods, and cultures (Miller 1978). It invokes parallel structures and processes that apply across seven levels of systems: cell, organ, individual, group, community, society, and supranational system. If, as LST suggests, there are deep laws of individual and social behavior that are of wide applicability, our knowledge of biological and social systems on Earth gives us a starting place for organizing our thinking about life elsewhere. More recently, Harrison turned his attention to the interplay of science, religion, and folklore in shaping people's views of the universe and our place within it (Harrison 2007). He suggests that we live in a time when almost anything seems possible, but many intriguing ideas will fall by the wayside in light of new scientific discoveries.

Historian Steven J. Dick's *The Biological Universe: The Twentieth Century Extraterrestrial Life Debate and the Limits of Science* (1996) extends his earlier review of the debate from ancient Greece into the Renaissance (1982). In *The Biological Universe* he advances the thesis that, even as principles of physics and chemistry hold true throughout the universe, so do principles of biology. Dick's work is scholarly, comprehensive, and nuanced; places many contemporary SETI-related issues within their historical contexts; and explores ramifications for science, religion, and society.

A long-range interdisciplinary effort that was initiated prior to and influenced *After Contact* but published afterward is John Billingham and colleagues' *Social Implications of the Detection of an Extraterrestrial Civilization* (1999). Billingham, a physician who originally specialized in human adaptation to spaceflight, was largely responsible for ensuring that behavioral and social sciences remained prominent in SETI (Dick 2006). Stemming from a series of workshops in the early 1990s and originally presented as a working paper in 1994, this monograph distilled three decades of work into a brief but definitive overview of the cultural aspects of SETI.

An interdisciplinary workshop, sponsored in 1999 by the Bellevue, Washington-centered Foundation For the Future, focused on the long-term (thousand-year) implications of SETI. The report of this workshop includes papers on such diverse topics as Roman Catholic views of extraterrestrial intelligence, cosmic humanity, interstellar networking, novel search strategies, and how the discovery might affect our self-assessments (Tough 2000). That same year, the NASA Ames Research Center was the site of a conference on the societal implications of astrobiology (Harrison and Connell 2000). Panelists noted that scientific training should not cause researchers to overlook how people use religion to cope with new threats, and they urged astrobiologists to quit delivering speeches on the topic and engage the public in a true dialogue.

Also in 1999, a privately funded Contact Planning Group developed a broad spectrum of planning scenarios and outlined multiple strategies for managing relations with non-human intelligence (Harrison 2007). The framework for this planning involved three critical uncertainties (familiarity of the intelligence, the speed with which contact unfolds, and the favorableness of the anticipated net effects), five societal sectors (government, business, religion, science, and the media), and four response strategies (cooperation, adaptation, containment, and defense). Each strategy includes shaping public perceptions of the situation, maintaining social cohesion and international stability, and assembling and positioning the resources to mount an effective response.

Discussions of the psychological, societal, and cultural aspects of SETI have become a regular feature at annual conferences of the International Academy of Astronautics (IAA). Typically, these events include a half-day session on the technical aspects of the search and a half-day session on the human implications. Every few years, a selection of these papers appears in a special issue of the IAA's refereed journal *Acta Astronautica*. Slowly, sessions devoted to the human side of SETI are spreading to other venues. For example, symposia on SETI took place at three recent annual meetings of the American Anthropological Association (Vakoch 2004, 2005, 2006, 2009).

One of the most recent books on the societal dimensions of SETI is Michael A. G. Michaud's *Contact with Alien Civilizations: Our Hopes and Fears about Encountering Extraterrestrials* (2006). A former foreign service officer, Michaud is more concerned about the possible risks of SETI than many other authors. He notes that we are hampered by optimistic and pessimistic biases, as well as tendencies to anthropomorphize or impute human characteristics to extraterrestrials. We are also limited by the assumptions that astronomers will make the discovery, that extraterrestrial societies will have either no impact or extreme impact on our own civilization, that they will speak the language of science, and that they will be prepared for us even if we are not prepared for them. He urges us to ferret out hidden assumptions, illuminate blindspots, and challenge foregone conclusions. Here it is worth repeating one of Michaud's (1974: 33) early observations:

> In our thinking about alien intelligence, we reveal ourselves. We are variously hostile, intolerant, hopeful, naïve: influenced by science fiction, we see the aliens as implacable, grotesque conquerors, or as benign, altruistic teachers who can save us from ourselves. Usually, we think of them as superior to us in some way: either their miraculous but malevolently applied technology must be overcome by simpler virtues, or we must accept them as gods who will raise humanity from its fallen condition. Here we display fear, insecurity, wishful thinking, defeatism, even self-loathing, everything but the calm maturity appropriate for our emergence into the galactic community. We are not ready.

Research Questions and Approaches

A white paper on the role of the social sciences in SETI identifies ten areas where SETI could benefit from social science, broadly defined (Harrison et al. 2000). These are:

(1) attitudes and public support; (2) conduct and expansion of the search; (3) composing a model reply from Earth; (4) decryption and interpretation; (5) news dissemination and rumor control; (6) other preparations and readiness for contact; (7) short-term impact and (8) long-term consequences for societies, institutions. Under some circumstances, social scientists may be helpful for (9) the analysis of extraterrestrial organisms and civilizations; and (10) the initiation and conduct of relations with extraterrestrial civilizations. (Harrison, et al. 2000: 73)

This is, of course, quite a range of topics, and whereas we have the tools we need to address some of these issues empirically (for example, attitudes and public support), others—such as the comparative analyses of extraterrestrial civilizations—await a hypothetical future. Yet even if we are alone in the universe, thinking about extraterrestrial intelligence can still serve useful purposes, since it provides a looking glass in which we can learn about ourselves (Maruyama and Harkins 1977). As Michael Ruse writes:

> Exploring the possibility of life elsewhere in the universe is full of philosophical interest. Such exploration puts a bright light on our own powers and limitations. ... By speculating on what other forms of life would be, we see more clearly the nature and extent of our own knowledge.... Such fairy story telling does not prove anything empirically that we do not already know, but it does force us to think about ourselves from a novel perspective. (1985: 71)

Anthropologists, psychologists, political scientists, and sociologists bring different strengths to the table. Despite its literal definition as "the study of humans," anthropology is well equipped to offer its own distinctive perspective on organisms that share neither our heredity nor our environment but that show signs of intelligence and culture. Areas where we see obvious links between SETI and anthropology include: (1) helping SETI researchers identify and "work through" anthropocentric and ethnocentric thinking that could hamper the search and undermine interstellar communication; (2) decryption, translation, and interpretation of extraterrestrial messages; (3) cross-cultural studies, with special attention to religion, myth, and magic; and (4) analyses of intercultural contact and the diffusion of ideas.

To approach such topics we can conduct thought experiments, develop scenarios, conduct simulations, and analyze historical events. Indeed, history can be construed as a large number of experiments, conducted under widely varying conditions (Dick 2000b). Although we have yet to discover extraterrestrial intelligence, there have been episodes where numerous people believed that this had occurred. This includes a successful hoax in

1835 that convinced large numbers of newspaper readers that a powerful telescope made it possible to see "bat men" on the Moon, a period bridging the late nineteenth and early twentieth centuries when it was inferred from illusory "canals" on Mars that the red planet was home to a dying civilization, the famous Orson Welles's "War of the Worlds" broadcast of 1938 that led many radio listeners to believe that the United States had been invaded by Martians, and a brief period in the 1960s when astronomers discovered quasars and pulsars but initially misinterpreted these as intelligently controlled (Harrison 1997). And, of course, a fairly sizeable and stable portion of the population believes that extraterrestrials are visiting Earth right now (Barkun 2003).

Then, too, we can look to analogous or "analogue" situations that resemble, but are more accessible than, the situation of interest. This is common in studies of human adaptation to spaceflight; since astronauts and spacecraft are relatively inaccessible, we turn to places like Antarctica, submarines, and other environments characterized by isolation, confinement, deprivation, and risk (Bishop 2011). Thus, the arrival of the Europeans in America and the diffusion of Arab science in the Mediterranean may be useful prototypes of analogues for understanding the effects of contact. Whereas we have yet to be contacted by extraterrestrials, there are many incidents where, with little or no advanced warning, very different cultures have come across one another. If we follow this track, we must be very mindful that analogues are only rough approximations of the phenomenon that interests us.

Overcoming Human Biases

Our expectations regarding extraterrestrial civilizations are shaped by our cognitive abilities and our cultures. Working assumptions that "the other" is similar to us may limit our search and, indeed, blind us to radically different forms of intelligence.

There are multiple paths to multiple realities, and the Western scientific version is only one example (Maruyama and Harkins 1975; Harrison 2007). Social science can help enlighten us as to our hidden assumptions and biases.

As Iosif Shklovskiĭ and Carl Sagan write, "We do not know what hidden assumptions lie in our communication channel, assumptions which we are unable to evaluate because they are so intimately woven into the fabric of our thinking" (1966: 439). One of the reasons that aliens may be so elusive is that due to differences in time of origin and rates of biological and cultural evolution, there may be only a brief window in time when two civilizations can recognize each other (Duric and Field 2003). Perhaps social scientists can help stretch open this window.

Signal Decryption and Interpretation

Social scientists can draw upon archaeology, animal communication, linguistics, and cultural anthropology to decrypt and interpret messages. Conspicuous here are efforts to decipher long-dead languages, including Egyptian and Mayan hieroglyphics and Linear B. Similarly, we might learn from efforts to communicate with our own descendents. Framing messages for progeny thousands of years from now would require overcoming many of the hurdles associated with communicating with extraterrestrial civilizations. An example of this is the effort to warn people away from sites that will remain dangerously radioactive over the next ten thousand years (Benford 1999).

Active SETI, which involves launching probes or transmitting radio signals to distant solar systems (Vakoch 2011a, 2011b), offers the opportunity to compose intelligible interstellar messages. If we enter into communication, anthropologists can help us minimize misunderstandings. As astronomer Ian Ridpath has stated, we may benefit from professionals who can serve as intermediaries to make sure that neither culture offends the other (Ridpath 1978: 139–140). An essay by David Samuels demonstrates how anthropologists could help assemble a representative sample of materials for transmission, link languages to realities, and expose fake or bogus alien tongues (2005).

Cross-Cultural Studies

Several types of cross-cultural studies could benefit SETI. The first type, which can be initiated right now, is cross-cultural studies of human beliefs about extraterrestrial life (e.g., Vakoch and Lee 2000). These beliefs come in rich variety, sometimes intermingling, and sometimes independent. Variations are important, because they affect attitudes toward the search, and they are likely to influence reactions if extraterrestrial life is discovered. We might expect very different reactions from scientists who acknowledge the possibility of extraterrestrial life, from religious fundamentalists, and from people who are heavily immersed in UFO folklore. Most of the research conducted so far focuses on North America, Europe, and to a somewhat lesser extent Russia. Apart from a few case histories developed by psychiatrist John Mack, very little research has been done on the likely reactions of indigenous populations in Africa, South America, and Asia (1999).

Magic, myth, and religion are three important topics. Magic is significant because highly advanced technologies may be so far ahead of our own that they seem like magic to us. How will we interpret technology that is beyond our understanding? Could we become a cargo cult, deifying a civilization that we at best partially understand? Could their functional equivalent of a World War II C-3 cargo vessel become for us a magical religious artifact?

Myths require attention because of their great potential for influencing interpretations of extraterrestrial civilizations. Relevant here are ancient myths that are found in all corners of the world, and more recent myths in which transcendental sky gods are replaced by advanced technocrats who began meddling in human evolution and culture in the distant past (Colavito 2005). Myths about extraterrestrial life enter into new religious movements centering on ancient astronauts, flying saucers, and alien abductions. Are these myths divergent, parallel, or convergent, and what does this mean for the SETI enterprise (Harrison 2007)? Recently, anthropologists (Battaglia 2005) have joined the sociologists who study flying saucer religions (Lewis 1995; Partridge 2003; Tumminia 2005, 2007).

The authors of the Brookings Report, mentioned at the beginning of this introduction, were concerned that the discovery would have a devastating effect on religion, because it would contradict narratives that depend heavily on events that transpired on Earth, such as Christ's birth and redemption (Committee on Science and Astronautics 1961). Today, some scientists view the discovery as the capstone of the Copernican and Darwinian revolutions, proof once and for all of the superiority of naturalistic explanations (Chaisson 2001). Yet the overall picture is complicated and nuanced. Generally, theologians with strong academic credentials are more open to the discovery than are those who interpret the Bible literally. Religions that are geocentric and homocentric are expected to be particularly resistant to the discovery; on the other hand, there are religions that are very open to the possibility of life on other worlds (Harrison and Dick 2000). Ted Peters (2009) recently found that approximately 83 to 94 percent of his respondents (depending on religious affiliation) strongly disagreed with the statement that "Official confirmation of the discovery of an advanced extraterrestrial civilization would so undercut my religious beliefs that my beliefs would face a crisis." They were slightly less confident of their religious tradition's ability to withstand the discovery, but still 99 percent of the mainline Protestants, 73 percent of the evangelical Protestants, and 67 percent of the Catholics strongly disagreed with the proposition that the discovery would cause a crisis within their faiths. Respondents were less confident that other people's religions could withstand the discovery. It was the agnostics and atheists, not people affiliated with religious groups, who thought that the discovery would be catastrophic for religion. It is useful to keep in mind that Peters's study did not assess people's views on the likelihood that extraterrestrial intelligence exists, or that it would be discovered by scientists; these are separate questions.

Some new approaches to religion, such as Steven J. Dick's cosmotheology (2000c) and Diarmuid O'Murchu's quantum theology (2004), are geared for a universe full of life, a universe where in comparison to others we ourselves are at best mediocre.

Many of the scientists involved in the search expect that vastly older civilizations will have worked through the troubles of their adolescence and be benign or even benevolent. Others point to situations on Earth in which the meeting of different cultures resulted in disaster. Thus, we have images of deceptively friendly colonizers waiting only until they get sufficient military reinforcements to massacre indigenous tribes; fun-loving explorers donning facemasks or using cheap magic tricks to terrorize the natives; and bullies making natives wear silly outfits, getting them drunk, seducing them, and using bayonets to force religious conversions. But, as Reed Riner cautions, there are counter-examples where there have been sustained, mutually beneficial outcomes (2000). He cites three conspicuous examples: potlatching on the Northwest Coast of North America, the Kula Ring in the Melanesian Pacific; and the symbiotic relationship among the Kohistanis, Pathans, and Gujars in the Pakistani State of Swat. The real problem, Riner points out, is identifying the different conditions that yield different patterns of outcomes. In his analysis, the nation-state form of organization is conducive to hostile interactions.

Cultural diffusion is another important area. Because SETI scientists expect that contact—if it occurs—will take place at a distance, we are particularly interested in the diffusion of ideas. Prototypes include the Arabs' transmission of Greek science to the Latin West in the twelfth and thirteenth centuries, the introduction of Copernican theory during the sixteenth century, the "galactocentric" revolution of the early twentieth century, and reactions to the Darwinian theory of evolution (Dick 1996).

If we do enter into communication with extraterrestrial civilizations, we may be able to initiate a new generation of cross-cultural studies. Harrison and Elms (1990) point out that we have only a limited number of data points to conduct cross-species and cross-cultural research and finding new samples would provide new answers to old questions. Finney (2000) observes that the discovery would offer an unparalleled opportunity to explore the co-evolution of genes and culture, pointing to answers to many of the most fundamental questions in anthropology. He writes: "A science of civilizations is required, one that would compare and contrast a wide variety of independent cases in order to investigate how diverse societies and cultures developed from their respective biological bases and how these in turn are linked to fundamental physical laws and principles" (2000: 141). The distance of Finney's vision is revealed in his view that if extraterrestrial civilizations do not exist, given enough time our descendants will colonize the stars; their biological and cultural evolution will provide the anticipated database. Further, this "would have the advantage of methodological control, for each new outpost would spring from the common biocultural bases of terrestrial humanity" (2000: 142).

Intelligence and the Longevity of Civilizations

As we turn to a preview of the rest of this book, Part I uses multiple disciplinary perspectives to examine the question "Does extraterrestrial life exist?" In the first chapter, "Are We Alone? Estimating the Prevalence of Extraterrestrial Intelligence," astronomer Seth Shostak recounts the major reasons that so many people are optimistic about the existence of extraterrestrial civilizations. After summarizing the argument that the universe must contain intelligent aliens *somewhere*, Shostak details recent discoveries that add substance to this stance. Even if we assume that extraterrestrial life requires liquid water, there are a half dozen bodies in our solar system alone where this basic necessity for life might be found. Beyond our solar system, hundreds of planets have been discovered circling other stars. While the first extrasolar planets that were detected are large Jupiter- and Saturn-like planets, as planet-hunting technologies improve astronomers are able to discover increasingly Earth-like planets. NASA's Kepler satellite, launched in 2009, completed its planned search for terrestrial-sized planets before finally ending observations in May 2013. Its data continue to be analyzed for evidence of other Earths.

Regardless of how many habitable planets exist around other stars, unless intelligence evolves there will be no other civilizations to contact. Shostak emphasizes that while the evolution of *Homo sapiens* on another planet is unlikely, functionally equivalent forms of intelligence may exist, albeit looking far different from the intelligence we know on Earth. Similarly, to make contact, that intelligence will need to survive long enough to co-exist with our civilization. Shostak introduces the relevant variables using the Drake Equation, a heuristic for estimating the prevalence of intelligent civilizations by considering key astronomical, biological, and cultural prerequisites to the development of technology capable of interstellar communication. Two of the terms of the Drake Equation that we will see in other chapters are f_l, the fraction of life-bearing planets on which intelligent life evolves, and L, the average longevity of civilizations, measured in the number of years they broadcast their existence into space.

In "Encountering Alternative Intelligences: Cognitive Archaeology and SETI," archaeologist Paul K. Wason asks whether his discipline's study of the evolution of human intelligence has implications for understanding intelligence on other worlds, or whether the conclusions of archaeology apply only to humankind. Wason focuses on the encounter between Neanderthals and modern humans, and he examines intelligence as multifaced, consisting of specific modules or mental operations, such as social intelligence, technical intelligence, and natural history intelligence. Neanderthals likely had high intelligence in multiple domains: skillfully interacting with other Neanderthals (social intelligence), manipulating their environment to create technologies like stone tools (technical intelligence), and being savvy about their natural environments (natural history intelligence).

But high intelligence, Wason argues, is not sufficient to ensure meaningful exchanges between species. Neanderthals may have built fires, but they would have been oblivious to *Homo sapiens*'s penchant for keeping the cooking area of a home separate from other areas. The interrelationships between social intelligence and technical intelligence found in modern humans would be opaque to Neanderthals, and so the specialized demarcations of modern human living spaces would be invisible to Neanderthals. Both species were highly intelligent, Wason argues, but the differences in the form of their intelligence would have posed an obstacle for clear comprehension. The implication for SETI is sobering. If two such closely related species as Neanderthals and *Homo sapiens* would have had difficulty understanding one another, Wason concludes that meaningfully engaging with an independently evolved extraterrestrial would almost certainly be more difficult. Rather than expecting to understand another species fully, he suggests that a more reasonable goal is to identify the intentionality in their signals. Though we may not understand exactly *what* they are saying, we may be able to understand *that* they are saying *something*.

Astronomer Alan Penny examines the final term in the Drake Equation, L, in his chapter "The Lifetimes of Scientific Civilizations and the Genetic Evolution of the Brain." Before an extraterrestrial civilization can make itself known to us across interstellar distances, it must possess a technology for sending a detectable signal of its existence. Penny argues that this in turn presupposes a science on which such technology is based. While others have considered the biological and cultural prerequisites for the development of such science, Penny's approach is novel in SETI circles insofar as he focuses on the specifically genetic events that make scientific thinking possible. And if, as he conjectures, science is made possible by a genetic change, then subsequent genetic events might undo this capacity for scientific thinking. The time between these genetic changes— one change making scientific thinking possible, the other making it impossible—serves as Penny's estimate of L. Unless a civilization intervenes to override or compensate for such a genetic "off switch" for scientific thinking, genetic changes may limit its technological longevity.

To support his argument, Penny analyzes the history of genetic changes as well as the history of thinking in the genus *Homo*. He proposes three successive modes of modern human thinking separated by two genetic events. In the first mode, "early" thinking, thoughts and actions remain unconnected. With "transitional" thinking, the link between thoughts and actions is evident, but the third mode, "conceptual" thinking, is required before this connection is seen as an abstract whole. By Penny's review of the evidence, "conceptual" thinking arose a mere three thousand years ago. If future genetic changes to the human brain should "undo" the change that made "conceptual" thinking possible, humankind's scientific thinking would end, eliminating the scientific foundation for interstellar communication.

Archaeologist Kathryn Denning takes a radically different approach to the longevity of civilizations in her chapter "'L' on Earth." Contrary to many who have contemplated the lifetimes of extraterrestrial civilizations, Denning foregoes the attempt to provide a numerical estimate of L, in part because she rejects the common bias that a quantified solution is the most scientific way of grappling with the longevity of cultures beyond Earth. Rather than using the historical record of terrestrial civilizations as data for calculating L, she considers the types of information that can be garnered from this record, as well as the assumptions that may need to be revised in the process. In particular, Denning advocates a reexamination of the theoretical frameworks by which we explain the evolution of civilizations, and she proposes the formulation of hypotheses about the evolution of civilizations that can be examined using data gathered by archaeologists, anthropologists, and historians.

One common assumption of SETI scientists, says Denning, is that social evolution on other worlds will be unilinear. Whereas nineteenth-century anthropologists tended to characterize societies in terms of a uniform progression from primitive barbarians to advanced civilizations, by the twentieth century they recognized the problems of ranking diverse societies by the complexity of their political systems and technologies. Today anthropologists emphasize the need to understand each society in its own historical specificity. Likewise, Denning argues for caution in assuming that extraterrestrial civilizations will have gone through the same critical events that terrestrial cultures have.

As one example, some SETI scientists have suggested that long-lived extraterrestrial civilizations will have avoided the threat of self-destruction that humankind now faces; if extraterrestrials do not overcome such dangers, they would not exist long enough to make contact. Denning questions the implicit assumption behind this idea, which is that extraterrestrial societies will follow the same path as on Earth, with technologies of mass destruction tied to technologies allowing interstellar communication. Indeed, she questions whether this presumed connection between the capacity to make contact with other civilizations and the military use of technology is a necessary link even on Earth; she advocates turning to data from diverse terrestrial civilizations to examine this hypothesis as well as other assumptions that guide our thinking about the longevity of civilizations beyond Earth.

Impact of a Discovery on Humanity

Suppose we *do* discover extraterrestrial life—either microbial life within our solar system, or intelligent life through SETI. Part II of this book examines how humankind would respond to such a discovery. As sociologist Donald E. Tarter details in "Can SETI Fulfill the Value Agenda of Cultural Anthropology?" the Apollo Lunar Program of the 1960s gave us a new perspective on our place in the universe. An increasing sense of human unity was fostered by the stunning photographs of Earth against the backdrop of space. These photos showed one globe with no national or state boundaries and very interlocking ecosystems. The great planetary expeditions of the 1970s and beyond, with their more distant photographs of planet Earth, reinforced our collective self-image as a small and fragile planet whose inhabitants shared a collective heritage and future. This sense of unity was shattered by the events of September 11, 2001, says Tarter. Since then humanity has drifted back toward the days of ancient ethnic tensions and hostilities.

By Tarter's analysis, SETI offers us another opportunity to regain our sense of human unity, ironically through a cosmic analogue to anthropology's emphasis on the value of appreciating the diversity of terrestrial cultures. In this analogy, our appreciation of cultural diversity comes as we understand that humankind is only one of many civilizations in the universe. If we are able to detect evidence of other civilizations in space, we may once again find it easier to envision ourselves as one civilization among many. We may embark on the adventure of cataloguing and seeking to understand intelligent creatures far different from ourselves and in so doing evolve a deeper appreciation of our place in the universe.

Tarter attempts to anticipate the various consequences of detecting life beyond Earth. Working on the assumption that an initial detection of extraterrestrials may tell us little about their civilization due to the tremendous challenges of decoding their messages, he suggests that humankind will feel a sense of "cosmic anxiety" in the face of many unknowns. He anticipates the rise of an "interpretation industry" that attempts to make sense of the messages coming in, and he calls for establishing groups responsible for helping the general public understand which of the many, often-competing claims is plausible. Though in reality Earth may face few security risks by detecting extraterrestrials, due to the buffer of interstellar space, Tarter expects this will not be immediately obvious to many people, and there may be a call for space-based weapons systems. The detection of a single extraterrestrial civilization would lead to increased funding for a range of further SETI projects, which could be as ambitious as establishing a radio observatory on the far side of the Moon or launching a gravitational lens to enhance search capabilities, to more far-future prospects like quantum communication.

As a complement to theoretical approaches to predicting the consequences of contact, other researchers have empirically studied the issue, as exemplified in survey expert George Pettinico's "American Attitudes about Life beyond Earth: Beliefs, Concerns, and the Role of Education and Religion in Shaping Public Perceptions." In this telephone survey of one thousand randomly selected Americans who were representative of the national adult population, Pettinico discovered two key demographic variables that influence people's attitudes about extraterrestrial life: their highest level of education and their religiosity, as measured by how often they attended religious services. More religious people were twice as likely than less religious people to reject the possibility of extraterrestrial life. Of those who did not believe extraterrestrial life exists, the most frequent reason given was that it contradicts their religious beliefs.

Those in Pettinico's study who are open to the possibility of extraterrestrial life *existing* were also sanguine about humankind eventually *discovering* that it exists. People who were open to the possibility of extraterrestrial life were generally excited and hopeful about the prospect of learning of its existence. Level of education played a major role in determining people's anticipated responses to detection, with those who had a high school degree or less being over two and a half times more likely to be afraid and nervous than those with a college education. Even those who expected extraterrestrial life to exist, however, suspect it will be rare in the universe.

Pettinico's study also has implications for post-detection activities, suggesting there would be strong support for a reply from Earth. Of those who believed extraterrestrial life is likely, fully 90 percent said that if we receive a signal from extraterrestrials, humans should respond. This was the most nearly unanimous finding in the entire survey. Only half of the respondents answered affirmatively to the question "If beings from another planet sent a message to us through deep space, do you think we would be able to figure out what they were saying?" Though this is more skeptical than the views of many SETI scientists, who have long argued for the universality of science and mathematics as a common language for interstellar communication, it is consistent with some of the challenges of creating intelligible messages raised in more recent scholarship (e.g., Dunér 2011).

An alternative survey approach was employed in William Sims Bainbridge's "Cultural Beliefs about Extraterrestrials: A Questionnaire Study." By using an online questionnaire, he was able to recruit nearly four thousand participants while asking a long list of questions. Although there is no guarantee that the results can extrapolate to the population as a whole because sampling was not random, past studies suggest that such online questionnaires are good at comparing the answers of subgroups of respondents, as well as exploring relationships between variables—the latter being one of the priorities identified during a series of workshops on the cultural aspects of SETI (Billingham et al. 1999). Among the thirty questions that Bainbridge asked participants about science, technology, and pseudoscience, two addressed life beyond Earth: "Intelligent life probably does not exist on any planet but our own" and "Some UFOs (Unidentified Flying Objects) are probably spaceships from other worlds." While a significant majority believed that intelligent life probably exists beyond Earth, just over a fifth of the respondents agreed that UFOs are probably spaceships. Even more interesting, however, is how the responses to these questions were related to answers to other questions. There was a strong connection between believing that UFOs are spaceships and belief in astrology, but no meaningful connection between belief in extraterrestrial intelligence and belief in astrology. This supports Bainbridge's interpretation that a belief that UFOs are spaceships is connected to New Age beliefs, but belief in extraterrestrial intelligence is not.

To learn more about these beliefs, Bainbridge categorized people according to whether they believed extraterrestrial intelligence exists and whether some UFOs are spacecraft, considering these two questions together. "Geocentrists" rejected the possibility that intelligence exists on other planets, and logically following this, rejected the claim that some UFOs are spacecraft. Another group accepted the possibility of extraterrestrial intelligence, but not the possibility that some UFOs are spacecraft. Bainbridge calls the second group "allopatrists," based on a term that population biologists use to refer to geographically separated gene pools; he suggests that these people may have been aware of the vast distances between stars, and thus they concluded that even if extraterrestrial intelligence exists, it may not be able to visit Earth. Finally, he considers the "ufophiles," who contended that some UFOs could be spaceships, and thus logically, that extraterrestrial intelligence is possible.

Consistent with Pettinico's study, Bainbridge found that education and religiosity helped differentiate these groups. Nearly 70 percent of allopatrists had graduated from college, while just under half of ufophiles had. Geocentrists were more religious than average, while allopatrists were less religious. Interestingly, a large fraction of ufophiles were only moderately religious or identified themselves as "neither religious nor non-religious." Bainbridge suggests that this semi-religiosity of ufophiles is consistent with sociological studies showing involvement in New Age phenomena among those who are positive toward the supernatural but who have weak ties to traditional religious groups. Thus, belief that UFOs are from other worlds may help meet a religious need among ufophiles. Bainbridge's study provides a compelling reminder that studies on people's attitudes about life beyond Earth need to be clear in the specific questions being asked. A survey on beliefs about alien visitation may shed little light on people's likely reaction to a SETI signal detection (Vakoch and Lee 2000).

In "The Science and Politics of SETI: How to Succeed in an Era of Make-Believe History and Pseudoscience," psychologist Albert A. Harrison explains that to maintain their credibility within the community of science, astronomers who became engaged in SETI sought to distance themselves from widespread popular beliefs about UFOs and alien visitation. They achieved this in part by relentless emphasis on scientific methods with meticulous attention to replication and verification. Early on, SETI scientists enlisted the support of prominent senior scientists from NASA and elsewhere. Through a series of conferences and other activities they were able to build strong ties that cut across national boundaries and disciplines and led to recognition and acceptance within prominent professional associations. Many of the benefits of astronomy are humanistic, in the sense that they pique the intellectual curiosity and hopes of the public.

Three of the strategies available to scientists to create boundaries between SETI and UFOlogy are bashing, silence, and education. Because it tends to escalate conflicts, Harrison says, bashing is often ineffective or counterproductive, and while evading the issue allows the scientists to work in peace, it leaves the public at the mercy of people of lesser judgment. Harrison contends that although in an age of declining scientific literacy and sensationalism, education is an uphill battle, it remains the most promising strategy for minimizing confusion in the public mind.

Messages to Other Civilizations

After considering the likelihood that life beyond Earth exists, then attempting to anticipate the societal response, in Part III, the final section of the book, we examine the challenges of creating messages that will be comprehensible to an alien civilization. In "Cultural Aspects of Interstellar Communication," mathematician Carl L. DeVito asks what we can presuppose humans and extraterrestrials to have in common, assuming we have made contact. The answer, he says, is technology; without that, there would be no signals to detect. Given that SETI projects currently search for radio signals or brief laser pulses, at a minimum we can assume that the other civilization has the capacity to generate electromagnetic waves. And that, says DeVito, presupposes an understanding of some of the same scientific principles that humans know. Because humans and extraterrestrials share a common physical reality, their independent attempts to understand that reality through science will converge, he concludes.

Similarly, DeVito argues for the universality of at least *some* mathematical concepts. He stresses that we need not assume *much* overlap in terrestrial and extraterrestrial mathematics to provide a starting point for an interstellar conversation. Taking an incremental approach, he explains that by starting with the natural numbers (1, 2, 3, ...), we can begin to discuss chemistry. Extraterrestrial chemists will know as well as humans do that there are ninety-two naturally occurring elements in the universe, he argues, and even if they do not themselves use the Periodic Table of Elements to organize their thinking, they should be able to recognize its significance by their familiarity with the properties of each element. Using chemistry as a subject matter, and mathematics as a "language," we can go on to introduce such concepts as mass, heat, and pressure.

Science and mathematics have an additional virtue as the starting points of an interstellar conversation, in DeVito's view: they resist interpretations as being morally or religiously significant, and thus they are unlikely to offend or upset people. Throughout his chapter DeVito argues that teams tasked with creating or decoding interstellar messages should be multidisciplinary, with cross-cultural researchers being especially important in helping the broader public prepare to deal with the new knowledge that other civilizations exist.

In "Cosmic Storytelling: Primitive Observables as Rosetta Analogies," Harry Letaw, Jr., makes the case that we human beings are a species of storytellers. We sing our poetry, decorate cave walls, and use each medium as it emerges to communicate our stories to any who will attend. Human societies, generation after generation, pass down their precious stories. Storytelling teaches and reinforces our most highly prized behaviors and truths while disclosing the pitfalls of contrary actions. We craft stories for very young children as well as for mature, sophisticated audiences. It seems only fitting, Letaw concludes, to begin our messages to extraterrestrials with this same reliance on storytelling.

Contrary to some who argue that a message must begin with symbols that can be arranged in an arbitrary manner, Letaw argues for the importance of pictures in interstellar messages—including stories. Whether or not extraterrestrials can themselves directly see, civilizations that attempt contact via radio waves or laser pulses should be familiar with electromagnetic radiation, which makes vision possible.

Letaw points out that the interpretation of a story relies on a familiarity with cultural conventions. Given the independent origins of humans and extraterrestrials, and the assumption that there will be no face-to-face contact in SETI scenarios, that means the sender will need to teach those conventions to the recipient. To accomplish this, Letaw suggests ways we might represent human activities in interstellar messages. Primitive observables may serve as the foundation for an "interstellar Rosetta Stone," an analogue of the slab of basalt that provided a key to Europeans learning ancient Egyptian hieroglyphics. Physical observables, the first type of primitive observables, consist of such elements as light and shadow, changes of state, and fluid flow. Simple machines and tools include, for example, levers, ropes, pulleys, hammers, and saws. Among the basic physical activities Letaw suggests are lifting, climbing, running, and walking. More complex domestic pursuits include erecting shelters, weaving, and hunting. Beyond the initial stages of storytelling, which rely on these primitive observables, Letaw anticipates adding more complex technologies and activities. Using redundant images across the story provides continuity and should increase intelligibility. By using storytelling to introduce human beings relating to other humans, inanimate objects, and other animals, Letaw suggests we can begin to communicate something as elusive as human thoughts.

In "Direct Contact with Extraterrestrials via Computer Emulation," sociologist William Sims Bainbridge suggests that cognitive science and information technology are progressing in a direction that will make it possible to transmit realistic avatars of individual human beings to extraterrestrial civilizations. The first step is personality capture, the process of gathering sufficient information about a human being's memories, thoughts, and feelings to allow emulation of the person in a computer, information system, or robot. Bainbridge estimates that a single personality could be copied with medium to high fidelity with less than a gigabyte of data. The computer code to create an artificial intelligence system capable of emulating personality would add several more gigabytes—still remaining within the size limits of plausible interstellar messages (Shostak 2011). As the number of different personalities to be emulated increases, the fidelity of each avatar could increase due to improvements in the artificial intelligence technology.

Personality capture must employ culturogenic measures, Bainbridge emphasizes, because personalities arise in a particular cultural context. Once recorded, personalities can be delivered to the stars in Starbase interstellar database probes or via radio given the willingness of a recipient civilization. Embassies from multiple civilizations can be situated in a virtual reality Cosmopolis, where computer-generated avatars emulate the original biological beings in social interaction, trade, and cultural innovation. Bainbridge closes with ideas about practical steps we might undertake to fund, develop, and apply the needed technology.

In "The Inscrutable Names of God: The Jesuit Missions of New France as a Model for SETI-Related Spiritual Questions," historian Jason T. Kuznicki challenges the standard argument of SETI researchers that by virtue of their communicative abilities, intelligent aliens will necessarily share a certain set of concepts with humans, such as mathematics and logic. Although extraterrestrials may be alien in all other respects, it has been argued, these qualities will be universal—at least among those extraterrestrials with technologies sufficiently similar to ours to make contact with us in the first place.

Likewise, says Kuznicki, some might reason that at least some abstract notions of spirituality are also shared across civilizations, albeit in quite different forms than on Earth. Using evidence from another first contact, between French Jesuits and the Montagnais, Huron, and Iroquois peoples of what is now eastern Canada, he challenges this notion. Contrary to Saint Thomas Aquinas's argument that natural reason alone would lead one to the concepts of the soul and of God, this was not borne out in encounters between Europeans and these natives of North America.

The Jesuits expected that their interlocutors would conceive of the soul as immortal and unitary. On the contrary, the Iroquois viewed people as having several separate attributes that the Jesuits would see as all unified into a single soul, with transformations of these various "souls" occurring at different times and in different ways. Similarly, reports that most native North American religions call upon a "Great Spirit" in some way analogous to God is more likely a reflection of later syncretic beliefs than native spirituality in its original form.

Finally, Kuznicki notes that even in more mundane descriptions of the world, native and European linguistic categories carry with them philosophical assumptions about the nature of the objects or actions to which they refer. Kuznicki concludes that in interstellar communication as well, the categories that seem foundational to one culture may not even be conceived in another culture. If two strands of humankind with a shared genetic heritage have such tremendous difficulties understanding one another with face-to-face contact, we should expect our encounters with extraterrestrial civilizations to be fraught with mutual confusion, often about concepts that had been considered unproblematic beforehand.

In the spirit of biologist Richard Dawkins's (1983) arguments for "universal Darwinism," anthropologists Kathryn Coe, Craig T. Palmer, and Christina Pomianek examine the relevance of evolutionary theory for SETI in "ET Phone Darwin: What Can an Evolutionary Understanding of Animal Communication and Art Contribute to Our Understanding of Methods for Interstellar Communication?" They ask what lessons can be learned for communicating with independently evolved intelligence on other worlds by considering the evolution of social behavior on Earth, especially in the form of communication. Focusing particularly on sight and hearing, these authors argue that there are sound evolutionary reasons to believe these senses will be found on other worlds as well. They observe that both vision and audition have evolved multiple times independently on Earth, arguing that this bodes well for similar convergent evolution on other planets. Having earlier defined art as the modification of a body or object to attract attention (Coe 1992), in this chapter Coe, Palmer, and Pomianek suggest that messages such as those borne on the Pioneer spacecraft (Sagan, Salzman Sagan, and Drake 1972) may well serve the fundamental goal of art as seen in evolutionary perspective: to proclaim they are artifacts intended to attract the recipient's attention.

Coe, Palmer, and Pomianek propose that evolutionary theory can help us think about whether we should send messages to other worlds, and if we do, help clarify both the appropriate content and our motivations for transmitting. Given that life evolves through competition, they ask whether we should be wary of making contact with extraterrestrials, who may view us as competitors. And if we decide to communicate, for example, that we are altruistic, could we do so and still be honest? Or are there scenarios, they ask, in which we would want intentionally to deceive the recipients, such as portraying ourselves as having greater capabilities than we do to dissuade aliens from coming to Earth to exploit our natural resources?

In the final chapter, "A Journalistic Perspective on SETI-Related Message Composition," writer and space analyst Morris Jones argues that although historically SETI scientists have had good relationships with journalists, these have been one-sided, with the scientists providing material for the journalists' stories. Jones proposes that the SETI community could benefit by encouraging input in the opposite direction—from journalists and media specialists *to* SETI scientists—when contemplating how to create interstellar messages.

At one level, any interstellar message is a bearer of news: that its sender exists—something not known previously to the recipient, unless it had detected the sender earlier through accidental leakage radiation or other manifestations of life on its planet. So too might the message's content tell of new forms of life, not previously encountered. And if, as some have argued, science progresses differently on other worlds (Vakoch 2011a), even accounts of scientific concepts that seem foundational to the senders may be novel to the recipients. Even if some aspects of messages about shared understandings are intelligible to other civilizations, Jones suggests that the sort of content typically associated with news, which relies on a deep familiarity with social and historical context, may be inaccessible to extraterrestrials.

In many ways, interstellar messages have been designed in ways that diverge considerably from standard news stories. Typically interstellar messages have been conceived as "one-off" attempts to communicate, rather than a series of missives sent on a regular timetable, as is typical of terrestrial news media, whether broadcast or print. Interstellar messages have often been "sanitized" to emphasize those aspects of humankind of which we are most proud; thus, the creators of the Voyager interstellar recording intentionally excluded images of war, disease, and poverty (Lomberg 1978). In contrast, Jones emphasizes, negative content represents a significant portion of terrestrial news. In short, by thinking of interstellar messages in comparison to news, we have another opportunity to consider whether traditional assumptions about interstellar communication are warranted, or whether other alternatives are preferable, such as also presenting those aspects of humanity of which we are less proud.

Conclusion

In 1959, C. P. Snow published his famous essay *The Two Cultures and the Scientific Revolution* that described a growing schism between scientists and humanists. Snow, an eminent scientist and writer who helped recruit about four thousand scientists and engineers during World War II, complained that between the 1930s and 1950s, scientists and humanists quit smiling at each other and began making faces instead. Snow foresaw that atomic energy, electronics, and automation would be among the primary driving technological forces over the next few decades. A dialogue between scientists and humanists would expand each constituency's breadth of thinking and help ease us into the future. This dialogue, he thought, would help reduce the growing division between the rich and the poor, protect the free world from being outpaced by the communists, and reduce the threat of war. British, American, and Russian educational systems each had their strengths, Snow observed, but one of the strengths of the Russian system was that it expected students of science and students of literature to become acquainted with each other's ideas.

Ben Finney notes that SETI is a perfect meeting ground for the physical, biological, and social sciences, and the humanities (2000). He proclaims that the discovery of extraterrestrial civilizations would provide a welcome wake-up call: "We need extraterrestrial civilizations to introduce us to an array of possibilities and variations beyond our past experience and also to shock us out of such parochialisms as regarding ourselves as the summit and final goal of evolution" (2000: 141). Social science can help develop the scientific base and practical information that would help guide humanity through the major transformations that are likely to follow. A satisfactory overall research program would be broad, structured to permit meaningful quantitative comparisons as possible, and enable cogent explanations of the findings. More social-science involvement should be welcomed not only by physical and biological scientists but also by policy makers and the public.

Bibliography

Baird, John. 1987. *The Inner Limits of Outer Space*. Hanover, NH: The University Press of New England.

Barkun, Michael. 2003. *A Culture of Conspiracy: Apocalyptic Visions in Contemporary America*. Berkeley, CA: University of California Press.

Battaglia, Debora. 2005. *ET Cultures: Anthropology in Outerspaces*. Durham, NC: Duke University Press.

Benford, Gregory. 1999. *Deep Time: How Humanity Communicates across the Millennia*. New York: Perennial.

Billingham, John, et al., eds. 1999. *Social Implications of the Detection of an Extraterrestrial Civilization: A Report of the Workshops on the Cultural Aspects of SETI Held in October 1991, May 1992, and September 1992*. Mountain View, CA: SETI Press.

Billings, Linda, Pamela Conrad, and Janet Siefert. 2011. "Foreword." In *Communication with Extraterrestrial Intelligence*, ed. Douglas A. Vakoch, xiii–xv. Albany, NY: State University of New York Press.

Bishop, Sheryl L. 2011. "From Earth Analogs to Space: Getting There from Here." In *Psychology of Space Exploration: Contemporary Research in Historical Perspective*, NASA SP-2011-4411, ed. Douglas A. Vakoch, 47–77. Washington, DC: National Aeronautics and Space Administration.

Black, D. C., and M. A. Stull. 1977. "The Science of SETI." In *The Search for Extraterrestrial Intelligence*, NASA Publication SP-419, eds. Philip Morrison, John Billingham, and John Wolfe, 93–120. Washington, DC: National Aeronautics and Space Administration.

Chaisson, Eric J. 2001. *Cosmic Evolution: The Rise of Complexity in Nature*. Cambridge, MA: Harvard University Press.

Coe, Kathryn. 1992. "Art: The Replicable Unit. An Inquiry into the Origin of Art as a Social Behavior." *Journal of Social and Evolutionary Systems* 1: 217–234.

Colavito, Jason. 2005. *The Cult of Alien Gods: H. P. Lovecraft and Extraterrestrial Pop Culture*. Amherst, NY: Prometheus.

Committee on Science and Astronautics. 1961. *Proposed Studies on the Implications of Peaceful Space Activities for Human Affairs*. Prepared for the National Aeronautics and Space Administration by the Brookings Institute and presented to the US House of Representatives, Eighty-Seventh Congress, 24 March 1961.

Connors, Mary M. 1976a. "The Consequences of Detecting Extraterrestrial Intelligence for Telecommunications Policy." Unpublished paper. NASA Ames Research Center.

———. 1976b. "The Role of the Social Scientist in the Search for Extraterrestrial Intelligence." Unpublished paper. NASA Ames Research Center.

Connors, Mary M., Albert A. Harrison, and Faren R. Akins. 1985. *Living Aloft: Human Requirements for Extended Spaceflight*, NASA SP-483. Washington, DC: National Aeronautics and Space Administration.

Dawkins, Richard. 1983. "Universal Darwinism." In *Evolution from Microbes to Men*, ed. D. S. Bendall, 403–425. Cambridge: Cambridge University Press.

Denzler, Brenda. 2001. *The Lure of the Edge: Scientific Passions, Religious Beliefs, and the Pursuit of UFOs*. Berkeley: University of California Press.

Dick, Steven J. 1996. *The Biological Universe: The Twentieth Century Extraterrestrial Life Debate and the Limits of Science*. Cambridge: Cambridge University Press.

———. 2000a. "Cosmotheology: Theological Implications of the New Universe." In *Many Worlds: The New Universe, Extraterrestrial Life, & the Theological Implication*, ed. Steven J. Dick, 191–211. Radnor, PA: The John Templeton Foundation Press.

———. 2000b. "Cultural Aspects of Astrobiology." In *If SETI Succeeds: The Impact of High Information Contact*, ed. Allen Tough, 145–152. Bellevue, WA: Foundation For the Future.

———, ed. 2000c. *Many Worlds: The New Universe, Extraterrestrial Life, & the Theological Implications*. Radnor, PA: The John Templeton Foundation Press.

———. 2006. "Anthropology and the Search for Extraterrestrial Intelligence." *Anthropology Today* 22, 2: 3–7.

Drake, Frank. 1960. "How Can We Detect Radio Transmissions from Distant Planetary Systems?" *Sky and Telescope* 19: 140–143.

Dunér, David. 2011. "Cognitive Foundations of Interstellar Communication." In *Communication with Extraterrestrial Intelligence*, ed. Douglas A. Vakoch, 449–467. Albany, NY: State University of New York Press.

Duric, N., and L. Field. 2003. "On the Detectability of Intelligent Civilizations in the Galaxy." *Serbian Astronomy Journal* no. 167: 1–10.

Finney, Ben. 2000. "SETI, Consilience and the Unity of Knowledge." In *If SETI Succeeds: The Impact of High Information Contact*, ed. Allen Tough, 139–144. Bellevue, WA: Foundation For the Future.

Finney, Ben, and Eric Jones. 1984. *Interstellar Migration and the Human Experience*. Berkeley, CA: University of California Press.

Harrison, Albert A. 1997. *After Contact: The Human Response to Extraterrestrial Life*. New York: Plenum.

———. 2007. *Starstruck: Cosmic Visions in Science, Religion, and Folklore*. New York: Berghahn Books.

———. 2010. "The ETI Myth: Idolatrous Fantasy or Plausible Inference." *Science and Theology* 9, no. 1: 51–67.

Harrison, Albert A., et al. 2000. "The Role of the Social Sciences in SETI." In *If SETI Succeeds: The Impact of High Information Contact*, ed. Allen Tough, 105–119. Bellevue, WA: Foundation For the Future.

Harrison, Albert A., and Kathleen Connell. 2000. *Workshop on the Societal Implications of Astrobiology*, Final Report. NASA Ames Research Center. http://astrobiology.arc.nasa.gov/workshops/societal/societal_report.pdf. Accessed on 18 April 2011.

Harrison, Albert A., Kathleen Connell, and Gregory K. Schmidt. 2002. "Rethinking our Place in the Universe: Exploring the Societal Implications of NASA's Astrobiology Program." *Space Times*, January–February, 4–9.

Harrison, Albert A., and Steven J. Dick. 2000. "Contact: Long-Term Implications for Humanity." In *If SETI Succeeds: The Impact of High Information Contact*, ed. Allen Tough, 35–60. Bellevue, WA: Foundation For the Future.

Harrison, Albert A., and Alan C. Elms. 1990. "Psychology and the Search for Extraterrestrial Intelligence." *Behavioral Science* 35: 3.

Lewis, James R., ed. 1995. *The Gods Have Landed: New Religions from Other Worlds*. Albany, NY: State University of New York Press.

Lomberg, Jon. 1978. "Pictures of Earth." In *Murmurs of Earth*, ed. Carl Sagan, 71–121. New York: Random House.

Mack, John E. 1999. *Passport to the Cosmos: Human Transformation and Alien Encounter*. New York: Crown.

Maruyama, Magorah, and Arthur Harkins, eds. *Cultures beyond Earth: The Role of Anthropology in Outer Space*. New York: Vintage Books.

Mead, Curtis, and Paul Horowitz. 2011. "Harvard's Advanced All-Sky Optical SETI." In *Communication with Extraterrestrial Intelligence*, ed. Douglas A. Vakoch, 125–135. Albany, NY: State University of New York Press.

Michaud, Michael A. G. 1974. "On Communicating with Aliens." *Foreign Service Journal* June: 10–14, 29–30.

———. 2000. *Contact with Alien Civilizations: Our Hopes and Fears about Encountering Extraterrestrials*. New York: Springer.

Morrison, Philip, John Billingham, and John Wolfe, eds. 1977. *The Search for Extraterrestrial Intelligence*, NASA Publication SP-419. Washington, DC: National Aeronautics and Space Administration.

Norris, Ray P. 2000. "How Old Is ET?" In *If SETI Succeeds: The Impact of High Information Contact*, ed. Allen Tough, 103–106. Bellevue, WA: Foundation For the Future.

O'Murchu, Diarmuid. 2004. *Quantum Theology: Spiritual Implications of the New Physics*. New York: Crossroad Publishing Company.

Palmer, Susan J. 2004. *Aliens Adored: Rael's UFO Religion*. New Brunswick, NJ: Rutgers University Press.

Partridge, Christopher, ed. 2003. *UFO Religions*. London: Routledge.

Peters, Ted. 2009. "Astrotheology and the ETI Myth." *Theology and Science* 7, no. 1: 3–29.

Ridpath, Ian. 1978. *Messages from the Stars: Communication with Extraterrestrial Life*. New York: Harper and Row.

Riner, Reed D. 2000. "The Contact Hypothesis: On the Impossibility of Sustained and Mutually Beneficial Contact between Aliens, and Two Proofs to the Contrary." In *If SETI Succeeds: The Impact of High Information Contact*, ed. Allen Tough, 127–137. Bellevue, WA: Foundation For the Future.

Ruse, Michael. 1985. "Is Rape Wrong on Andromeda? An Introduction to Extraterrestrial Evolution, Science, and Morality." In *Extraterrestrials: Science and Alien Intelligence*, ed. Edward Regis, 43–78. New York: Cambridge University Press.

Sagan, Carl. 1973. *Communication with Extraterrestrial Intelligence*. Cambridge, MA: MIT Press.

Sagan, Carl, Linda Salzman Sagan, and Frank Drake. 1972. "A Message from Earth." *Science* 175: 881–884.

Samuels, David. 2005. "Alien Tongues." In *ET Cultures: Anthropology in Outerspace*, ed. Debora Battaglia, 94–129. Durham, NC: Duke University Press.

Shostak, Seth. 2011. "Limits on Interstellar Messages." In *Communication with Extraterrestrial Intelligence*, ed. Douglas A. Vakoch, 357–369. Albany, NY: State University of New York Press.

Siemion, Andrew, et al. 2011. "Current and Nascent SETI Instruments in the Radio and Optical." In *Communication with Extraterrestrial Intelligence*, ed. Douglas A. Vakoch, 19–35. Albany, NY: State University of New York Press.

Shklovskiĭ, Iosif S., and Carl Sagan. 1966. *Intelligent Life in the Universe*. San Francisco: Holden-Day.

Snow, C. P. 1959. *The Two Cultures and the Scientific Revolution*. Cambridge: Cambridge University Press.

Tarter, Jill C. 2011. "Exoplanets, Extremophiles, and the Search for Extraterrestrial Intelligence." In *Communication with Extraterrestrial Intelligence*, ed. Douglas A. Vakoch, 3–18. Albany, NY: State University of New York Press.

Tough, Allen, ed. 2000. *If SETI Succeeds: The Impact of High Information Contact*. Bellevue, WA: Foundation for the Future.

Tumminia, Diane E. 2005. *When Prophecy Never Fails: Myth and Reality in a Flying Saucer Group*. New York: Oxford University Press.

———. 2007. *Alien Worlds: Social and Religious Dimensions of Extraterrestrial Contact*. Syracuse, NY: Syracuse University Press.

Vakoch, Douglas A. 2009. "Anthropological Contributions to the Search for Extraterrestrial Intelligence." In *Bioastronomy 2007: Molecules, Microbes, and Extraterrestrial Life*, eds. Karen J. Meech, et al., 421–427. San Francisco: Astronomical Society of the Pacific.

———. 2011a. "Asymmetry in Active SETI: A Case for Transmissions from Earth." *Acta Astronautica*, 68: 476–488.

———. 2011b. "Responsibility, Capability, and Active SETI: Policy, Law, Ethics, and Communication with Extraterrestrial Intelligence." *Acta Astronautica*, 68: 512–519.

Vakoch, Douglas A., and Yuh-Shiow Lee. 2000. "Reactions to Receipt of a Message from

Extraterrestrial Intelligence: A Cross-Cultural Empirical Study," *Acta Astronautica*, 46: 737–744.

Vakoch, Douglas A., chair. 2004. Session on Anthropology, Archaeology, and Interstellar Communication: Science and the Knowledge of Distant Worlds, Annual Meeting of the American Anthropological Association, Atlanta, GA.

———. 2005. Session on Historical Perspectives on Anthropology and the Search for Extraterrestrial Intelligence (SETI), Annual Meeting of the American Anthropological Association, Washington, DC.

———. 2006. Session on Culture, Anthropology, and the Search for Extraterrestrial Intelligence (SETI), Annual Meeting of the American Anthropological Association, San Jose, CA.

White, Frank. 1990. *The SETI Factor*. New York: Walker and Company.

Part I

DOES EXTRATERRESTRIAL LIFE EXIST?

Chapter 1

ARE WE ALONE?
Estimating the Prevalence of Extraterrestrial Intelligence

Seth Shostak

The idea that other thinking beings inhabit the cosmos is surely more popular today than ever before. "Aliens" (the routine shorthand for extraterrestrial sentients) infest books, movies, and television dramas. Recent polls of the American public show that more than half the citizenry believes they infest deep space as well (Pettinico 2011).

The proposal that other beings exist on other worlds dates back at least 2,400 years. To the classical Greeks, the cosmos consisted of everything they could see: the Sun, planets, and naked-eye stars. But the Greeks had the temerity to suggest that there might be other cosmoses, other complete universes.

What Motivates the Hypothesis That Intelligent Beings Might Be Widespread?

By definition, these other cosmoses could not be observed. However, this fact hardly inhibited speculation, as the Greeks were generally more disposed to theory than experiment. The postulated existence of other universes was a spin-off from the Greek atomic theory that Democritus and others were proposing around 400 BCE. According to these early savants, our world was created from whirling atoms that collided and coalesced after swarming in from infinity. But since the number of atoms itself was believed to be infinite (an assumption that modern scientists are unsure about adopting), and as only a finite number of atoms are necessary to construct our own cosmos, the Greeks concluded that an infinite number of parallel cosmoses also exist. Curiously, this virtually unprovable philosophical notion has its modern-day counterpart. Some theoreticians have speculated that our own universe is but one of an endless number of parallel, but non-interacting universes (Kaku 2005).

In an infinite number of cosmoses, anything that *can* happen, *has* happened—over and over. If physics does not preclude the creation of life, then we should expect it in abundance, at least if the universe is large, or "semi-infinite," enough. This is simply the fecund and unavoidable consequence of "infinite."

Aristotle offered an alternative to this expansive, multi-world scenario, insisting that our cosmos was unique. Earth—and its mantle of life—was deemed the nexus of creation, the focus of existence. Aristotle's view dominated thought in the western world for almost two millennia. Only when the discoveries of the Renaissance dethroned our spinning, planetary perch from its central position in the solar system did the possibility of other beings come back into vogue. Copernicus's *De revolutionibus* was published in 1543, barely half a century after Columbus's voyage to the new world, and it is difficult to say which event more radically altered European minds. With the proof of a Sun-centered universe, the Earth had become merely another heavenly body, and *a priori* no more privileged than Venus, Mars, or Jupiter. The question naturally arose: if Earth is merely one planet among many, why couldn't earthly life be only one biota among many?

In the four centuries since the invention of the telescope, our concept of the universe has expanded greatly: from a clutch of planets separated from one another by a few light-hours, to a stupefyingly vast omneity that is tens of billions of light-years across. Admittedly, this is not the infinite cosmoses envisioned by the Greeks, but the latter's hypothesis of inhabited worlds still seems reasonable in view of the universe's immense size. The visible galaxies are home to approximately 10^{22} stars, and many scientists find it difficult to believe that in such a mammoth expanse of celestial real estate, only Earth has produced both life and its most recent incarnation, technically sophisticated life.

This "argument from large numbers" is perhaps the strongest motivation for those who search for beings beyond our planet. It may be that planets only occasionally spawn biology, and possibly only a small percentage of these worlds witness the emergence of intelligence. But even small probabilities produce many successes when the number of trials is large.

In addition to this probabilistic argument, a number of recent discoveries in astronomy and biology give credence to the suggestion that worlds with life could be common, and that the evolution of thinking beings might be a frequent occurrence. We will discuss some of these discoveries below. But here, in the bottom line of this section, it is well to state the bottom line of our search for extraterrestrial biology to date: not a single, confirmed bit of life (including the fossilized remains of life) from another world has yet been found.

Habitats That Might Spawn Intelligence

It is the general (and often unstated) assumption of those who search for extraterrestrial beings that such life will have evolved on a planet (or a moon). This seemingly obvious postulate derives from the nature of earthly life's building blocks: the organic molecules that are the consequence of carbon's affinity for other atoms. These molecules are assembled into yet more complex structures: proteins, for example, or the DNA molecules that are the blueprints for organisms. At temperatures even modestly above what we consider comfortable, these molecules break apart. At the surface temperature of stars (5,500 C in the case of the Sun), few molecules of any kind can remain intact. At the gelid, bitter temperatures of interstellar space, there is another problem: chemical reactions are slow, and the sort of rapid metabolism we associate with intelligent creatures is impossible. Only planets, which have the possibility for relatively moderate temperatures, seem suitable candidates for the evolution of advanced life.

One might argue that these assumptions reflect a lack of imagination and are unduly anthropocentric. This may be true. The possibilities for sophisticated life in less familiar environments, such as the cold expanses of an interstellar cloud (Hoyle 1957) or the surface of a neutron star (Forward 1980), have been explored by technically adept authors, albeit in works of fiction. Nonetheless, the usual modus operandi of astrobiologists (scientists who busy themselves with the matter of extraterrestrial life) is to be conservative, to be unabashedly terracentric. Many things might be possible, and Nature is undoubtedly ingenious beyond our imaginings. But by assuming that complex life needs the type of environments found on Earth, we can be sure that our postulates have not exceeded the possible. In addition, using the single example of intelligent life that we know (us) provides guidance in what to search for, and where.

Liquid water seems to be a necessity for biology of any type. A fluid environment dissolves organic molecules, so that they can interact in the chemical dance of life as compounds enter and leave cells. Metabolic reactions within cells are also facilitated by an aqueous environment. While other liquids might serve these functions, water remains fluid over a wider range of temperatures than the alternatives that would likely be found on other worlds (ammonia, methane, and ethane). Most astrobiologists opine that liquid water is the *sine qua non* of life.

There are, even within the provincial confines of our own solar system, at least six worlds other than Earth where liquid water might be found: Venus, Mars, Europa, Callisto, Ganymede, and Enceladus (the last four are moons of the outer solar system). However, these nearby bodies of water, if they exist, do not bestraddle the surface of their worlds; rather, they are sequestered underground (Mars), in the atmosphere (Venus), or beneath thick crusts of hard ice (the moons of Jupiter and Saturn). While life may arise and even thrive in hidden aquifers (for example, microbes exist in rock kilometers deep on Earth [Pedersen 1997]), it seems reasonable to assume that complex, intelligent life would only develop on the surface. The surface, after all, is exposed to stellar radiation, an abundant source of energy. In the case of the Earth, this amounts to about 1,370 watts/m^2 above the atmosphere. By comparison, the flux of energy from Jupiter's interior is 250 times less (and this flux is still 1.7 times greater than the amount of energy the giant planet absorbs from sunlight [Hanel et al. 1981]). Without a source of radiant, stellar energy, which on our planet drives photosynthesis—which is the root of the food chain for nearly all terrestrial life—biological abundance and diversity would be less, and consequently the chance that intelligent beings would evolve would also be less.

Maintaining a surface liquid ocean requires the insulation of a reasonably thick atmosphere. Atmospheric gases are used for respiration by both planets and animals on our planet, and in the last two billion years, oxygen has become a plentiful component of Earth's air. Oxygen is highly reactive and has fostered the high metabolic rates we associate with agile, complex animal life. It may be a requirement for intelligent life on other worlds as well.

Liquid, surface oceans and atmospheres containing oxygen are only some of the possible requirements for the development of intelligent beings, but even these few necessities suggest that sentient beings would most likely be found on worlds that are not only Earth-size (which allows them to retain an atmosphere) but also Earth-like.

As of late July 2013, 925 planets had been found orbiting other, main-sequence, hydrogen-burning stars (Extrasolar Planets Encyclopaedia n.d.)

While the overwhelming majority of these are giant worlds, the preponderance of big planets is thought to be the inevitable consequence of the detection technique used for discovery. Most of these bodies are found by measuring the slight changes in the forward-and-back motions of their host stars, caused as both star and planet orbit their common center of mass.

Indeed, two lines of evidence suggest that small worlds, approximately the size of Earth, might be quite common. As the ability to find less weighty worlds has improved, the fraction of small planets found using the "wobble" technique has increased. Less massive worlds are now reliably inferred to outnumber the giant planets that have dominated the planet discoveries of the past. Furthermore, early results from NASA's Kepler telescope (Kepler Mission n.d.) have already included more than fifty candidate planets that might not only be similar to Earth in mass, but also situated in the "habitable zone" of their solar systems: orbital distances from their suns that would allow them to support liquid water (Borucki et al. 2011). Extrapolation of these first Kepler results suggests that the number of planets in the Milky Way that might be suitable worlds for life numbers in the hundreds of millions, at least.

While most researchers continue to bet on small planets as the most likely locales for intelligent beings, such terrestrial analogs are no longer the only game in town. As mentioned, there is growing evidence that several moons of the outer solar system, most notably Europa, sport hidden oceans. This has opened our eyes to an entirely new class of water-washed habitats in which life might develop. Note that these satellites are far beyond that happy orbital zone where water will neither permanently freeze nor endlessly boil—the so-called "habitable zone." These promising worlds are warmed not by starlight, but by the changing gravitational tug of their host planets during the course of their orbits, a process known as tidal heating.

Simply on the basis of energetics arguments, it is unlikely that very large, very complex life will evolve in the pitch-dark oceans of a moon-like Europa. But calculations suggest that far larger moons—the size of Earth—could be tidally heated at a hundred times the rate of the jovian moons (Sharf 2006). If moons this size exist around some of the large, extrasolar planets that astronomers continue to uncover, they might be sufficiently Earth-like at their surfaces to permit the emergence of a diverse biota, possibly including intelligent life.

Today, we know something that we could only guess at a decade ago: that planets around stars are commonplace. Indeed, it is reasonable to estimate that there are at least as many planets in the cosmos as there are stars. Within the next half-decade, we will learn if Earth-size planets are frequent or few, with most researchers guessing that the former will prove to be true. Additionally, the realization that moons can be habitable has increased the odds that there are numerous places—many billions in our galaxy alone—where life could have emerged and evolved.

The Evolution of Intelligence

Even if life is copiously abundant, it is not self-evident that intelligence frequently arises. For at least 3.5 billion years, Earth has been carpeted with life—but for all but the most recent sliver of time, that life was beastly and brainless. Intelligence is a very recent development, and some paleontologists would argue that it was also a very *unlikely* development.

Clearly, biology must reach a certain minimum level of complexity before sentient creatures can take the stage. Multicellular creatures (which only appeared on Earth after several billion years) are an obvious requirement. As we have noted, it is likely that an oxygen atmosphere—with its ability to supercharge metabolism—is also a necessity for intelligence. Competitive environments and social animals seem to be favored in the evolution of sentience. In addition to such positive circumstances, there is also the proviso that life, to evolve intelligence, must be spared routine, dramatic devastation from wild shifts in the poles, incoming comets and asteroids, nearby supernova explosions, or gamma-ray bursts.

The laundry list of the requirements for sophisticated life has led some to argue that Earth is extraordinarily special—that our world is exceptionally endowed with just the right set of circumstances to permit the evolution of the sort of complex animals we see stuffed and mounted in our museums (Ward and Brownlee 2000). However, this argument is countered by the fact that none of these circumstances is either unique to Earth or expected to be rare for the overwhelming majority of other worlds. Without doubt, most planets will be unsuitable for the evolution of intelligence, but in a galaxy in which habitable worlds could easily number in the billions, it requires heroic pessimism to argue that *only* Earth has the *mise en place* for cooking up thinking beings.

Environmental requirements aside, some paleontologists have argued against the frequent emergence of intelligence on the basis of evolution itself (Mayr 1985). The creation of new species is the result of happenstance and contingency: if the dinosaurs and their contemporaries had not been rudely taken off Earth's stage by an errant rock 65 million years ago, we would likely not be here now. *Homo sapiens* is the consequence of many forks in the evolutionary road, and if any one of the other forks had been taken, our species would not have appeared.

However, the question is not whether *Homo sapiens* is likely to arise, but whether functionally similar intelligence will do so. Evolution is, after all, unpredictable and shaped by the environmental circumstances of the moment. We should only expect intelligent beings elsewhere if we can convince ourselves that the evolution of intelligence is probable. As it is, there is a well-recognized mechanism, convergent evolution, that ensures that similar environments will produce similar adaptations, even in unrelated organisms. A simple example is the streamlining of ocean predators. The torpedo-shaped body plan of barracuda and dolphins is simply good engineering for a species whose survival depends on getting through the water quickly. These two species are only very distantly related; their similar silhouettes are the consequence of convergent evolution.

For some complex animals, particularly those that are highly social, there is clearly a benefit in being smarter than the fellow members of your species. Birds, octopuses, and simians are some of the creatures that display above-average intelligence. A study of dolphins and toothed whales from the last 50 million years shows that some (but not all) species have dramatically increased their intelligence, at least as gauged by the ratio of brain to body mass (Marino et al. 2004). The fact that several species have upped their cognitive abilities suggests that convergent evolution is at work, adapting to the niche market for high-IQ animals. While the mechanism for the development of human-level sentience is still unsure, this research suggests that intelligence may be a frequent evolutionary development, and hardly a fluke. However, proving the suggestion may not occur until, and unless, we find intelligence elsewhere in the Galaxy.

The Drake Equation

Our discussion so far has surveyed the manifold parameters, both astronomical and biological, that determine the prevalence (or paucity) of sentient species. These parameters were first summarized in 1961 by astronomer Frank Drake, who collected them into an equation that bears his name. This famous formulation was concocted as an agenda for a meeting to discuss how sensible it was to search for evidence of extraterrestrials many light-years distant.

The meeting was prompted by an experiment Drake had conducted only a year earlier in the same locale, the then-new National Radio Astronomy Observatory in Green Bank, West Virginia. For two weeks, Drake had commandeered an 85-foot diameter antenna at the observatory, alternately pointing it at the stars Tau Ceti and Epsilon Eridani. These are nearby cousins to our Sun, roughly a dozen light-years away and conceivably the stellar centerpieces to worlds populated by thinking beings. *Project Ozma*, as Drake christened this pioneering experiment, was an effort to eavesdrop on radio broadcasts either deliberately sent our way, or inadvertently leaking off an alien world.

Drake used his equation as an organizational tool. It is a simple product of seven terms yielding N, the number of galactic civilizations we could pick up with our telescopes. The equation, which can be found on trucks and T-shirts, is simple and linear:

$$N = R_* f_p n_e f_l f_i f_c L$$

The logic of the equation is straightforward. To calculate how many worlds in the Galaxy are outfitted with active transmitters (the N in the formula), break the equation into two parts: (a) how many societies per year cross the threshold into technical competence, constructing transmitters we could hear, and (b) how long do they stay on the air? This is analogous to estimating the number of students at Princeton University. It is the rate at which new students are admitted (freshmen per year), multiplied by the length of time they stay (four years).

The first six terms in the Drake Equation yield the rate at which technical societies arise, and the last (L) is the number of years their transmitters remain active. In 1961, only a handful of the terms could be reliably estimated, and only one of them—R_*—was actually known (and then, only approximately). As a consequence, estimates for N varied widely; optimists, such as Carl Sagan, thought there might be millions of detectable worlds churning through the Milky Way's stellar arms. Pessimists felt the number might be near zero (Dick 1996).

At the 1961 Green Bank meeting, attendees tried to estimate values for each of the terms of the formula (producing what is known in the trade as "educated guesses"). They were sanguine about the chances that life, including clever life, is abundant, although that is hardly surprising given their willing presence at the meeting. Very briefly, here is a listing of the factors in the equation, together with estimates of their values:

R_* is the number of stars born each year in the Galaxy that are suitable for hosting habitable planets. A crude estimate can be made by noting that the Galaxy is approximately 13 billion years old and contains several hundred billion stars. Consequently, R_* is roughly 10 stars per year. Refinements to this calculation take account of the fact that not all stars are suitable (in particular, giant stars burn out quickly, and therefore cannot sustain the long development we assume is necessary to foster intelligence) and that star formation in general has tapered off as the Galaxy has aged. Nonetheless, even our back-of-the-envelope appraisal of R_* is probably more accurate than estimates for any of the other terms in the equation.

f_p is the fraction of suitable stars that are girded by planets. The current detection rate for planet surveys runs between 5 and 10 percent, but the actual percentage of stars with orbiting worlds is certainly greater. Attendees at the 1961 meeting estimated f_p as about one-half; a guess without observational foundation. Today we can say that the guess was tolerably good. Recent results suggest that at least 70 to 80 percent of stars are accompanied by planets.

n_e is the average number of planets per solar system with the conditions necessary to give rise to intelligence. These conditions are often assumed to be similar to those of our own world. A recent analysis of Kepler data for red dwarf stars suggests that approximately 15 percent of these very numerous stars have a planet in the habitable zone.

f_l and f_i are, respectively, the fraction of suitable planets that actually develop life and the fraction of such bio-worlds where intelligent beings eventually emerge. Life on Earth is known to have flourished by, at the latest, 3.4 billion years ago (Allwood et al. 2006). This is a mere few hundred million years after the easing of the late, heavy bombardment—a rain of rocks that presumably would have been devastating to any biota. Put another way, life began on Earth practically as soon as it could, suggesting that the probability of its appearance was high. f_l was, and is, unknown, but if—in the coming two decades—we find evidence for life on any of the nearby worlds of our solar system, life whose genesis was independent of that life on Earth, we will know that it has a value near one. In contrast, f_i may prove far harder to establish.

f_c and L are the terms of the Drake Equation that dwell in the realms of the social sciences. The first, f_c, is the fraction of planets sporting sentient beings that develop a technological civilization, and L is the length of time that a civilization broadcasts into space (its "lifetime"). While it is not hard to imagine that, sooner or later, any intelligent species will discover science and its gratifying spin-off, technology, the durability of societies adept at exploiting the laws of nature, is thoroughly unknown. The invention of the atomic bomb followed the invention of radio by a half-century, which suggests that any culture able to reveal its presence will also be capable of self-destruction. But whether capability generally leads to consummation is unsure. Pundits frequently and solemnly intone that *Homo sapiens* is doomed to imminent annihilation by its own hand. Whether this is true (and is true for other societies as well) is a question for which we have no answer.

The Value of N and the Prognosis for Detecting a Signal

It should be evident to even a nonchalant reader that there is no "solution" to the Drake Equation. Knowing a few terms reasonably well does not help to constrain the value of N. As noted above, various researchers in the field have ventured guesses for N that range from zero (we are alone) to millions. Frank Drake himself has frequently cited N = 10,000 as a realistic estimate. If this is so, and if societies are spread uniformly through the Galaxy, then the distance to the nearest other civilization is approximately 1,000 light-years.

Since the local average density of stars is 0.004 per cubic light-year (Cox 2000), there are approximately 13 million stars within 1,000 light-years (assuming a local, galactic disk thickness of 1,000 light-years). Not all of these stars will be suitable for hosting the types of planets we think necessary for sentient life, but if half of them are, then SETI searches need to examine on the order of 6 million targets to have a reasonable chance of detecting an extraterrestrial society.

This simple calculation—admittedly based solely on Drake's middle-of-the-road estimate for N—is revealing for the following:

1. It is neither a surprise nor a discouragement that in the four decades since *Project Ozma*, SETI has failed to find a signal. The number of star systems examined with high sensitivity and over a wide swath of spectrum is less than a thousand (Tarter 1997). This is nearly four orders of magnitude fewer than required by our example.

2. Historically, the average speed of SETI searches (stars per year) has increased in lock-step with Moore's Law for the improvement of digital electronics (Moore 1965), namely, a doubling of computational capability per dollar every 18 months. New telescopes being built for SETI—in particular, the Allen Telescope Array—are designed to take advantage of this exponential improvement in digital speed. When operational, this instrument could examine 6 million star systems by the year 2030.

3. This example shows that a detection of a signal could quite conceivably happen in the lifetime of this generation (Shostak 2004). Ergo, and especially relevant to the present volume, a consideration of the social implications of learning that we are not alone in the Galaxy is a justified endeavor.

Although the Drake Equation was formulated a half century ago, it is still the basis for most discussion regarding the probability of finding extraterrestrial intelligence. There are, however, some obvious scenarios under which the formula might be an inaccurate gauge for the prevalence of technically advanced societies.

For example, the equation assumes that a civilization, once "on the air," remains in a transmitting and detectable state for L years, where L is the (average) technological lifetime. However, it could be that a society quickly adopts highly efficient transmitting schemes that reduce its "leakage" into space. For example, large television-type transmitters that belch megawatts into space are replaced with fiber optics or direct-broadcast satellite schemes. Carrier-based transmissions are supplanted by spread-spectrum modulation. Both of these technical developments are underway on Earth, even though radio is an invention scarcely more than a century old. Such a natural progression toward efficiency could mean that, despite being technologically "alive," advanced societies do not betray their presence unless they undertake deliberate signaling to the cosmos. This is an example of how the Drake Equation—at least in its conventional interpretation—may overestimate the number of detectable societies.

In other respects, the equation might be too cautious. It assumes that all transmitting cultures are still located in the solar system of their birth. This ignores the possibility of colonization of other star systems (difficult, but not forbidden by physics), or the possible deployment of transmitting facilities far from home. In addition, it does not deal with the development of synthetic intelligence—thinking machines that would not be constrained to watery worlds orbiting long-lasting stars. In short, it makes the assumption that "they" are much like "us."

Summary

In our brief review of the factors that govern both the existence and detectability of other sentient societies, we have uncovered several reasons why this subject—even aside from its great popularity with the public and the media—should be accorded attention by the social sciences. In particular, several of the crucial factors that govern the number of signaling societies are sociological (f_c and L). In the case of L, greater study should prove useful in charting our own path into the future, even without consideration of its benefit in estimating the chances for finding extraterrestrials. In addition, it is possible that the exponentially increasing capability of SETI searches will produce a confirmed signal detection within the next several decades.

It is generally acknowledged that proof of thinking beings beyond Earth would be one of the most profound discoveries ever. While scientists and engineers are working hard at making such a discovery possible, it is the social scientists who can tell us what will happen if they succeed.

Bibliography

Allwood, Abigail C., et al. 2006. "Stromatolite Reef from the Early Archaean Era of Australia." *Nature* 441: 714–718.

Borucki, William J., et al. 2011. "Characteristics of Planetary Candidates Observed by Kepler, II: Analysis of the First Four Months of Data." http://arxiv.org/abs/1102.0541v2. Accessed on 18 April 2011.

Cox, Arthur, ed. 2000. *Allen's Astrophysical Quantities*. New York: AIP Press, Springer-Verlag.

Dick, Steven J. 1996. *The Biological Universe*. Cambridge: Cambridge University Press.

The Extrasolar Planets Encyclopaedia. http://exoplanet.eu/. Accessed on 18 April 2011.

Forward, Robert L. 1980. *Dragon's Egg*. New York: Del Rey.

Hanel, R., et al. 1981. "Albedo, Internal Heat, and Energy Balance of Jupiter—Preliminary Results of the Voyager Infrared Investigation." *Journal of Geophysical Research* 86: 8705–8712.

Hoyle, Fred. 1957. *The Black Cloud*. New York: Harper and Brothers.

Kaku, Michio. 2005. *Parallel Worlds*. New York: Doubleday.

"Kepler Mission" (NASA). http://kepler.nasa.gov/. Accessed on 18 April 2011.

Marino, Lori, Daniel McShea, and Mark Uhen. 2004. "Origin and Evolution of Large Brains in Toothed Whales." *The Anatomical Record*, Part A, 281A, 1247–1255.

Mayr, Ernst. 1985. "The Probability of Extraterrestrial Intelligent Life." In *Extraterrestrials: Science and Alien Intelligence*, ed. Edward Regis, Jr. Cambridge: Cambridge University Press.

Moore, Gordon E. 1965. "Cramming More Components onto Integrated Circuits." *Electronics* 38, no. 8 (19 April). ftp://download.intel.com/research/silicon/moorespaper.pdf. Accessed on 18 April 2011.

Pedersen, K. 1997. "Microbial Life in Deep Granitic Rock." *FEMS Microbiology Reviews* 20: 399–414.

Pettinico, George. 2011. "American Attitudes about Life beyond Earth: Beliefs, Concerns, and the Role of Education and Religion in Shaping Public Perceptions." In *Civilizations Beyond Earth: Extraterrestrial Life and Society*, eds. Douglas A. Vakoch and Albert A. Harrison. New York: Berghahn Books.

Scharf, Caleb A. 2006. "The Potential for Tidally Heated Icy and Temperate Moons around Exoplanets." *Astrophysical Journal* 648: 1196–1205.

Shostak, G. Seth. 2004. "When Will We Detect the Extraterrestrials?" *Acta Astronautica* 55: 753–758.

Tarter, Jill. 1997. "Results from Project Phoenix: Looking Up from Down Under." In *Astronomical and Biochemical Origins and the Search for Life in the Universe*, eds. B. Comovici, S. Bowyer, and Dan Werthimer, 633–643. Bologna: Editrice Compositori.

Ward, Peter D., and Donald Brownlee. 2000. *Rare Earth*. New York: Copernicus.

Chapter 2

Encountering Alternative Intelligences
Cognitive Archaeology and SETI

Paul K. Wason

The study of human cognitive evolution has long been an important interest of archaeologists. My questions concern whether there are any insights gained from this experience that might be of value in the search for alternative intelligences from other planets, or whether archaeological study really is just about *uniquely human* cognition.

The answer is some of each, I think, and for this chapter I wish to approach the matter by examining the encounter between modern humans and Neanderthals. Of course, that encounter itself is known only by indirect inference and creative reconstruction. Evidence for actual encounters is indirect. There continues to be strong disagreement concerning what Neanderthal thinking was like. It is difficult to study intelligence even in living creatures. Everything is compounded by limited archaeological data. And it is only after all this that we can begin to ask about relevance to potential contact with extraterrestrial intelligence (ETI).

Why bother? Why not use instead a comparative study of the interactions among living animals of different cognitive abilities? Or why not study cultural contact experiences of contemporary and historical human groups?

First, I would certainly advocate doing all of the above. But for all its uncertainties, a Neanderthal–Cro-Magnon encounter offers something different from either alternative. They were far more different from each other than any differences to be found among living human groups. The latter are primarily cultural whereas Neanderthals and Cro-Magnon appear to have differed some in brain size and organization as well.[1] And in this case, both Neanderthals and Cro-Magnons are more cognitively complex than any living animal interactions we might study. This contact would therefore be more like any plausible interplanetary communication than encounters among different human cultures, or encounters between other animals.

There remains, of course, a range of opinion on just how different *Homo sapiens neanderthalensis* was from *Homo sapiens sapiens*. But I begin with a perspective somewhat like that of David Lewis-Williams, who said:

> If a couple of trained anthropologists who had worked with small-scale communities in various parts of the world were to be transported back in time to the Middle Paleolithic and given the opportunity to live with, study and learn the language of the Neanderthals, I believe they would be at a loss, marooned in an incomprehensible world. But were the same anthropologists allowed to move forward just a few thousand years to the early Upper Paleolithic, they would immediately set about learning the language, studying kinship systems … and even the religion of their hosts. In short, they would be "at home" every bit as much as they would be "at home" among human community anywhere in the world today. (2002: 40)

Similarly, Ian Tattersall argues that we are no longer justified in using modern humans as ethnographic analogues for trying to make sense of Neanderthals. "When we look at *Homo neanderthalensis*," he observes, "we are looking at a creature possessed of another sensibility entirely" (1995: 153). Altogether, we might well expect any encounter between Neanderthals and Cro-Magnons to have been a difficult and ineffective affair, fraught with misunderstanding.

Models of Cognitive Evolution:
Better Understanding the Encounter

There are many ways of studying intelligence and cognition generally, and several of these have been put to good use in the study of human cognitive evolution. Particularly useful, I think, have been Merlin Donald's four stages of development and analyses making use of Jean Piaget's model of intellectual development in human children, both of which, though rich and complex, are clear and easily summarized.

Merlin Donald (1991) proposes a four-stage cognitive development in human evolution, each stage separated by a substantial transition period. *Episodic culture*, characteristic of primate cognition, represented improved self-awareness and event-sensitivity. *Mimetic culture* was that characteristic of *Homo erectus*, but presumably also Neanderthals, and involved non-verbal action modeling, a true revolution in skill, gesture (including vocal), non-verbal communication, and shared attention. He calls this phase mimetic, as you might easily guess, because of the ability to mime or imitate and reenact events. The next phase, *linguistic or mythic culture*, was characteristic of early *Homo sapiens*, and encompasses the Upper Paleolithic, Mesolithic, and Neolithic. What was new at this time in Donald's model is high-speed phonology, oral language, and many other things that go with it. The final phase (so far) is *theoretic culture* utilizing external symbolic storage (Donald 1998: 14; Renfrew 1998: 2).

A number of detailed studies have attempted to organize human cognitive evolution on the basis of Piaget's models of cognitive development in modern children. This has obvious attractions, since it is a sensible, widely accepted model of cognitive growth and also because it is very concrete and fairly easily operationalized for use with data like that found in archaeological contexts. To take one interesting example, James Russell argues, based on the view that the artistic accomplishments of the Upper Paleolithic represent our planet's first symbolic expressions, that this period "represents the first attainment of a level of cognitive development equivalent to that of the human child at the transition between Piaget's sensorimotor and preoperational stages" (in Gibson and Mellars 1996: 5). This suggests that an encounter with a Neanderthal would be something more difficult than the meeting of minds of a modern adult human with his 18-month-old child. Although at first rather unnerving, especially given the sturdy build of an adult Neanderthal compared to most toddlers, we are, of course, speaking of intellectual skill, not emotional maturity.

I should add that other Piaget-informed studies have come up with somewhat different results. Kathleen Gibson suggested that the creation of handaxes originally devised long before Neanderthal times, "exhibited cognitive levels equivalent to Piaget's third stage, that of concrete operations, which emerges at about seven to eight years of age" (Gibson and Mellars 1996: 5; see Gibson 1985). This is no small difference. It has mainly to do with whether one emphasizes (as Russell did) art as the primary evidence of symbolic capacity or whether one can see more advanced abilities in the symmetry and spatial proportions of stone tools.[2]

Approaches of this kind (like any other approach I know of so far) are very helpful but also face some problems. One difficulty of attempting to fit prehistoric cognitive evolution into categories developed from a study of individual development of young human children is that in modern humans these abilities develop in a coordinated and largely predictable way, while in the course of human evolution they may well have developed separately and at different times. An issue that cuts rather more deeply is that in any case the connection, if there is one, between the cognitive development of the individual child and the evolution of species-wide cognition is one of analogy only. That is, there is no demonstrable sense in which, in the nineteenth-century phrase, "ontogeny recapitulates phylogeny." Nevertheless it is a popular idea in human evolution that a study of child development can offer suggestions concerning evolution even though the two are not really connected. And we haven't even considered the fact, mentioned above, that studies using a Piagetan analogy seem to yield wildly differing conclusions.

But without pretending that Piagetan models are necessarily a dead end, I nevertheless prefer to make use of the model developed by Steven Mithen. Drawing on the multiple intelligence theory of Howard Gardner (1983), on primate studies (e.g., Cheney and Seyfarth's 1990 study), and perhaps especially evolutionary psychology (Barkow et al. 1992; Buss 2004), Mithen makes use of a modular view of the human mind in his extensive studies of the mind's prehistory (1996: 219).

The idea in general is very helpful—to the extent that natural selection helped shape the mind[3] one would expect mental abilities to be related to problems to solve. Sometimes fairly specific mental operations or modules are discussed such as the "agency detection device" that figures so importantly in Justin Barrett's cognitive model of religion (Barrett 2004). But the three major "domains" of intelligence that Mithen emphasizes in his article on the Neanderthals—social intelligence, technical intelligence, and natural history intelligence—break things down more usefully, I think, at least given the kinds of evidence we have to work with.[4]

Social intelligence, being that element needed for interacting with conspecifics, is no doubt the most important domain of intelligence for social primates generally and humans specifically. Technical intelligence concerns sensorimotor skills, particularly, given Neanderthal evidence, in the making of stone tools, and natural history intelligence involves knowledge and ability to think about the natural environment, especially as needed to adapt and survive.

Mithen argues that among the Neanderthals all three of these domains of intelligence were well developed. Even monkeys are known to show high levels of social intelligence, and the group living of Neanderthals surely shows the same. Mithen also makes the case that technical intelligence was well developed, based on the complexity of the manufacturing process involved in making handaxes which exhibit an imposed form and symmetry—"the goal of the knapper making a handaxe is not to simply obtain a sharp cutting edge but to extricate an integral shape from a nodule, independent from the starting shape of the nodule" (Mithen 1996a: 221). His main argument that natural history intelligence was also well developed (for example, understanding the spatial and temporal distribution of suitable food sources) is based on their success in living in severe environments with limited technology. Hand axes may have involved planned sequences of actions and an aesthetic sense of some kind but Neanderthals didn't make a great variety of specialized tools.

The modern human mind is also modular, and this, evolutionary psychologists will argue, not only helps explain what we are capable of doing but what we find difficult. Studies have indicated, for example, that we have well-developed social intelligences: "When problems which share the same logical structure are framed in social terms rather than with reference to abstract entities, people appear to solve them with much greater ease" (Mithen 1996: 219; referring to a study by Cosmides).

Mithen argues there really is a dramatic cognitive difference between fully modern humans and any previous hominid, this being an increased accessibility between cognitive domains and the consequent creation of a generalized intelligence on top of (so to speak), not instead of, social intelligence and other domains. Presumably it is not an all-or-nothing matter, but with much greater accessibility of one domain to another, and far-stronger generalized intelligence, modern humans are capable of thinking thoughts a Neanderthal could never think no matter how much more advanced they had become in each domain.

According to this model, the Neanderthals could make fine quality tools and they also knew a great deal about the natural environment, but it was difficult for them to think about using technology to solve problems raised by their natural history intelligence. This would account for the fact that they could make tools like handaxes with skill, but they didn't think to make many new kinds of tools. The model of a modular mind has its problems like any other approach, but it does help solve problems like this where we seem to be getting contradictory information about Neanderthal intelligence (high skill in what they make but lack of creativity and variety).

They would also have found it difficult to think creatively about using tools to address social problems. We are quite different. It seems to come natural even for teenagers to think of technological solutions to social problems, such as males choosing automobiles as a means of enhancing their ability to attract the attention of females. One can only guess how Neanderthals approached such matters, but this model suggests they would have been totally mystified by our way of life—and that as they got used to it, they might well have found it easier to learn how an automobile works mechanically than how it works in the world of young men and young women.

Cognitive Accessibility and the Neanderthal–Cro-Magnon Encounter

How can all this help us understand the encounter of these different minds, the Neanderthal and the Cro-Magnon? And can anything we learn in this way possibly be of interest in the search for extraterrestrial intelligence? I will review several example areas of culture in which archaeologists have noted important differences between Neanderthals (as represented by the Middle Paleolithic Mousterian of Europe—and, very importantly, the Chatelperronian sites) and modern humans of the Upper Paleolithic (UP). For each I ask how this might relate to Mithen's general distinction between Neanderthal and modern human minds and also how this might affect an encounter between these two types of hominids.

But first, a little background and one important caveat: Modern human behaviors are known from at least 70,000 years ago at places like Blombos Cave in South Africa. And anatomically modern humans date from much longer ago—we are reaching back closer and closer to 200,000 years ago. Modern humans were found in the Near East perhaps 100,000 years ago and may have overlapped with Neanderthals for some time. It is likely that Neanderthals and *Homo sapiens* shared the Levant for some 60,000 years, though evidence of their ever living side by side is not clear.[5] Upper Paleolithic industries came to the area about 45kya (45,000 years ago) and Neanderthals were gone by 40kya (if we assume Amud is the most recent Neanderthal date in the region). Modern humans did not enter Europe until about 40,000 years ago (and the first ones to come brought UP, specifically Aurignatian industries with them) but because Neanderthals did not die out there until about 30,000 or 32,000 years ago, there was considerable time for overlap. The database for Europe is richer, consisting of dozens of sites; it is not just Eurocentrism that leads archaeologists to rely more on this data.

As for the caveat, you will notice I have stayed away from the contentious issue of language. I haven't studied the massive literature on this, and will only say that what seem like good arguments are being put forth both for the idea that language developed long before this stage, on the one hand, and that true language awaited (and maybe helped cause) the creative explosion found among modern humans some 40,000 years ago. It is an immensely important question, ultimately, but for present purposes it is worth pointing out that there is considerable evidence for cognitive differences between Neanderthals and modern humans without worrying about language. Mithen believes language developed some time before the Neanderthals and that it is one of the major (but separate) domains of intelligence. Some additional differences I don't have space to discuss include the fact that social groups were never large—a dozen adults roughly. It appears that they sometimes provided support for some disadvantaged individuals (not unknown of course among other social animals like elephants). It is also the case, and probably very important too, that the people of the Upper Paleolithic made much more efficient use of fire than the Neanderthals did—including animal fat lamps with wicks and kilns for firing clay by 26kya.

Living areas

Mousterian sites are generally simple, without the structured use of space typical of behaviorally modern humans. Traces of structures are usually nonexistent (Le Lazaret and Combe Grenal perhaps being exceptions). Traces of "structure" or organization of sites is also limited. Lewis Binford has argued that the lack of organization (such as activity areas) in Mousterian sites suggests foraging rather than true hunting and gathering, by beings not used to (or capable of) forward planning as we are.[6] How this kind of conclusion squares with the steps involved in making handaxes, I am not sure. In contrast, at Upper Paleolithic sites we see substantial living structures, including cobble pavements and food storage (Tattersall 1995: 189). There is also organization in the sense of often clearly discernable activity areas. UP sites also varied greatly in size, implying different kinds of social groups.

Mithen observes that typically among contemporary humans the use of space is social. Neanderthals might well have carried out a range of activities in their living areas, but these are not well defined, spatially. They certainly used fire, for example, but hearths are extremely rare. This might, but does not necessarily mean that Neanderthals had radically different social interactions as Binford had suggested. Rather they might have had similar social interactions, but the lack of special organization instead would be "a further reflection of a domain-specific intelligence in which thought about social interaction was only marginally integrated with thought about the use of space [an important and well-developed element of natural history intelligence]" (Mithen 1996: 225).

Neanderthals would have difficulty interpreting the lives of modern humans. If a modern human visited a Neanderthal home or camp it might seem strangely chaotic with a mix of things that seem superficially logical (certain social interactions, for example) along with oddities, like building a fire where someone had slept the previous evening. What of a Neanderthal visiting a modern human living place? My guess is that a Neanderthal would be even more at a loss to interpret their surroundings, but wouldn't realize it. That is, he or she perhaps wouldn't recognize the "real" special order of the site, and if asked to build a fire would be completely surprised and mystified when later berated by these strange gracile humans for having built it in someone's bed.

Here's another way of expressing the difference I am trying to get at. To mention Lewis Binford again, he is surely one of the most creative of *Homo sapiens* now living. We may wonder how he ever thought of this idea or that, or even wish we had thought of it ourselves. But we do understand his creative suggestions when we hear them. My guess is that the Neanderthals would be amazed at some of the things modern humans did but wouldn't always know what to make of it (the Chatelperronian being a likely exception as I note in a moment).

Tool traditions

Neanderthals made their tools well, generally, but couldn't begin to compare with the skill and equipment of Upper Paleolithic hunters. The latter used spear throwers, barbed harpoons, and later bows and arrows and a sophisticated knowledge of the environment. Another element is that *Neanderthals used local materials.* There is little evidence for exchanges over long distances (though this is true of human sites during the same time periods). Non-local stone was never from more than a few miles away. They might well have been isolated. Upper Paleolithic toolmakers used cores and techniques that yielded far more tools per pound of material. They were much pickier as well about the kind of stone used.

Mousterian tools have proven difficult to classify. UP tools are much easier to categorize and they also fit into many more categories, suggesting that the final form of each specialized type of tool existed as a specific image in the minds of the UP toolmakers. By contrast, Middle Paleolithic craftsmen may simply have been using tested techniques to produce a particular attribute, such as a point or a broad scraping surface.

While some Neanderthals probably used their stone tools to work wood, bone and antler were hardly ever used and never for specialized implements. But in the UP, bone, antler, and ivory were widely carved and polished into a wide range of useful and decorative forms. One of the greatest differences is the enormous variation among UP industries. While Mousterian cultures were not as static as sometimes portrayed, in the UP, variety expands dramatically.

Mithen had argued that Neanderthals must have had a very extensive knowledge of the environment ("natural history intelligence"). It is also the case that tools they used were sometimes of high quality. Mithen's view that their thinking represented limited accessibility among domains could be a way of explaining this—they had the motor and other skills needed to make tools, and they had a good knowledge of the natural environment, but the idea of creating new tools as a way of working with the environment did not come easily. This required engaging technological intelligence to solve problems raised by natural history intelligence. It was a struggle to think through the idea, however obvious it is for us, of making a new kind of tool for solving a food-getting problem.

Variation among Mousterian tools appears to us random and irrational, and no less an archaeologist than François Bordes is said to have concluded "they made beautiful tools stupidly." Well, maybe. I'm not here to defend Neanderthal applications to the Mensa society. But more likely there was a kind of logic to it that we simply don't (and perhaps can't) understand. Very likely there was a "process" to tool making, even a philosophy to Neanderthal technological intelligence that was quite different from what we imagine would be going through a flintknapper's mind. Even though the products sometimes have a ring of familiarity, we would be mistaken to assume we understand the deeper thinking behind it.

Symbolic behavior

Neanderthals made limited use of symbolism. The evidence for symbolic behavior is not so good as we once thought. The evidence for bear cults (as at Drachenloch and Regourdou), for example, have not withstood close study. Similarly, the other accounts of ritual (beheading and brain eating as suggested for Monte Circeo) have been put into serious doubt. Yet at least sometimes, *they did bury their dead*, which is probably the only evidence that Neanderthals engaged in ritual activity (which of course is an important form of symbolic behavior). They were the first archaic humans known to do even this, so this is not a trivial matter.

The big difference with Upper Paleolithic peoples is not that they uniquely dug graves, but in the number and range of items they included

in the grave along with the body.[7] Things found in graves with Neanderthals were mostly everyday objects (random tools and animal bones)
that could well have fallen unintentionally into the fill.[8] But in contrast, burial became a regular cultural feature for UP people, often elaborate and thus suggesting interment was accompanied by ceremony and
ritual.

It is unlikely to have the same symbolic significance that it does for us.
It may have been no more than a matter of getting rid of unpleasant dead
bodies, or it might have had a significance for them quite different from
any view of the world we are familiar with. For most modern humans,
the ritual involved in burial engages social factors as well as cosmologi-
cal ideas and technological elements. It may be that these elements fit
together differently for Neanderthals, if they fit together well at all. From
the multiple domain approach to intelligence we might expect Neanderthals to seriously mourn the loss of a fellow member of the society but not
elaborate technological ways of expressing it.

As one more example of evidences for symbolizing consider: *Examples of
cut marks on bone are mostly difficult to show as anything but random.* However, there are a few examples of perforated bone and teeth from Mousterian sites, and a limestone block with pecked circular depressions was
found at La Ferrassie. The site of Quneitia in the Golan Heights yielded
a plaque with engraving which seems to be deliberate. This is a Mousterian site, but the association of Neanderthals with Mousterian in the
Near Eastern sites is not as clear. The contrast with the UP is dramatic,
of course.

Aesthetic sensibility. Mousterian sites have yielded invertebrate shells,
fossilized mollusks, and several kinds of pigments that suggest to some
scholars that they engaged in symbolic behavior, perhaps painting. This
is possible, but questionable. What does seem clear, though, is that Neanderthals possessed some kind of aesthetic sensibility. This was already
noted for tools; many hand axes exhibit bifacial symmetry, which could
well suggest an aesthetic sense also.

Upper Paleolithic art is very different. It includes, indeed, bone flutes and
whistles. Some of this was in the time period of overlap with Neanderthals, though of course the highly developed work of the Magdalenian
(18–10kya) was much later (Lascaux, Font de Gaume, Altamira, Rouf-
finac). Compared to any of their predecessors, the people of the Upper
Paleolithic were complex, inventive, and creative with a subtle understanding of the world around them.

While there is virtually no accepted evidence that Neanderthals engaged in artistic activity, painting, music, or whatever else, it does seem that they possessed an aesthetic sensibility. This doesn't make much sense to us—well, to me, anyway—and seems to be another way in which Neanderthal and Cro-Magnon thinking would have led to misunderstandings of each other.

Evidence of contact and imitation?

The Châtelperronian of Western France is a short-lived industry (ca. 36–32kya) of the Neanderthals,[9] following the arrival of Upper Paleolithic folk. It likely resulted from the contact, that is, it evolved from the Mousterian industry under the inspiration of contact with and imitation of modern humans..This industry was characterized by a high proportion of blades struck from cylindrical cores. At the French sites of Arcy-sur-Cure, a carved bone pendant, pierced animal teeth, and probably the foundation of a hut all were found in the Chatelperronian layer. Such things were virtually absent from the Mousterian but completely typical for Upper Paleolithic cultures. Interaction is further suggested by the fact that a few sites are interlayered with Aurignacian (earliest UP in the area), which represents fully modern humans. While some sites have, reasonably enough, been questioned, Brad Gravina and Paul Mellars recently re-studied finds from the 1950s excavations of Grotte de Fées and found somewhat more conclusive evidence of interstratification—Mousterian, followed by Chatelperonnian (40kya), followed by an Aurignatian layer (39–36kya), and then another Chatelperronian occupation (36kya)

How would these two cognitively divergent populations have communicated? Mousterians learned well by imitation (as indicated by their consistent craftsmanship). Tattersall says "Perhaps it is not too far fetched to imagine that only the cleverest Neanderthals could have managed such contacts successfully and passed their new found knowledge on to others" (1995: 201–202).

Contact was not terribly prolonged (short-term replacement of Mousterian by UP was very consistent), but the very existence of the Chatelperronian indicates that not all contact was destructive. Yet these sites are few (a handful of them over a four thousand–year period) compared to the more numerous preceding Mousterian. Populations declined any way you look at it.

In addition, the Neanderthals understood enough of what the modern humans were doing to copy some of it. I can't help thinking that they had a different idea of what they were doing in making personal adornment than the Cro-Magnon people they imitated, and that similarities are superficial. Yet, it does indicate some, one might say positive, impact of the contact and communication, that whatever the extent of mutual incomprehension, there really was some kind of meeting of the minds.

Some Points of Relevance for the Search for Extraterrestrials

Our meetings with fellow humans are fraught with confusion at many levels. Mutual incomprehension is common when cultures meet. The fact that men and women so regularly speak past each other may be the source of endless jokes but it is no less real for that. And at an individual level most people have felt completely misunderstood at one time or another even by those closest to them.

But the meeting of Neanderthals with modern humans would be of a different kind. We would not just experience all the same confusions, only more so. In addition, it is very likely that it would have been impossible to get over the initial confusions. With enough study anthropologists, and even open-minded and thoughtful traders or missionaries, can figure out what is going on and learn to predict how those of another culture will react and what they will do.

I expect that neither Neanderthals nor early modern humans would ever be able to sort out their differences. It is not that Neanderthals are, say, unused to organizing their camps with defined hearths, working and sleeping areas, and need only be introduced to this enlightened concept. Much more likely, they wouldn't be able to recognize what is happening even when seeing it.

All of this reminds us of a point we probably agree with anyway, that there is no simple, linear scale of intelligence on which Neanderthals sit, further toward the stupid end, and we scholars also sit, just further toward the other end. Even within our own species there are different kinds of intelligence and if we compare ourselves with fellow primates and extinct hominids like Neanderthals this becomes even more dramatic.

What, then, of extraterrestrial intelligence? It seems fair to assume that if closely related minds, having evolved together through most of their history and only recently branched, can be so different as that of the Neanderthal and the Cro-Magnon, an encounter between a human and an ETI would almost certainly be more difficult. We can expect there to be large areas of incomprehension, relieved by small elements that seem to make sense. And we can expect that many of these seeming points of contact and real understanding—like a finished Mousterian hand axe—unfortunately, would turn out to be superficial similarities masking deeper differences.

When discussing tools I suggested that the Neanderthals may have a more-developed technological intelligence than Bordes gave them credit for, but this does not mean we know what's going on. Indeed, the fact that some of their tools are so familiar, sensible, well made, and aesthetically pleasing is surely a point of cognitive connection, but at the same time there are hints that it is a "false friend," as my language teacher used to say—it lulls us into thinking we know what is going on when we really very much do not. That would become clear soon enough when we try to predict behaviors, ideas, or conclusions and turn out to be wrong. When we use our mental capacity for putting ourselves in the place of another mind, we will get in trouble.

But Neanderthals and Cro-Magnons may well have had "productive" interactions even if from my hypothetical outsider's view, there almost certainly was more confusion than communication. A Cro-Magnon might never have imagined that Neanderthals had a philosophy of tool making, and certainly wouldn't have understood that philosophy, but they would have recognized these hand axes as tools, the products of purposive agency and not of rocks getting chipped as they rolled down a hillside.

Similarly, communication with extraterrestrials can't be anything but immensely difficult and fraught with misunderstanding, but we are likely to be able to recognize such communications when we see them as the products of purposeful, intentional agents. And that in itself would be something quite remarkable.

In a previous paper I argued that while human intelligence would be unique, due if nothing else to our unique evolutionary history on one real planet and not another one, there may well be points of contact with otherwise very different beings because there are certain elements common to intelligence such as purpose-seeking and -making behavior, agency, meaning, and no doubt many others (Wason forthcoming).

There is reason to believe Neanderthals had different things going through their minds when they set out to make a hand axe than modern humans did when making their tools, but this activity still drew on purpose—different purposes, goals, motivations, and so on, but purposive behavior nonetheless. Humans can recognize those elements of intelligence and do not need to know what a Neanderthal or an ETI thought their purposes were to realize that their results—stone tools or encoded electromagnetic waves—are purposeful, and that we are communicating with an intelligent agent.

In addition, carefully thinking such things through is of no small value. Like Lewis-Williams I am inclined to believe that Neanderthals were, cognitively, very different from modern humans, but I do disagree with him on one point. If a trained anthropologist, especially one familiar with cognitive studies, were to visit a Neanderthal site, I think she could make very good progress in figuring out what is going on. It is true that it might be a little more like ethology than ethnography, but the study of animal behavior is one that we have made great progress on as well, for all its difficulty.

I am not certain Steven Mithen or I am right in all this. But to the extent that we are, I find it interesting that the breakthrough came through advances in understanding how our own minds work. Could it be also that one of the best ways of preparing for interstellar communication with other intelligences would be to engage in more study of how human intelligence works?

The more we know about our own cognition, and about the range of intelligences found among life on Earth, the more chance we would have of figuring out what kind of intelligence we are meeting, should a message cross our paths. Neanderthal tool kits (especially the fact that they have so few tools, yet those are mostly well made) make more sense to us on the assumption of a modular mind, without having found any new archaeological sites. Methodologically, then, theoretical models of intelligence can be very important in attempts to make sense of empirical data. And as mentioned, the actual content of a message is not the only thing we would want to know about it. Experience with figuring out Neanderthal cognition, as well as more recent finds, suggests that archaeology is much better at these "subtext" issues than in reading the symbolism of the ancients.

There have been some good works of fiction in anthropology—I think especially of Bjorn Kurten's *Dance of the Tiger*, or Elizabeth Marshall Thomas's *The Animal Wife*—in which scholars have taken up the creative task of imagining other worlds and possibilities concerning Neanderthals. There is also a good deal of additional prehistoric fiction that is interesting, sometimes quite valuable, and a great deal of fun, but not written by anthropologists or paleontologists. We need all of this to help us consider what is possible "out there" in the deep past and not be stuck too closely to contemporary ethnographic models.

And Vice Versa

What are some ways in which the SETI project can, in turn, be an aid to archaeology? Kathleen Gibson and Paul Mellars argue (1996) that a productive approach to modeling the evolution of the human mind engages a wide range of cognitive disciplines. While the purpose of this chapter is to see how anthropology and archaeology might help the search for extraterrestrial intelligence, surely this is reciprocal.

Scholars studying the possibility of communication beyond our solar system have had to content themselves with imagining and working through scenarios and possibilities. What are the limits of life? That is, what could beings on another planet *possibly* be like? Or better yet, what could they not possibly be like? What can we expect about their similarity to or difference from ourselves?

Can these attempts to tease out the limits of possibility be of any help to archaeologists? Or more mundanely, couldn't science fiction about space and time be as valuable as anthropological fiction in working out plausible scenarios? It is always difficult to think the impossible but we must—we must realize that in the past there were ways of thinking for which we do not have contemporary ethnographic analogy, and it may be that archaeologists studying SETI research could help us recognize something from the past that we had not imagined before.

Notes

1. Modern humans and Neanderthals were more cognitively divergent than any other known case of hominid contact except perhaps modern humans and *Homo floresiensis*.
2. One reviewer of this chapter objected to my including this line of argument on grounds that it was a major legitimation for colonialism. This objection founders on the fact that colonialism was in full swing long before such arguments were put forward. Even if the reviewer were correct about the historical associations, the fact that an idea can be used for ill does not tell us much about whether it is true or useful for other purposes. Charles Darwin's idea of natural selection has been used to justify great evils, but many of us think it is true and helpful nonetheless. To be consistent, the reviewer would have to reject natural selection as well, and this I think would be a great loss. So I must maintain that my own concerns about the analogical nature of the connection are far more important.
3. It is not necessarily the case that all of human cognitive development was directly adaptive. For example, the mind could be, in large part, a "spandrel"—not directly selected for but a by-product of other elements that were. Or perhaps culture was a major element—certainly culture took on a major iterative role at some point.
4. Linguistic intelligence is another major domain discussed in his book. Of immense importance for any full understanding of human cognitive evolution, it raises too many complicated issues for present purposes.
5. Recent studies of the Neanderthal genome (Burbano et al. 2010, Green et al. 2010) offer strong evidence for interbreeding with *Homo sapiens*, so there was some contact, but the nature of cultural interaction remains unclear.
6. Kebara is another exception, with hearths and activity areas, but this was also rather unusual in being a Mousterian site with modern human skeletal remains.
7. What were these burials like? There are a small number of cases of the de-fleshing of bones, which could mean secondary burial, a significantly more complex set of practices than simple interment. The famous Shanidar "flower people" burials have,

of course, been questioned. But while there may be alternate ways the pollen could have gotten there besides intentional interment with flowers, the case *against* complex ritual here isn't strong.

8. Ian Tattersall (1995: 170) says the best evidence for grave goods comes from the Mousterian graves at Qafzeh and Skhul, but these are modern human burials. Nothing is simple I guess.

9. At Saint-Cesaire a burial clearly identifies the Chatelperronian toolmakers as Neanderthals.

Bibliography

Barkow, Jerome H., Leda Cosmides, and John Tooby, eds. 1992. *The Adapted Mind: Evolutionary Psychology and the Generation of Culture*. New York: Oxford University Press.

Barrett, Justin L. 2004. *Why Would Anyone Believe in God*. Walnut Creek, CA: Altamira Press.

Burbano, Hernán A., et al. 2010. "Targeted Investigation of the Neandertal Genome by Array-Based Sequence Capture." *Science* 328: 723–725.

Buss, David M. 2004. *Evolutionary Psychology: The New Science of the Mind*. Boston: Pearson Education, Inc.

Cheney, Dorothy L., and Robert M. Seyforth. 1990. *How Monkeys See the World: Inside the Mind of Another Species*. Chicago: University of Chicago Press.

Donald, Merlin. 1991. *Origins of the Modern Mind: Three Stages in the Evolution of Culture and Cognition*. Cambridge: Harvard University Press.

———. 1998. "Hominid Enculturation and Cognitive Evolution." In *Cognition and Material Culture: The Archaeology of Symbolic Storage*, ed. Colin Renfew and Chris Scarre, 1–6. Cambridge: McDonald Institute for Archaeological Research.

Gardner, Howard. 1983. *Frames of Mind: The Theory of Multiple Intelligences*. New York: Basic Books.

Gibson, Kathleen R. 1985. "Has the Evolution of Intelligence Stagnated since Neanderthal Man?" In *Evolution and Developmental Psychology*, ed. G. Butterworth, J. Rutkowska, and M. Scaife, 102–114. Brighton, England: Harvester Press.

Gibson, Kathleen, and Paul Mellars. 1996. "Introduction: Approaches to Modelling Early Human Minds." In *Modelling the Early Human Mind*, ed. Paul Mellars and Kathleen Gibson, 1–8. Cambridge: McDonald Institute for Archaeological Research.

Green, Richard E., et al. 2010. "A Draft Sequence of the Neandertal Genome." *Science* 328: 710–722.

Klein, Richard G., and Blake Edgar. 2002. *The Dawn of Human Culture: A Bold New Theory on What Sparked the "Big Bang" of Human Consciousness*. New York: John Wiley & Sons, Inc.

Lewis-Williams, David. 2002. *The Mind in the Cave: Consciousness and the Origins of Art*. London: Thames and Hudson, Ltd.

Mellars, Paul. 1996. *The Neanderthal Legacy: An Archaeological Perspective from Western Europe*. Princeton, NJ: Princeton University Press.

Mellars, Paul, and Kathleen Gibson. 1996. *Modelling the Early Human Mind*. Cambridge: McDonald Institute for Archaeological Research.

Mithen, Steven J. 1996a. *The Prehistory of the Mind: A Search for the Origins of Art, Religion and Science*. London: Thames and Hudson.

———. 1996b. "Domain-Specific Intelligence and the Neanderthal Mind." In *Modelling the Early Human Mind*, ed. Paul Mellars and Kathleen Gibson, 217–229. Cambridge: McDonald Institute for Archaeological Research.

———. 2005. *The Singing Neanderthals: The Origins of Music, Language, Mind and Body*. London: Weidenfield & Nicolson.

Renfrew, Colin. 1998. "Mind and Matter: Cognitive Archaeology and External Symbolic Storage." In *Cognition and Material Culture: The Archaeology of Symbolic Storage*, eds. Colin Renfrew and Chris Scarre, 1–6. Cambridge: McDonald Institute for Archaeological Research.

Russell, James. 1996. "Development and Evolution of the Symbolic Function: The Role of Working Memory." In *Modelling the Early Human Mind*, eds. Paul Mellars and Kathleen Gibson, 159–170. Cambridge, McDonald Institute for Archaeological Research.

Sever, Megan. 2005. "Neanderthal Neighbors." *Geotimes* November. http://www.geotimes.org/nov05/NN_neanderthalneighbors.html. Accessed on 18 April 2011.

Tattersall, Ian. 1995. *The Last Neanderthal: The Rise, Success, and Mysterious Extinction of Our Closest Human Relatives*. New York: Macmillan

Trinkaus, Erik, and Pat Shipman. 1993. *The Neanderthals: Changing the Image of Mankind*. New York: Alfred A. Knopf.

Wason, Paul K. 1994. *The Archaeology of Rank*. Cambridge: Cambridge University Press.

———. 2003. "Culture, Origins of." In *Encyclopedia of Science and Religion Volume 1*, ed. J. Wenzel Vrede van Huyssteen, 193–196. New York: Macmillan Reference USA.

———. Forthcoming. "Inferring Intelligence: Prehistoric and Extraterrestrial." In *Archaeology, Anthropology, and Interstellar Communication*, ed. Douglas A. Vakoch. Washington, DC: NASA History Series.

Chapter 3

The Lifetimes of Scientific Civilizations and the Genetic Evolution of the Brain

Alan Penny

In considering the design of present and future Search for Extraterrestrial Intelligence (SETI) searches and the interpretation of their (so far) negative results, an important factor is the estimated probability of detecting electromagnetic (EM) radiation from a civilization. This factor depends on the parameters of the search itself and on the probable number of civilizations emitting EM radiation in a manner and at a level that a search would detect it. In estimating the number of such civilizations, an important factor is the average length of time that any such civilization does emit such EM radiation. This lifetime is the L in the Drake Equation (Drake 1965), which has had estimates as divergent as 10 years to 100 million years. This lifetime is a complex concept. It is commonly thought of as being less than or equal to the lifetime of the actual civilization itself, but various factors can modify that limit. Thus an estimate of 420 years (Shermer 2002) based on the average lifetime of past human civilizations such as the Roman and British Empires can be criticized as not being relevant to the SETI "civilization." The SETI "civilization" is not the political entity, but rather the type of civilization that emits EM radiation. And so, for example, the presumed future ending of the current American Empire will not automatically bring EM radiations from Earth to an end. Similarly, if a civilization constructs von Neumann machines (von Neumann 1966), they could continue to emit EM radiation after the civilization itself has ceased to exist.

Estimates for L commonly take our present "human" civilization as being the only known example of a civilization emitting EM radiation at levels relevant to SETI searches, and then try to estimate the time to the end of "our" EM radiation. Reasons for such an end, and thus likely lifetimes, tend (see, e.g., Rees 2003) to fall into two groups: cultural (such as blowing ourselves up) and external (such as being wiped out by an asteroid). All estimates of L are necessarily speculative, but a full discussion of a new type of estimate is worthwhile as L is such a critical number for SETI.

This chapter proposes a novel lifetime estimate. If, as is argued below, it is a plausible hypothesis that for a civilization to emit significant EM radiation, it is essential that "science" be practiced, then the genetic structure of the brains of the members of that civilization must permit the mode of thinking that makes such "science" possible. As the members of any such civilization would have almost inescapably emerged by genetic evolution from simpler lifeforms, incapable of such thinking, there must have been a genetic event through which such thinking became possible. (Although there would then be an interval, perhaps very long or even too long, before any EM radiation would start.) As genetic changes would continue and if other events—for example, cultural or external changes—did not intervene, then such further genetic changes might result in an end of such thinking.

The chapter then argues that there is evidence for just such a scenario, based on the history of genetic changes and the history of thinking in members of the *Homo* genus, and it further proposes that such a "genetic" lifetime could be as short as a few thousand years. The short lifetime and genetic origin concept is based on an interpretation that our "conceptual" thinking only started some three thousand years before the present (3 kya), at a time roughly coincident with the recently discovered mutation age of a gene that influences brain size, and thus that future genetic changes to our brains could occur on a similar timescale, leading to the end of "scientific" thinking and so of significant EM radiation.

To support this positing of such a recent advent of the present "conceptual" thinking, this chapter claims there are significant differences between three successive modes of modern human thinking, separated by two genetic events, modes which are herein called "early," "transitional," and "conceptual." In "early" thinking, little understanding is shown of the actions made; connections are not made between, for example, the thought "this is a tool" and the thought "other tools could be made." In "transitional" thinking, thoughts and actions are understood and connected, but not perceived as part of an abstract whole. In "conceptual" thinking the full abstract underpinning of thoughts and actions are perceived. Admittedly, the contention that a future genetic change would produce a way of thinking that would replace rather than supplement present "conceptual" thinking is merely a possibility.

The concept that genetic changes are needed for "conceptual" thinking to start also has implications for another factor in the Drake Equation, f_c, the fraction of planets with intelligent life that are willing and able to communicate. However these implications are not discussed here.

The Relationship between "Science" and Modes of Thinking

This chapter adopts the approach that a significant difference exists between the thinking that permits technology and that which permits both technology and science—that science concerns itself with the abstract concepts that can explain and predict the properties of the natural world, while technology deals with using tools to manipulate and investigate that natural world. Thus a brain incapable of abstract thinking would not be able to do "science." The chapter then posits that some areas of technology—crucially for SETI, which includes radio transmitters—depend on a prior development of the relevant science.

An example of the difference between the "transitional" and "conceptual" modes of thinking is the "technology" of the use of the 3, 4, 5 triangle by the Ancient Egyptians to construct right angles before the relevant "scientific" concept in geometry—that the length of the hypotenuse of a right-angled triangle can be deduced as a general rule from the other two lengths—was known. Another example is the use of metallurgical technology before the underlying scientific concepts of atoms, molecules, and atomic structure were developed. The technology was sometimes successful—by 6 kya, copper and tin were being melted together to make bronze—and sometimes unsuccessful, as in the medieval efforts of alchemists to turn lead into gold.

The transmutation of elements is an example of the second proposition, that there are fields of technology that seem unlikely to develop before the relevant science is known. The enterprise failed because the alchemists did not understand the atomic and sub-atomic nature of matter. This understanding only came after the scientific desire arose to develop concepts of the structure of matter, which was a necessary element of the nineteenth- and twentieth-century investigations of the existence and nature of atoms. Without those scientific investigations the realization that only the use of devices working at the sub-atomic level ("atom smashers") would accomplish transmutations seems unlikely to have come about.

Is "Science" Needed for Emitting Electromagnetic Radiation?

The assumption of this chapter is that the EM radiation, that SETI looks for, is a field where "science" must precede technology. Of course, this can only be exactly that, an assumption. It is certainly possible to envisage a non-scientific but still technological civilization that is capable of emitting significant EM radiation. Taking our own history, a possible route would be for early technological investigations of electricity—such as Volta's and Franklin's—to have led to the construction of banks of batteries giving sufficient voltages to produce a spark across a gap. At some point by chance such a bank of batteries could have been observed producing a spark across a nearby gapped metal loop, and from this a technology of EM communication may have developed, with no understanding of what the sparks were or how the transmission between the loops was occurring.

However, this is not how it actually happened. The development of electricity and EM radiation occurred after a series of scientific developments. A particular example was that Heinrich Hertz only found the transmission effect after it had been predicted on theoretical grounds by James Maxwell, even though sparks had been produced artificially for over a hundred years. Further, it is difficult to see the subsequent development of high-power EM radiation happening without the theoretical concepts of electric currents and radiation.

One counter-argument to this hypothesis is that if science does not emerge then technology still may have millions of years to produce EM radiation, and that it is rather presumptuous to assert that it could not. Another counter-argument is that this discussion is based on our own experience of having science and technology intertwined for centuries, and thus it could be only a lack of imagination that makes us unable to see that technology alone could suffice.

But taking our own experience, at least a reasonable case can be made that science is indeed needed for emitting significant EM radiation.

The Development of Modes of Thinking in Humans

This section discusses the evidence for the modes of thinking in humans and pre-humans can be divided into successive phases. Specifically for humans it proposes that there was first an "early" mode of thinking that permitted only limited technology, then a "transitional" phase that was characterized by significant technology, and finally a "conceptual" phase that now permits science and that this phase only arose in *Homo sapiens* and in them only at about 3 kya. It should be borne in mind that in these discussions the extent of the anthropological and archeological evidence that will be used to deduce the modes of thinking is limited. The deductions will be at best cautious and at worst speculative. Many efforts have been made to make such deductions, for example, by André Leroi-Gourhan, but such efforts have as often been criticized. However, it seems possible to say that the interpretation given herein is, at a minimum, a possible one which is backed up by the evidence to some extent.

Pre-humans

There is no doubt that technology emerged much earlier than 3 kya. Even some animals that are primitive by human standards have technology. Perhaps the most famous example is the New Caledonian crow (Wier, Chappel, and Kaceink 2002) that, without training or prior example, spontaneously bent a straight piece of wire into the hook needed to retrieve food set in a bucket at the bottom of another container. Similar tool-making behavior is seen in the great apes, among which such skills are sometimes also taught to offspring by parents. However, it is unlikely that crows or apes have theoretical concepts of nature.

Early humans

It is likely that when the first humans diverged from the other hominids some 7 million years ago (7 Mka), they had tool-making abilities similar to those other hominids. But as has been pointed out (see, e.g., Mithen 1996), almost the whole subsequent development of tool-making technology in humans shows little evidence of theoretical concepts. (No artifacts other than tools, such as scratches on those tools or stones with holes in them, have been found that can be used to discuss the thinking modes of pre-humans.) Good examples of tools are the handaxes made by *Homo erectus* in the Early and Middle Acheulean (1.6–0.5 Mka). These are sophisticated designs that take substantial skill and time to manufacture. However, no other types of tools were made and the basic design changed little over one million years or fifty thousand generations. *Homo erectus* must have had no general concept of "a tool," and in effect had much the same relation to their tools as the New Caledonian crow has to its bent hook. A change in the tool-making only occurs with a change in species, with *Homo neanderthalensis*—Neanderthals (230–30 kya)—making a wider range of tools. But again Neanderthal tools show little sign of evolution with time (Klein 2003), except at the very end, when it seems that some making of artifacts similar to those of *Homo sapiens* occurred (Hublin et al. 1996).

Homo sapiens

150–40 kya

It is only with the coming of *Homo sapiens* at about 150 kya that tool design develops significantly within a species. However, the extent to which this tool-making technology by itself is proof of connected thinking is unclear. Further, the evidence for connected thinking from other archaeological sources of evidence is less clear than one might think. The earliest evidence for *Homo sapiens'* connected thinking is the two small blocks of ochre with inscribed cross-hatched lines found in the Blombos Cave on the southern South Africa coast and dated to 80 kya (Henshilwood et al. 2002). However, it is difficult to see this as clear evidence for connected thinking. Until about 40 kya there is very little other evidence for such thinking, although claims have been made (see, e.g., McBreaty and Brooks 2000) that holes found in some shells and bone segments can be interpreted as deliberate designs. However, the limited and contentious extent of this evidence can only point to, at most, limited connected thinking. It is thus classified here as "early" thinking.

40–10 kya

The situation seems to change drastically at about 40 kya, with the emergence of sophisticated cave art and complex figurines—the now-contentious "cultural explosion." But while this must show connected thinking, the evidence for complex abstract thinking on a level with present-day humans is unclear. As has been pointed out by Nicholas Humphrey (1998), the cave paintings—although complex and containing advanced artistic concepts such as perspective—have a limited range of subjects, and similar artwork can be produced by autistic children less than four years old. This is not to say that the cave painters were autistic, but rather that it cannot be inferred from the paintings themselves that at 40–20 kya *Homo sapiens* had modern abstract thinking. Similarly, the evidence from figurines is limited. All the full-length figurines with human bodies have animal or stylized human heads, very similar to the sketchy human (the "bird-man," the "dead man," in the "Shaft of the Dead Man" [see the Lascaux web site]) found in the cave paintings at Lascaux dated at 19 kya. (There are claims [Rappenglueck 1999] for the existence of star charts, but these claims seem deeply unconvincing.) Whatever these people were thinking, it was not fully modern thinking, and is thus classified here as "transitional."

10–3 kya

With the advent of cities and substantial cultural artifacts at 10 kya, and especially writing (5.5 kya) and literature and mathematics (circa 4.5 kya), it might be thought that modern abstract thinking was definitely present. However, the evidence points to a mode of thinking that was still significantly different from the modern mode.

In mathematics, it is currently thought that Egyptian and Babylonian mathematics only used abstract entities to a very limited extent. Egyptian examples are the Rhind (British Museum) and Moscow (Museum of Fine Arts, Moscow) papyri of about 3.8 kya. There were "8 cows" and "8 cubits," but little concept of an entity "8." A Babylonian example is the Plimpton 322 tablet (A. Plimpton Collection at Columbia University), dated at 3.9–3.6 kya and one of about four hundred known Babylonian mathematical tablets. The tablet contains a table of three columns that seem to contain the lengths of two sides of different right-angle triangles and a complicated number related to one of the angles, the derivation of which seems to imply knowledge of the abstract Pythagorean theorem for these triangles. But in this tablet and in all the others, there is no evidence pointing to such abstract knowledge, just the tabulations themselves

Another difference from modern thought has been pointed out by Julian Jaynes (1976) in the oldest literature. The only significant literature definitely from before 3 kya is *The Epic of Gilgamesh*, parts of which exist on Babylonian tablets from 4.5 kya. Jaynes also suggests that *The Iliad* and the E and J sections of the *Pentateuch*, although both composed after 3 kya, contain pre–3 kya elements. (The Chinese *Book of Songs* contains some verses that point to a circa 3.5 kya origin [see, e.g., Owen 1996: xv], but these verses are so limited and indeed gnomic that dating and interpretation are uncertain.) Jaynes points out that the pre–3 kya Greek and Middle Eastern literature is strikingly different from modern works. People take their ideas from dreams and talks with gods—the ideas come from "outside." There seems little concept of an interior abstract self. This matches other non-literary evidence for thought processes, such as the claim by King Gudea (2164–2144 BCE, circa 4.2 kya) that the design of the temple at Lagash was given to him in a dream by the god Ningirsu (Thureau-Dangin 1907).

In both mathematics and literature, there must have actually been abstract thinking—somebody had to conceive of the Pythagorean triangle and design a ziggurat—but this did not seem to be directly accessible to the thinkers themselves. An analogy with present-day experience is that of schizophrenics. Some schizophrenics perceive some of their own thinking as voices coming from outside. Their thinking is not integrated. This is not to say that the pre–3 kya humans were schizophrenic, but that as such disconnected thinking is possible in humans, then it is possible that their thinking was in fact not fully integrated, in the manner proposed by Steven Mithen for the earlier stages of human development. It was this lack of access to the "concepts" that prevented the development of significant modern abstract thinking. Thus, the mode of thinking from 10 to 3 kya is here classified similar to the "transitional" thinking of the 40 to 10 kya period.

3 kya–present

The first clear evidence for modern abstract thinking appears at about 3 kya, with evidence from Greek literature (as Jaynes pointed out) such as *The Odyssey* (circa 2.8 kya), from Hellenic Greek mathematics, and from Chinese literature. This "conceptual" thinking permits what we think of as "modern" thinking, seeing ourselves as independent entities and having abstract concepts of the world. There seems to have been little conceptual change in modes of thinking since then, in those locations where written records survive—mainly the arc from Europe through the Middle East and India to China. There is unfortunately no evidence available for other regions of the world as to their modes of thinking either before 3 kya or in the period soon thereafter.

Genetic Changes and Their Effects on the *Homo sapiens* Brain

Genetic changes within the last 40,000 years

Two papers (Evans et al. 2005 and Mekel-Bobrov et al. 2005) reported evidence of changes in the genes controlling brain size and structure. Using phylogenetic analysis, an origin of 37 (95 percent confidence 60–14) kya for the gene *Microcephalin* and an origin of 5.8 (95 percent confidence 14–0.5) kya for the gene *ASPM* was established. Both genes regulate brain size. In present-day *Homo sapiens* the gene *Microcephalin* is distributed fairly worldwide, except there is a lower incidence in sub-Saharan Africa. The gene *ASPM* is more limited to the band from Europe to China. The authors allude to a correlation for the age of the *Microcephalin* gene with the "dramatic" shift in modern human behavior in the "Upper Paleolithic revolution," and of the age of gene *ASPM* with the start of domestication of animals, cities, and writing. The coalescence ages of other relevant chromosomes are (the very different) 1.7 Mya and 0.8 Mya, respectively.

Correlations between genetic changes in *Homo sapiens* brains and modes of thinking

There are striking correlations between the times of genetic changes with times of substantial behavioral changes that, coupled with evidence for the relative constancy of behavior between those times of genetic changes, point to a significant effect of gene change on behavior. For *Homo erectus* and *H. neanderthalensis*, the onset and ending of modes of thinking and the little change within those times is clear. The onset of *Homo sapiens* is clearly a genetic event. More controversial is the claim above for the relative constancy of behavior over the first 100,000 years. Even more controversial are the claims above for significant changes in thinking at 40 kya and 3 kya, and that these events were due to the recently discovered genetic changes at those times.

So it seems it is at least possible that the behavioral changes were indeed caused by genetic changes.

Arguments against the gene changes causing the behavioral changes

The question naturally arises of whether there is a need to posit a genetic change to account for the behavioral changes in *Homo sapiens* over the last 150,000 years. Could not these changes merely reflect different cultural backgrounds (as is a commonly held opinion)? Could such genetic changes that are posited lead to such significant behavioral changes? Isn't there a larger genetic variation within modern-day *Homo sapiens* without any evidence for such inherent differences?

With the assumption that the above arguments for behavioral and gene changes and dates are accepted for *Homo sapiens*, then the most important doubts can be grouped into four classes: whether the genetic changes were in fact coincident with the cultural changes, whether the cultural changes were not caused by the genetic changes, whether the gene changes could in fact effect such significant behavior changes, and the fact that possession of the relevant genes does not seem to be a necessary condition for a given mode of thinking.

Is there a correlation?

Work on genetic changes in the brain is so far very limited, and so it is possible that further work could show that many more genetic change events have occurred, and that these two present correlations with behavioral changes are mere coincidences—that genetic changes happen continuously, with little influence on the behavioral changes.

Behavior changes caused by cultural changes alone?

An example of a large behavioral change with little evidence for genetic change is the case discussed above when late *Homo neanderthalensis* adopted some *Homo sapiens* tool-making skills when they were in contact in Europe in the time 45–30 kya. But this has been argued to be a "copying" rather than a real change in inherent capabilities. Also, although there is little evidence (see, e.g., Klein 2003, but also note Wolpoff et al. 2004) for genetic mixing between the two species, it is possible that this tool-making change in *Homo neanderthalensis* was due to some small, but crucial, genetic influx from *H. sapiens*. Another example is the present-day *Homo sapiens* group of the Amazonian Pirahã tribe (Everett 2005), who seem to have little concept of number, amongst other things, that we associate with "scientific" thinking. (While it has been claimed in a study [Dehaene et al. 2006] of another Amazonian tribe, the Mundurukú, that although they have similar verbal limitations, they still posses such knowledge "innately," as shown up in intelligence tests, it is precisely this lack of internal awareness that we are considering.) Here there is no evidence for significant genetic difference, although it is interesting to note the variation in the present-day geographical incidence of the 3.8-kya-old *Microcephalin* gene (see fig. 3 in Evans et al. 2005), which Patrick D. Evans and colleagues speculatively link to the onset of writing.

Genetic changes capable of causing cultural changes?

The relation of brain size and structure with cognitive ability and cognitive resources is complex and ill-defined. There is some evidence that brain size and structure, which to some extent have genetic determinants, are correlated to some extent, with cognitive ability (see, e.g., Andreasen et al. 1993) perhaps accounting for 26 percent of the variation in ability. But this is clearly no proof that even substantial physical differences permit or deny modes of thinking. A famous counter example has been claimed to be that of the Nobel Prize winner Anatole France, who is said to have had a brain size in the range of that of *Homo erectus* (Gould 1981: 92). A more quantitative analysis (Geidd et al. 1996) found "normal" individuals with brain sizes in the *Homo erectus* range. Diet (Waterland and Jirtle 2004) and cultural effects (Weaver 2004) can affect brain genes. The brain size of *Homo sapiens* seems to have fallen by 10 percent in the last 30,000 years. The correlation of brain size with body mass (as in the "encephalization quotient") brings in yet another variable.

Thus it is certainly possible that cultural differences could account for the behavioral changes, and also that the genetic changes seen in *Homo sapiens* might not result in these behavioral changes.

Genes not needed for a mode of thinking

It is clear that many people do not have the *Microcephalin* and *ASPM* mutations, while most if not all of them have "conceptual" thinking. So how, if "conceptual" thinking did not occur before the mutations occurred, is that possible? It is proposed that the gene mutation events were "triggers," occurring in only some people. These people then instigated a culture of conceptual thinking wherein children are raised, and thus those without the gene acquire the ability for "conceptual" thinking by a process of "nurture" rather than "nature." Of course, those with the mutation would also undergo this "nurture" process. This would be similar to the process through which the last Neanderthals acquired "transitional" thinking.

Indeed, given the very rapid spread posited for "conceptual" thinking, less than 3 kya worldwide, such a "nurture" process would be essential.

The Rate and Effects of Future Genetic Changes

This chapter posits that a future genetic change could affect our mode of thinking, either by degrading the ability for "conceptual" thinking or by adding a new mode of thinking so that "conceptual" thinking was discarded. The factors to be considered are: likely length of time before such a genetic change, whether the new thinking merely supplemented "conceptual" thinking, and the likelihood that other changes would intervene before the genetic change occurred.

Rate of changes

The rate of change in genetic evolution depends on many factors. The default would be that it stays constant, and so we can expect the next change in a few thousand years. It has been suggested that *Homo sapiens* is reaching a phase where this change will slow, since medical advances mean that there is no selection based on survival rates, because practically all people born in the future will survive to old age. However, there are other selection pressures—number of children per couple, behavioral practices affecting reproductive rates, and diseases—that could drive evolution. Another hypothesis is that the rate will slow down as isolated small populations are favorable in allowing changes to propagate, and no such groups now exist. However, it is possible that the movement of groups into the solar system will occur over the next centuries and these could be isolated, and of a small size. There is no way to estimate these differing factors.

Supplement or replace?

For genetic changes to be relevant to the EM radiation lifetime, such changes must not only start the era (as has been argued above), but also bring it to a close. For example, a possible way that "conceptual" thinking might be brought to an end would be the reversion to a small brain size as has been suggested to have occurred (Morwood et al. 2004) to *Homo flore-siensis* from their *H. erectus* forebears. However, there are also reasons why an end might not happen in that the genetic change would merely bring on a mode of thinking that supplemented this thinking, just as the advent of this thinking did not replace the existing "transitional" thinking.

Intervening changes

For the occurrence of genetic changes to bring "conceptual" thinking to an end, then other changes must not occur first. It is quite possible that the thousands-of-years timescale envisaged here could be pre-empted, by, for example, events such as a comet collision, runaway nanomachines, bioterrorism, nuclear warfare, etc. (see, e.g., Rees 2003) that could all occur in the next hundred years. Some changes might also significantly alter the prospect for genetic changes, such as the replacement of humans by human-machine hybrids.

All that can be said is that the ending of EM radiation by the genetic change route is an additional possible route to those already propounded, but is not necessarily the most (or least) likely route.

Conclusion

There are significant lines of evidence that the "conceptual" mode of thinking is necessary for a civilization to emit the significant EM radiation that SETI searches could pick up, and that such thinking could be brought on and ended, within a few thousand years, by genetic changes.

Acknowledgments

This chapter has benefited from comments by John Campbell, Kathryn Denning, Douglas Vakoch, and an anonymous referee.

Bibliography

Andreasen, Nancy C., et al. 1993. "Intelligence and Brain Structure in Normal Individuals." *American Journal of Psychiatry* 150: 130–134.

Dhaene, Stanislas V., et al. 2006. "Core Knowledge of Geometry in an Amazonian Indigene Group." *Science* 311: 381–384.

Drake, Frank. 1965. "The Radio Search for Intelligent Extraterrestrial Life." In *Current Aspects of Astrobiology*, ed. G. Mamikunian and M. H. Briggs, 323. Oxford: Pergamon Press.

Evans, Patrick D., et al. 2005. "Microcephalin, a Gene Regulating Brain Size, Continues to Evolve Adaptively in Humans." *Science* 309: 1717–1720.

Everett, Daniel L. 2005. "Cultural Constraints on Grammar and Cognition in Pirahã." *Current Anthropology* 46: 621–646.

Giedd, Jay N., et al. 1996. "Quantitative Magnetic Resonance Imaging of Human Brain Development: Ages 4–18." *Cerebral Cortex* 6: 551–560.

Gould, Stephen J. 1981. *The Mismeasure of Man*. New York: W. W. Norton.

Henshilwood, Christopher S., et al. 2002. "Emergence of Modern Human Behavior: Middle Stone Age Engravings from South Africa." *Science* 295: 1278–1280.

Hublin, Jean-Jacques, et al. 1996. "A Late Neanderthal Associated with Upper Palaeolithic Artefacts" *Nature* 381: 224–226.

Humphrey, Nicholas. 1998. "Cave Art, Autism, and the Evolution of the Human Mind." *Cambridge Archaeological Journal* 8, no. 2: 165–191.

Jaynes, Julian. 1976. *The Origin of Consciousness in the Breakdown of the Bicameral Mind*. Boston, MA: Houghton Mifflin Company.

Klein, Richard G. 2003. "Whither the Neanderthals?" *Science* 299: 1525–1526.

Lascaux. www.culture.gouv.fr/culture/arcnat/lascaux/en/. Accessed on 18 April 2011.

McBrearty, Sally, and Alison S. Brooks. 2000. "The Revolution That Wasn't: A New Interpretation of the Origin of Modern Human Behavior." *Journal of Human Evolution* 39: 453–563.

Mekel-Bobrov, Nitzan S., et al. 2005. "Ongoing Adaptive Evolution of ASPM, a Brain Size Determinant in *Homo sapiens*." *Science* 309: 1720–1722.

Mithen, Steven. 1996. *The Prehistory of the Mind: The Cognitive Origins of Art, Religion and Science*. London: Thames and Hudson.

Morwood, Michael J., et al. 2004. "Archaeology and Age of a New Hominin from Flores in Eastern Indonesia." *Nature* 431: 1087–1091.

Owen, Stephen. 1996. In *The Book of Songs*, transl. Arthur Waley and Joseph R. Allen. New York: Grove Press.

Rappenglueck, Michael A. 1999. "Palaeolithic Timekeepers Looking at the Golden Gate of the Ecliptic; The Lunar Cycle and the Pleiades in the Cave of La-TETe-Du-Lion (Ardéche, France)—21,000 BP." *Earth, Moon, and Planets* 85/86: 391–404.

Rees, Martin. 2003. *Our Final Century?* London: William Heinemann.

Shermer, Michael. 2002. "Why ET Hasn't Called." *Scientific American* 285, no. 2: 33.

Thureau-Dangin, François. 1907. *Die sumerischen und akkadischen Königsinschriften.* Leipzig: J. C. Hinrichs.

von Neumann, John. 1966. *Theory of Self-Reproducing Automata.* Urbana, IL: University of Illinois Press.

Waterland, Robert A., and Randy L. Jirtle. 2004. "Early Nutrition, Epigenetic Changes at Transposons and Imprinted Genes, and Enhanced Susceptibility to Adult Chronic Diseases." *Nutrition* 20: 63–68.

Weaver, Ian C. G., et al. 2004. "Epigenetic Programming by Maternal Behavior." *Nature Neuroscience* 7: 847–854.

Weir, Alex A. S., Jackie Chappell, and Alex Kacelnik. 2002. "Shaping of Hooks in New Caledonian Crows." *Science* 297: 981.

Wolpoff, Milford H., et al. 2004. "Why Not the Neanderthals?" *World Archaeology* 36: 527–546.

Chapter 4

"L" on Earth

Kathryn Denning

This chapter proposes a renewed look from an anthropological perspective at the Drake factor L, the average lifetime of a communicative civilization. As an anthropologist and archaeologist with a particular interest in methods of reasoning about the past, I offer here not a new estimate of L, but some thoughts about how we might investigate this factor anthropologically.

There has been a great deal of provocative and useful thinking on L. It is a controversial term: some contend that we have no useful data on the subject, while others contend we do; some argue that L is very short, while others think it is enormously long. It is also a factor in which we are exceptionally emotionally invested, for our estimates of L are intertwined with our forecasts for our own civilization's end. It is, in short, a problem. I do not think it impossible to investigate, however. For this, we need to turn to the social sciences.

Contributions to SETI from the social sciences have been infrequent, compared to those from the physical and biological sciences (Kukla 2001), but they have been consistently present. For example, social scientists have contributed to SETI-related endeavors through assessment of the possible evolutionary paths to intelligence (Raybeck 2004), review of historical precedents for contact between civilizations and simulations of contact,[1] consideration of the challenges of interstellar message decipherment and composition (Vakoch 1998a, 1998b, 2000, 2004), the projected lifetime of advanced civilizations (Sagan 1973; Urbanowicz 1977), and the characterization of long-lived societies (Harrison 2000). It has been argued that there is much more to be contributed by social scientists (Finney 2000), and I concur.

Here, I will explore the potential use of anthropology. SETI scientists have often drawn from archaeological and anthropological analogues in thinking about what ETI might be like, what contact would involve, and whether or how meaningful communication might be possible. But an anthropological perspective can be used more extensively in SETI with helpful results.

In this chapter, I first explain why I am not attempting a new estimate of L, and then consider why it is worthwhile to examine Earth's civilizations, and what kinds of knowledge about them should count. I then consider what an anthropological perspective could bring to the study of L, specifically in revising the theoretical models we use for the evolution of civilizations, and in understanding why civilizations end.

Putting away the Calculator

I decided to write this chapter after reading an essay from 2002 in *Scientific American*, in which the author computed L by averaging the lifespans of sixty Earth civilizations, including the ancient societies of Mesopotamia, Egypt, Greece, Rome, China, Africa, India, Japan, Central and South America, and several modern states. The paper concluded that terrestrial data thus gives L a value of 420.6 years (or considering only the rather more technological societies, L = 304.5 years), and that this short duration may explain why we have heard no signals from the cosmos (Shermer 2002).

Unquestionably, it can be entertaining to trawl through an encyclopedia with a calculator at one's side. But I must confess to a negative bias here, because to an archaeologist, this is one of the most trivial uses imaginable of historical knowledge; we can glean more significant information from the encyclopedia. If all we learn from hard-won evidence concerning the collective human experience of sixty Earth civilizations on four continents over many thousands of years is that their average duration is 420.6 years, then it is a sad situation indeed.

In this chapter, I will not attempt to arrive at a new value for L for two reasons. First, I am not certain another estimate would help, because to my mind, whether L is small or large, and N is thus estimated to be two or two billion, the search should continue. Second, focusing too narrowly on the numbers misses the larger use of the Drake Equation, as a framework for inquiry into subjects pertinent to SETI. Scientists do not study the earliest microbes on Earth, or the processes of planet formation, solely to obtain values for Drake factors; they study to learn everything they can about these phenomena, because it is all relevant to the task of understanding life in the universe. This should also be the case for L, and for the closely related factor f_c, the fraction of civilizations that develop technology that SETI searches could detect.

Therefore, this chapter is devoted instead to considering the sorts of information that we might usefully retrieve from the historical record, and to considering the assumptions we may need to revise in order to do it. What can we know about lifetimes of civilizations, based on terrestrial experience? Are there patterns that might be helpful in anticipating extraterrestrial civilizations? Or, conversely, have we been making assumptions about extraterrestrial civilizations based on considerations that are likely to be unique to Earth, or even to our own current society?

Why Bother with Earth's Civilizations?

We might well ask, Do Earth-based examples really matter? In thinking about extraterrestrial civilizations, should we not be more concerned with machine-based intelligence, or with projections derived from physics, like Nikolai Kardashev's typology based on energy consumption, than with the history of our own humble world?

Perhaps. If one is seeking an estimate of L, then yes, one should probably pay the most attention to the possibilities of extremely long-lived civilizations, because they significantly skew the average (Drake 2003). It may also be that these "supercivilizations" (Kardashev 1985) are the ones that we are most likely to encounter. And, clearly, one needs to consider the spectrum of possibilities for communicative intelligences, in order to keep developing new search strategies.

It may even be that our notion of a "civilization"—an entity bound in space and time, with cultural vacuums or enemies at its frontiers—is completely embedded within recent Western thought, and profoundly unlikely to be applicable to societies elsewhere.

Obviously, those conjectures are important. However, I would argue that we should *also* make the most of the *data* we are fortunate to have at our disposal. This is, I think, one of the most laudable aspects of SETI-related science: the creative use of specific Earth cases to address more universal questions. For example—*Star Trek IV* notwithstanding—I doubt anyone imagines that we will find cetaceans swimming through interstellar space, but studies of dolphin vocalizations are certainly useful in learning about structured communications in sentient species. Similarly, although we do not expect to encounter extraterrestrial civilizations just like our own, we should be able to learn something of value from these Earth-bound examples. But what?

What Kinds of Knowledge Should Count?

Even before considering what we might learn from Earth's civilizations, we need to determine what kinds of knowledge will count. There is a bias in many scientific fields toward quantification and experimentally verifiable propositions. But we cannot meaningfully quantify or test all that we know about human thought, technology, or behavior, or about the development of civilizations. This disjunction routinely leads to interminable discussions, particularly in undergraduate classes, about whether archaeology and anthropology are scientific. Of course, the debate is partly semantic in nature, for the outcome depends on the precise definition of "science," and that varies. But the debate also reflects the genuine discomfort that some people, students and scientists alike, have with interpretations concerning irreducible human realities. To this I can only say that in recent years, philosophers of science have convincingly argued that reasoning in historical disciplines like archaeology and evolutionary biology, for example, is not necessarily inferior to reasoning in experimental and mathematical sciences. The reasoning is different, but the resulting knowledge is not necessarily less secure (Wylie 2002).

In what follows, then, I take it as given that an anthropological description of the social influences of radio technology is a form of knowledge as valid and useful as a graph describing the increasing power of receivers or transmitters over time. I also take it as given that the difficulty and importance of understanding subjects subsumed under *L* means that we should use everything in our analytical arsenal.

This then, brings us to the next question.

What is Human History Really Good for?

We have considerable information about the history of humanity at our disposal. It is useful to step back for a moment to ask how these data are being used in SETI discussions and how they might be most useful.

Information about human civilizations has been used in SETI thinking primarily in these ways:

- as a source of specific numerical values to be used in predictive models concerning civilizations' longevity and development;
- to generally project aspects of our own future;
- to illustrate different potential outcomes of contact between civilizations, with a view to human-extraterrestrial (ET) contact;
- to characterize the general evolution of ET civilizations up to and beyond a level of technology that is SETI-detectable and/or spacefaring;
- and to consider potential patterns of ET colonization.

These are certainly reasonable uses of the historical record, but are there deeper or more rigorous ways for SETI research to exploit the vast database of human history? Perhaps so. In particular, I propose that we may achieve useful understandings for SETI by adopting an anthropological approach, specifically:

- by reconsidering the theoretical frameworks through which we explain the evolution of civilizations;
- and by formulating hypotheses concerning the evolution of civilizations that we can evaluate by examining anthropological, historical, and archaeological data.

The Anthropological Perspective

It is clear that the disciplinary backgrounds that people bring to SETI questions can affect their perspectives. For example, physicists and biologists tend to have diverging opinions about the probability of intelligent life emerging on other worlds, because of their frames of reference and understanding of evolutionary processes (Schilling and MacRobert 2011). But as Christopher Chyba pointed out, this comes down to differing perceptions of the "comparative importance of contingency versus convergence in evolution"—and that *can* actually be studied (in Schilling and MacRobert 2011).

Similarly, there are SETI debates concerning civilizations that could be, if not resolved, then at least informed by further research. In this, the anthropological perspective could be invaluable. One of anthropology's strengths is its focus on cross-cultural comparisons and on the diversity of human experience. In addition to allowing us to see commonalities and differences across cultures, past and present, it also helps us to identify our own ethnocentric assumptions, which we surely need to minimize if we are seeking theories that may apply not only to other civilizations, but also to those on other worlds. Anthropology also provides a variety of theoretical models for understanding the development of civilizations, and this could be very useful to SETI questions.

Next, I will illustrate this through two examples pertaining to L: the first concerns the theoretical frameworks we use to explain evolutionary change, and the second concerns our explanations for why civilizations end.

An Implicit Bias in SETI toward Unilinear Social Evolution?

Anthropology has been largely responsible for two "great ideas" of the nineteenth and twentieth centuries: first, in the 1800s, the notion that given enough time, all societies progress through the same stages of development from savagery to barbarism to civilization; and second, in the 1900s, the realization that this model of unilinear social evolution is inaccurate and overly simplistic.

The former idea has taken root in popular Western thinking, while the latter remains specialist knowledge. Many anthropologists and archaeologists now consider that ranking societies according to their level of political and technological complexity is problematic, and that it is more useful to understand each society in its own context before comparing them. For example, Western history books have often portrayed native New World cultures as technologically inferior to Old World cultures because they did not use the wheel in transportation; however, given that in the Americas before the European invasions, there were no draft animals suitable for pulling wheeled carts, this omission is entirely logical. Thus, using the absence of the wheel as a cross-cultural measure of technological sophistication is nonsensical. Similarly, a culture may have an elaborate and effective system of keeping records and transmitting knowledge that does not involve writing—which means that the standard practice of using writing as a criterion for evaluating a society's degree of intellectual advancement is problematic. A contemporary anthropological or archaeological perspective demands that we understand this before attempting comparisons. Moreover, it favors an approach that fairly represents the diversity, rather than slotting every society into a simple framework.

This connects to L in a potentially significant way, so it is worthwhile to elaborate. The easiest example comes from human biological evolution. We probably all recall the famous 1970s "March of Progress" illustration of human evolution, with different species of hominid in a line. One species simply turns into the next. We can contrast this with a phylogenetic tree, a different convention of illustrating hominid evolution, which shows not only the species on the direct line to *Homo sapiens*, but others too. It represents each species in its own right, not only for what it became (Gould 1991). It may be even more fair to use an illustration that subtracts the firm lines between species, since these are inferences that change.

These represent different ways of describing and understanding an evolutionary process. We can look at the "March of Progress" and say X inevitably led to Y, which led to Z, but this is not, of course, how it really happens. This is a rhetorical trope. This is one way of writing history after the fact, rather than how it really happened. The reality is not linear, but filled with bifurcation points, and better described not as a simple progression, but as realms of "adjacent possibilities" (Kauffman 2000). The same is true for cultural evolution. There is an important connection here to SETI theorizing about L, in terms of the way that social evolution is understood.

Decades ago, Carl Sagan, greatly concerned about nuclear war on Earth, commented about the threat of civilizations self-immolating, observing that other communicative civilizations, like our own, could "take billions of years of tortuous evolution to arise, and then snuff themselves out in an instant of unforgivable neglect" (1980: 301). He urged us, however, to consider the hopeful possibility that at least some civilizations would survive this "technological adolescence," and concluded that if even 1 percent lived to maturity, then those civilizations would surely have immensely long lifespans. This in turn would ensure that we have many as-yet-undiscovered neighbors. More recently, Seth Shostak (2001) argued that rather than being on the road to self-destruction, we may merely be passing through a bottleneck—that is, a period during which we have the technological capacity to destroy ourselves, but have not yet bought our species the anti-extinction insurance policy of colonizing other worlds. Further, he proposed that this is necessarily a short phase through which many technological civilizations will pass.

Scenarios like these are both interesting and plausible. But underlying them are some assumptions that are intriguing both in content and in form. Arguments like these assume, variously,

- that most societies that become sufficiently technological for a SETI detection will also have weapons of mass destruction;
- that most societies that become sufficiently technological will also colonize planets beyond their home world;
- and that the threat of self-destruction, if not fulfilled, will pass either through conscious evolution (enlightenment), or through the colonization of other worlds.

There is a sense of entailment here, of a necessary movement from one stage to the next; the framework seems to be an essentially unilinear model of social evolution. And certainly, it *could* be so. But we may reasonably ask whether it is *necessarily* so, or *likely* to be so? And we might investigate those questions anthropologically, through cross-cultural research. For example, we might ask the following:

- It is clearly the case on our world that communications technology and space science are linked to military activity; but is this inherent to the technology, or a result of the particular cultural milieu in which it was developed?
- It is certainly true that some human societies have been active colonizers, and it is certainly likely that some members of our species will take up residence off-world soon; however, would this propensity for colonizing necessarily be universal or even frequent in extraterrestrial technological societies?

In other words, using an anthropological approach, we might explore the range of possibilities, rather than assuming similarities.

Consider the subject of technology in particular. Technology is frequently construed as existing because it provides a competitive advantage in endeavors of aggression and expansion—machines for conquest or defense. But can we not imagine a world in which radar was developed to track weather systems instead of enemy aircraft? And can we not imagine a world in which technology was developed solely for its social merit, instead of its power or the "sweetness" of the experiment? In fact, we may not need to imagine; an examination of technology's role in Earth's different societies may provide useful insights.

This brings me to the next example of the potential contribution of an anthropological perspective on *L*.

Why Do Civilizations End?

Most of us, living in our technologically advanced civilization, are culturally biased; although we may have some misgivings about technology, we tend to think that our way of living is good, and that it would be only natural to continue becoming ever more technologically sophisticated, unless we collectively experience a catastrophe. And those of us interested in SETI are necessarily biased toward technological civilizations, since they are the only ones we can hope to contact.

That is not a problem in itself. What is interesting, however, is a related assumption. We tend to assume that if a technological civilization ceases to be visible for SETI detection, that could only be the result of a shift to more advanced technology, or a disaster—a rupture in the natural course of social evolution, caused by a very destructive war, a terrible disease, or an asteroid impact. In turn, embedded within this is the notion that the only rational process for a society, once it has achieved technological status, is to keep going.

We conceive of civilizations ending because of catastrophe. But there may be times when the most intelligent, rational option is to downscale—to become less technological. This is one crucial understanding from archaeological studies of ancient societies that collapsed: that downshifting to a less energy-intensive form of social organization can be a successful, rational adaptation, rather than a failure (Tainter 1988).

What this means for SETI is a subject for further exploration, as are all the factors limiting L on Earth.

Conclusion

It has often been said of L that it is both the most influential variable in the Drake Equation, as well as the hardest to know anything about.

The former is clearly true, but as for the latter, I am not convinced. I think we can learn a great deal of relevance to L if we uncover our own assumptions about the evolution of civilizations, and check those by looking across cultures and through time, exploring the full depth and breadth of human societies. This would of course be a big project, but that has not stopped SETI before.

Notes

1. For example, the long-running annual conference, Contact. www.contact-conference.com

Bibliography

Drake, Frank. 2003. "The Drake Equation, Revisited, Part I." *Astrobiology*. www.astrobio.net/news/article610.html. Accessed on 18 April 2011.
Finney, Ben. 2000. "SETI, Consilience and the Unity of Knowledge." In *Bioastronomy 99: A New Era in the Search for Life, ASP Conference Series*, vol. 213, eds. G. Lemarchand and K. Meech. San Francisco, CA: Astronomical Society of the Pacific.

Gould, Stephen J. 1991. *Wonderful Life: The Burgess Shale and the Nature of History*. New York: Penguin.

Harrison, Albert A. 2000. "The Relative Stability of Belligerent and Peaceful Societies: Implications for SETI." *Acta Astronautica* 46, no. 10–12: 707–712.

Kardashev, Nikolai S. 1985. "On the Inevitability and Possible Structures of Supercivilizations." In *The Search for Extraterrestrial Life: Recent Developments*, ed. Michael D. Papagiannis, 497–504. Dordrecht: D. Reidel.

Kauffman, Stuart A. 2000. *Investigations*. Oxford: Oxford University Press.

Kukla, André. 2001. "SETI: On the Prospects and Pursuitworthiness of the Search for Extraterrestrial Intelligence." *Studies in History and Philosophy of Science* 32, no. 1: 31–67.

Raybeck, Douglas. 2004. "Predator-Prey Models and the Development of Intelligence." Paper presented at SETI Institute, Mountain View, CA.

Sagan, Carl, ed. 1973. *Communication with Extraterrestrial Intelligence (CETI)*. Cambridge, MA: MIT Press.

———. 1980. *Cosmos*. New York: Random House.

Schilling, Govert, and Alan M. MacRobert. 2011. "The Chance of Finding Aliens." *Sky and Telescope*. http://www.skyandtelescope.com/resources/seti/3304541.html. Accessed on 18 April 2011.

Shermer, Michael. 2002. "Why ET Hasn't Called." *Scientific American* 285, no. 2: 33.

Shostak, Seth. 2001. "The Lifetime of Technological Civilizations." International Astronautical Congress (IAA-01-IAA.9.1.06).

Tainter, Joseph A. 1988. *The Collapse of Complex Societies*. Cambridge: Cambridge University Press.

Urbanowicz, Charles F. 1977. "Evolution of Technological Civilizations: What is Evolution, Technology, and Civilization?" Paper presented at NASA. www.csuchico.edu/~curban/Unpub_Papers/1977SETIPaper.html. Accessed on 18 April 2011.

Vakoch, Douglas A. 1998a. "Constructing Messages to Extraterrestrials: An Exosemiotic Perspective." *Acta Astronautica* 42, no. 10–12: 697–704.

———. 1998b. "The Dialogic Model: Representing Human Diversity in Messages to Extraterrestrials." *Acta Astronautica* 42, no. 10–12: 705–710.

———. 2000. "The Conventionality of Pictorial Representation in Interstellar Messages." *Acta Astronautica* 46, no. 10–12: 733–736.

———. 2004. "The Art and Science of Interstellar Message Composition." *Leonardo* 37, no. 1: 33–34.

Wylie, Alison. 2002. *Thinking from Things: Essays in the Philosophy of Archaeology*. Berkeley, CA: University of California Press.

Part II

REACTIONS TO DISCOVERING LIFE BEYOND EARTH

Chapter 5

CAN SETI FULFILL THE VALUE AGENDA OF CULTURAL ANTHROPOLOGY?

Donald E. Tarter

Intellectual revolutions follow scientific and technological revolutions. That is what I thought and taught in courses about science, technology, and society at the University of Alabama in Huntsville. Huntsville is the home of NASA's largest field center, the George C. Marshall Space Flight Center. From the 1960s to the 1990s, Huntsville played a vital role in the Apollo Lunar Program, the Skylab program, the Hubble Space Telescope, and the International Space Station. During these decades I was able to observe at close range the dynamic interplay of scientific, technological, and sociological forces that were generated by our ventures in space.

In the early 1960s, figures of power came to Huntsville. President John F. Kennedy and Vice President Lyndon Johnson came to monitor progress on Kennedy's announced goal of "placing a man on the Moon and returning him safely to Earth before this decade is out." Opinion leaders such as Walter Cronkite and Walt Disney came to visit with Werner von Braun and members of his German rocket team. Science fiction writer Arthur C. Clarke came to draw on von Braun's visions in writing the script and novelization for *2001: A Space Odyssey*. Even after von Braun's death in 1975, the public maintained strong interest in the space program. Opinion leaders such as Hugh Downs of *ABC News*, James A. Mitchner, the famous novelist, and Carl Sagan of *Cosmos* fame came to speak and talk with the space pioneers in Huntsville.

On the national and international scene the culture seemed to be edging toward a new evolving enlightenment. The vast popularity of the aforementioned television science series *Cosmos* was encouraging. This series made SETI a central theme. The human progress in science and technology, which led up to SETI, was explored. A better and more humbling assessment of our place in the universe was the ultimate goal of *Cosmos*. The show depicted human beings as being poised to explore perhaps the most fundamental scientific mystery of all: Is there intelligent life elsewhere in the universe? If so, SETI might be able to provide us with contact and communication with our fellow conscious beings.

In the same time frame, the television and movie series *Star Trek* flourished. The "trekkies" became a cultural phenomenon combining serious scientific curiosity and adventure with a bit of silly pop culture. The *Star Wars* series by producer George Lucas and the story of *E.T.* given to us by Stephen Spielberg seemed to assure us that a broader human perspective awaited us. It was as if we were beginning to develop a true "cosmic consciousness." Carl Sagan's novel *Contact* (1985) set to the big screen showed us what might be in store if we truly met a civilization far in advance of our own. Such a collective frame of reference, I felt, would be healthy. It promised for the first time in human history a way we might begin to minimize our ancient hostile ethnic identities. As we gazed on those photos from the Moon showing the Earth rising as a bright blue sphere in the blackness of space, we did not see political boundaries, nor did we hear different languages. A few years later from a more remote perspective we again saw our planet from the spacecraft Voyager as a mere pale blue dot. In a book by that name Carl Sagan made the following moving assessment of that faint image of our Earth; there is perhaps no better expression of the philosophical perspective promoted by astronomy and human space travel:

> Look again at that dot. That's here. That's home. That's us. On it everyone you love, everyone you know, everyone you ever heard of, every human being who ever was, lived out their lives. The aggregate of our joy and suffering, thousands of confident religions, ideologies, and economic doctrines, every hunter and forager, every hero and coward, every creator and destroyer of civilizations, every King and peasant, every young couple in love, every mother and father, hopeful child, inventor and explorer, every teacher of morals, every corrupt politician, every "supreme leader," every saint and sinner in the history of our species lived here—on a mote of dust suspended in a sunbeam.... Our posturings, our imagined self-importance, the delusion that we have some privileged position in the Universe, are challenged by this point of pale blue light. Our planet is a lonely speck

in the great enveloping cosmic dark. In our obscurity in all this vastness, there is no hint that help will come from elsewhere to save us from ourselves. (1994: 8–9)

The overwhelming response to Sagan's cosmic perspective in the 1980s and 1990s seemed a promising indicator that humankind was on the verge of developing a liberating expanded ethos that would help us rid ourselves of our hostilities based on ethnic identifications. Millions of us were eagerly awaiting the arrival of the new and even more enlightened twenty-first century.

Our New Century

Less than a year into the twenty-first century the world changed. It changed in the way that was diametrically opposed to the way that I have described. September 11, 2001, brought us a drastic change in global politics that sent the world's populations back to the days of ethnic hatred. It would come to be described as "the war of civilizations." The Muslim world set itself against the Judeo-Christian world with the attack on and the destruction of the World Trade Center in New York City.

The long-standing hostility between Israel and Palestine had moved to a new level involving a much broader array of countries. The United States launched retaliatory strikes against Afghanistan. This soon spread to a wider front with the subsequent US invasion of Iraq. Subsequent terrorist attacks in England, Spain, and throughout the Middle East gave this "war of civilizations" a very dramatic and deadly profile in world politics. Ethnic identities hardened. The ancient and deadly dividing lines of history re-emerged. The infant identity of one people on a mote of dust floating in a sunbeam seemed to give way to different peoples clashing over ancient and tribal belief systems in the vicious traditions of our past.

The Saudi Arabian astronaut, Prince Sultan bin Salman bin Abdulaziz Al Saud, who flew aboard the shuttle Discovery in 1985, had said of his trip into space, "The first day or so, we all pointed to our countries. The third or fourth day we were pointing to our continents. By the fifth day, we were aware of only one Earth" (1985). This "overview effect," which had diminished dangerous human divisions in space, had not been transmitted to the nations of Earth. Here on Earth our nationalism and tribalism were again flourishing in their traditional destructive forms. We must ask ourselves, what can be done to give the broader cosmic perspective new life and make the cosmic experience permanent?

The Potential Impact of SETI Success

Cultural anthropology has always sought to explore and catalogue the diversity of human cultures. SETI seeks to explore and catalogue cultures of other intelligent beings in space. The agenda of cultural anthropology embraces certain values, namely that information about others of different cultures than our own will lead to an understanding and appreciation of the diverse behaviors of the people of planet Earth. SETI has a similar value agenda except its focus is on the cultures of extraterrestrial beings in space. So far the catalogues of SETI are empty, but the search is only a few decades old—it has just begun.

Human space travel has become a reality, but as far as we now know we remain alone in the universe. Much has been written about the impact of the discovery of another civilization in space. Most scholars believe that such a discovery would touch virtually every aspect of society (Billingham et al. 1999; Bova and Preiss 1990; Harrison 1997). For the purpose of this brief discussion I will focus on the question, Does the discovery of another civilization in space have implications that could enhance human understanding and cooperation on Earth? Can there be cultural anthropology of the cosmos?

No one knows what the first message from another civilization in space may be, but the prevailing assumption among SETI scientists has been that a threat is unlikely. It may take us quite some time to decipher the meaning to the message. If the message seems threatening it is probable the threat will be manufactured among the more paranoid of our own kind rather than malicious aliens.

To the contrary, there seems to be more agreement that if we indeed do achieve contact, that contact will reveal a peaceful and benign sender. This is based on the rationale that any civilization we discover would obviously be technologically and perhaps intellectually superior. The civilization we find would be much older than our own. We have only been doing radio astronomy for a few decades and the sending civilization must have mastered the art long before we did. If there is any truth to the fact that age equates with wisdom, perhaps long-standing civilizations have mastered the forces that lead to war and destruction. Only time and discovery will prove if this idea is correct. Assuming, then, that the SETI contact event is not likely to be threatening to our own kind, what might be some of the consequences we could expect from our discovery?

Carl Sagan insisted that the mere fact of a discovery would help us calibrate our place in the universe. In our infantile phase humans have always assumed their place was too important. Religions have almost universally postulated that they alone have truth and a special connection with their god or gods. Super patriotism is based on the notion of my country right or wrong. Closed-minded intolerance is one of the ugly hallmarks of humankind. Relatively few humans have been able to escape at least some portion of this mindset.

Astronomy, since the time of Copernicus and Galileo, began to pry open our closed minds and allow some enlightenment into the dark recesses of our egocentric and ethnocentric feelings. We reflect on the centuries that have passed since Galileo and Copernicus gave us their insights. Think of the millions of hours scientists have spent lecturing on and writing about our new view of where we are in the universe. Think of the thousands of miles of film and videotape invested in the effort to show humanity the true nature of our planetary home. All this effort, and still human arrogance, intolerance, and ethnic blindness dominate our international relations. For those who can see beyond the walls of a single culture, it appears that human enlightenment has not yet occurred.

Will achieving contact substantially improve the human condition? I have demonstrated how truly difficult that can be. Just as the human movement into space gave us a potential new perspective on their place in the greater order of things, it did not bring us a change in our old political, religious, and military habits. Can we expect the achievement of knowledge that there are other intelligent beings out there to take us any further?

A Realistic Contact Scenario

No one knows what the contact event will reveal. The exact nature of the message received could be debated endlessly. It is within the realm of possibility that the message could provide us with clear and concise instructions to do something or to build something that would vastly improve our live and provide us with new ways to communicate with our newly found neighbors. The movie *Contact* portrays such a scenario.

It would be far better, however, to propose a contact scenario based on the tried and true scientific practice of using Occam's Razor. The simplest explanation is most times the best explanation. The first step in this process is to assume that the signal will tell us very little about the sender's nature. It may be nothing more that a series of radio or laser pulses that are clearly designed to show intelligent origin, but which relay very little information that is immediately obvious. It may take time to decipher any deeper meaning—indeed it may take a very long time. Perhaps the deciphering task will be beyond our technological ability and all we are left with is the disquieting fact that there is something intelligent out there.

Meanwhile, here on Earth an intense debate will break out about how to reply to the signal. Several unauthorized groups with the technological capability may indeed jump the gun and send their own signals before an official "reply from Earth" can be sent. In order to avoid this, the International Academy of Astronautics has consistently advocated that the reply from Earth go through the offices of the United Nations. Yes, under minimal information conditions we still have these pulsing signals that come in just like a lighthouse. As Jill Tarter of the SETI Institute in Mountain View, California, has said, "What do you say to a lighthouse?"

If, as I suspect, the encounter with the signals from extraterrestrial beings will involve a prolonged period of confusion and inability to extract detailed information about the nature or the meaning of the signal, we can expect the human race to fall into an extended period of cosmic anxiety. This anxiety will be a nagging mixture of curiosity, hope, fear, and confusion about what should be done. Anxieties seek resolution and there will arise many individuals and institutions that will offer programs designed to play upon the new cosmic anxiety that afflicts our species.

An Emerging Interpretation Industry

Anthropologist Ben Finney has coined the phrase "interpretation industry" to describe the activities of all sorts of individuals and groups who will offer and perhaps push their interpretations of what unintelligible signals from a distant civilization might mean (1990). It is very likely that the scientific community will take a long while to understand the meaning of the signals they are receiving. In the meantime, interpretations of the signals will probably provide a major source of propaganda and profit for many different groups.

We can expect a very wide variety of individuals and organizations to spring forth offering their interpretations of the mysterious new reality that we have encountered. A contact event of this sort will provide everyone from televangelists to politicians to speak and find an audience for their take on the situation. Products will be sold, gods will be promoted, and policies will be pushed, all in direct response to those beings that are out there. Although much of this will be within the bounds a legitimate exchange of religious and political discussion, it seems likely that there are opportunities for excesses and socially damaging exploitation to occur. Given this fact it would seem prudent for the scientific community and more specifically the SETI community to have some mechanism to give considered scientific response and opinion to the many situations that could arise. Perhaps an officially appointed committee within the National Academy of Sciences coordinating closely with a special committee within the United Nations could serve as an anchor to reality for the multiplicity of rumors and unfounded information that is likely to exist within this age of extraterrestrial anxiety.

It will be very important for official governmental agencies and the scientific community to have a highly visible role during the period of signal interpretation. The public should be informed and educated about the difficulties and pitfalls that could stem from misinterpretation of the signal's message. Public rumor and panic could spread if official interpretation and analysis are overwhelmed by those who seek to exploit this sensational event for their own ends.

Security Considerations

As of now the Earth-shaking impact of a SETI success is being ignored by governments around the world. The idea seems to be just too fantastic or improbable. The impact of a SETI discovery has not been seriously considered in the planning and policy debates of current governmental structures. The SETI community has made repeated overtures to national and international agencies to engage in dialogue on this matter but little of substance has been accomplished.

But what a difference a day makes. That day is "acquisition day," the day the announcement is made that scientists here on Earth have acquired evidence of an intelligently designed technology from other beings in space. On that day government officials will be seeking out SETI scientists for information rather that vice versa.

Again, assuming the minimal-information scenario holds, what it is we will know about the sender is virtually nothing. Despite this, we will have to make decisions. Do we attempt to reply? Who will reply, or, as Carl Sagan said, "Who speaks for Earth?" Then we must ask, What do we say? Unfortunately, all these official questions are likely to be made moot by the fact that there are no controls over or binding agreements on reply policy. While radio astronomers of a more guarded and responsible nature are debating the above-mentioned questions, others of a more opportunistic bent will be using their facilities to send signals to the source of the discovery. They hope to be able to claim they are the first to communicate with beings from another world. Major issues concerning national and international security are likely to develop (Tarter 2000). Although scientists will assure the public and security agencies that the signal emanates from a very great distance and it will take a very long time for any threat, even if present, to manifest itself, the normal human propensity for fear will translate into constant security assessments. This will involve passing rules and regulations for scientists to obey and will lead to a great many issues involving scientific freedoms and security concerns. The unfolding of this debate and the policies initiated from it will have profound impacts on the human future even though no alien presence has been found nor even suspected.

Space Policy Implications

The signal from the extraterrestrials has given us very little to work with. We know almost for certain it is of intelligent design but as of yet we have not found a way to decipher its meaning. There could very well be a number of more information-rich scenarios we might construct, but whatever scenario we might wish to imagine, I believe any scenario would have the effect of bringing the human interest in space technology to its highest levels ever. From school children to the highest levels of world political leadership, interest would be riveted on our capabilities in space. Partly out of fear, partly out of curiosity, any contact scenario would have the effect of involving the whole of humanity in a common enterprise. This would no doubt serve to put human conflicts here on Earth in a new light. President Ronald Reagan, in a speech before the United Nations General Assembly in 2000 stated the situation thusly: "Perhaps we need some outside universal threat to make us recognize this common bond. I occasionally think how quickly our differences world wide would vanish if we were facing an alien threat from outside this world."

No doubt this is true, but is a direct threat necessary to bring us together as one people? Confirming that contact had been established would probably not end war here on Earth, but contact would make the common bond of humanity more apparent. In a way, however, contact might serve to push the agenda of a more heavily armed Earth. It very well could lead to a rebirth of the Strategic Defense Initiative, or the "Star Wars" program, as it is more commonly known. This was a space-based weapons program initiated in the Reagan administration. It envisioned a wide array of laser weapons and space-based missile systems, which could fight and perhaps prevent intercontinental warfare launched against America. Of course, it was enormously expensive. Many observers feel that the Soviet Union found it prohibitively expensive and thereby changed its domestic policies and shed its coat of communism.

The latter point is a matter of debate, but the fact of being vastly expensive is not. Not much reference is made to the "Star Wars" program anymore, although research and development continues along these lines. Progress on the exotic weapons system has proven more difficult than thought. It appears that it was an idea well ahead of its technological time. The contact event will almost immediately boost interest in investing heavily in space-based defenses. The enormous corporate support will almost certainly make such investments a reality. Many scientists would scoff at this buildup in space weaponry. They would note that the threat had not been proven. They would also note that it would take many years if not centuries before physical contact between our two civilizations is possible. Yet the human propensity for interpreting a presence as a potential threat would most likely prevail. If we have detected a presence of others in the universe, it would be wise to be prepared as well as possible. This argument will win the day.

SETI and Space Reconnaissance

The discovery of a single intelligently designed signal in space would obviate the need to do a full reconnaissance of the space environment to search for more intelligently designed signals from other civilizations. We have a very limited array of radio telescopes here on Earth and the vast majority of them are devoted to other types of radio observations. A single discovery would greatly stimulate calls for additional radio observatories both here on Earth and in space. SETI programs worldwide would acquire new and top-priority billing under conditions created by actual contact. Rather than being the orphan child of the space age, the fantastic proposition that we might be able to establish contact with other intelligent beings would have demonstrated its correctness. Money would pour into SETI programs from both public and private sources. It would be apparent that we must improve our capabilities in searching for other signs of extraterrestrial intelligence. It could be that radio astronomy would become the new glamour science. Just as human fascination with physical space flight dominated the last four decades of the twentieth century so the fascination with the electronic surveillance of outer space would come to the fore in literature, movies, and popular culture. Assuming that the initial contact event would continue to yield indecipherable signals for several years, it would be reasonable to predict that SETI programs would be accelerated to the point that some of its fondest dreams would be made into serious proposals and put into action. One such example is the implementation of an effort to turn the "Lunar Far Side Program" into reality.

Lunar Far Side Observatories

For decades radio astronomers have been urging the establishment of radio observatories on the far side of the lunar surface. Of course, such calls fell on deaf ears because there were so many other urgent demands on our national budgets. Our concerns here on Earth seem much more important than listening to the immense whispering of radio waves from far across the universe. The contact event will change that thinking forever.

It will become imperative that we listen to the whispers of radio waves with all the sophistication that we can muster. What was esoteric now becomes essential. What was some of the most remote, barren, and seemingly useless landscape in near-Earth space now becomes the most valuable piece of property available to the human race. The contact event will set in motion forces that will bring a bustling of human activity to a desolate landscape that has for eons lain silently with its dark face toward the distant stars. The far side of the Moon would be destined to become a busy place with bristling human activity. It will become our first line of intelligence about what is out there in the far darkness.

Why the lunar far side? The Moon always keeps the same face toward us as it rotates around Earth. The Moon's far side is a radio-quiet zone. It is the only place in the solar system that is not swamped by the noise of our radio-active Earth. We are indeed fortunate to have this physical advantage so close to home. A giant radio-quiet zone sits right next to us in space.

Radio noise is one of the most devastating problems faced by modern radio astronomy. The available radio spectrum is becoming increasingly saturated with private and commercial usage. The number of radio frequencies available for radio astronomy is drastically shrinking. Some have predicted that by the end of the second decade of this century radio astronomy may be nearly impossible.

Given these facts, radio astronomers have for a long time wanted to go to the far side of the Moon and build receiving equipment there. The United States government has on a regular basis indicated its intention to return to the Moon and stay there on a permanent basis. Growing budget deficits have made this possibility more and more difficult. The eminent SETI astronomer Frank Drake, anticipating that we might someday discover an intelligently designed signal from outer space, has spent a great deal of time developing a scenario for a lunar farside radio observatory. According to Drake, upon the first discovery of a signal: "We will tell the world at large what has happened, and that we are taking the next step by building better equipment to understand the message we have received. How I would love to have to go to Congress with a budget request for that project. I don't imagine I'd encounter much opposition" (Drake and Sobel 1992: 229–230). I doubt if Frank Drake, or any other radio astronomer, under the conditions that I have described would encounter much opposition in their efforts to fulfill the dreams of the radio astronomy community. Of course, the project would be international in nature and the money would be found. The lunar far side is an excellent site for really serious radio astronomy for other reasons besides reduction of radio noise. On the Moon more frequencies are available. There is no atmosphere to shield out the radio longwaves (ten meters plus). On Earth these frequencies are not observable.

Another advantage for far-side radio astronomy would be the lack of wind force. Radio telescopes on Earth have their receiving capabilities frequently distorted by wind forces on the dish. In a no-atmosphere environment this obviously would not be a problem. Likewise, huge dishes have to resist the force of gravity as they are steered toward their targets. The lower the gravity the less the dish is distorted in the steering activity. Since lunar surface gravity is only one sixth that of Earth's, distortion should be less.

The thousands of craters that are found on the backside of the Moon provide perfect terrain for large fixed Arecibo-type dishes. Arecibo, located on the island of Puerto Rico, is the world's largest semi-steerable radio/radar observatory. Frank Drake has suggested building an Arecibo-type dish thirty miles in diameter on the lunar far side (Drake and Sobel 1992). The real Arecibo dish is only a fifth of a mile in diameter. The lunar receiver would have one hundred and fifty times the diameter of the Earthly Arecibo and would have several thousand times the collecting area. Far-side craters are available for such a project. The receiver in this low-gravity environment could be suspended from cables and no wind or other elements would hamper its operation. Huge radio receivers on the lunar far side would vastly increase our sensitivity. It is possible that with these types of facilities we could pick up the stronger radio emissions from planets orbiting distant suns. We could, for the first time, monitor their radio and television emissions, or planetary leakage, as it is called. If we were confronted with a source that either does not know we are here or chooses not to communicate with us, this may be the best hope of investigating their capabilities or their intentions. Under conditions of having received a minimum information signal, such a monitoring of planetary leakage would be assumed absolutely necessary for those in the intelligence community and national security agencies.

Planetary Observations over Immense Distances

The contact event would spur interest in learning as much as possible about the star system from which the signal is emanating. After the system is identified and charted on celestial maps, Earth's most powerful telescopes would be trained on it. Our present observational telescopes, even the powerful Hubble Space Telescope, could probably tell us little about planets around the distant sun of the system we have identified. Demands will be forthcoming for more sophisticated observational telescopes. One such proposal might be able to utilize the principles of gravity and light as proposed by Albert Einstein.

Albert Einstein's work on gravity and light suggested that light itself was bent by the presence of massive gravitational fields. This theory was verified by bending the Sun's rays during a solar eclipse. A sun or a galaxy can actually bend light to focus a concentrated image upon a point. In effect, a sun or galaxy can serve as a telescope of immense power.

Several scientists have suggested that the gravity lens phenomenon may have practical application in tremendously enhancing our space-based telescopic abilities (Cohen 1988). One proposal particularly important to SETI has been advanced by Italian mathematician Claudio Maccone. This project, called SETISAIL, is designed to exploit the Sun's gravitational field in order to obtain extremely high-resolution images of distant stars (Maccone 1992). A photon collector would be placed aboard a spacecraft and flown to a distance of at least 550 astronomical units (AU) from the Sun (one AU is the mean distance of the Earth from the Sun—approximately 93 million miles). At this distance and even further out to one thousand AUs the Sun's lensing effects could be used to provide images not only of planets around stars, but perhaps relatively small surface features on those planets. This amazing instrument is within current technological capabilities. More recently, Maccone (2011) has highlighted the benefits of having gravitational lenses located both near our Sun and near the target star, providing significant amplification of radio signals. Gravitational lens missions would be high on the request list that would be presented to world scientific organizations following contact.

Interstellar Communication in the Deeper Future

One of the most exciting aspects of contact, even with a minimal-information source, is the stimulating effect it would have for research and development on advanced ideas for deep-space communication and observation. Distance and the limitations of the speed of light have been the greatest deterrents to having the scientific community take seriously the search for extraterrestrial intelligence.

The distance between worlds in the galactic system is so immense and the speed of light as the maximum speed limit allowed by nature is so slow that most scientists have ruled out any serious communications among the scattered worlds of our galaxy. Even SETI scientists have traditionally assumed that any interstellar communication would involve decades or centuries. Most have engaged in SETI to answer the philosophical question about life in the universe. Few have anticipated any practical benefit made possible by striking up a conversation with our distant neighbors. Is there any prospect that this dismal scenario might be overcome?

I have suggested this possibility in two publications in the *Journal of the British Interplanetary Society* (Tarter 1996, 1997). The reason that we have not discovered any evidence of radio communication among the stars just may be that there are much faster ways to conduct interstellar communication. Civilizations not far beyond our level of development may communicate in vastly more efficient ways while we are still looking for evidence of communication by primitive means. Perhaps we might be able to communicate instantly with distant civilizations by a method I call "quantum communication."

Quantum communication is a concept that has grown out of one of the strangest properties in nature, the so-called Einstein, Podolsky, and Rosen (EPR) effect first reported in 1935. This effect predicts that two photons simultaneously emitted will remain "entangled" no matter how far they move apart. Effects of the observation of one photon will produce instant effects for the observer of the twin photon whether it is in another room or another galaxy. In the strange world of the quantum there is not only zero time but also zero distance.

Einstein himself was so shocked at this realization that he refused to believe in its reality. Yet, since 1935, numerous thought experiments and now physical experiments have verified the reality of the EPR effect. Perhaps the most vivid demonstration of this effect has come from experimenters in Switzerland. Nicolas Gisin and a group of researchers at the University of Geneva have demonstrated that this effect holds over large distance. These scientists sent entangled photons via fiber-optic lines to two small villages 10.9 kilometers apart. There was the demonstration of the properties of entangled photons to instantly react over substantial distances.

The EPR effect has been empirically demonstrated. Many other enabling technologies and strategies must be developed before this can be of use for deep space communication. Sophisticated photon traps would be needed. These traps would grab and store the photons for polarization measurement. We must also develop and transmit information keys that would be sent out ahead of our photon stream so as to give the receiver a hint as to how to read our message. The information we transmit would be carried in the changing polarization of the photon stream. Our receiving civilization would have to understand this. It would be somewhat akin to transmitting a cosmic Morse code.

The need for information keys sent out at the classical speed limit to make the procedure work demonstrates that this technique does not really violate the universal peed limit of light speed. When two civilizations have entangled photons in their position, instant communication would be possible. The initial contact, however, would be made at classical light speed.

We might imagine very old and very advanced civilizations in remote galaxies using massive and distant cosmic phenomena such as gamma-ray bursts to carry their quantum keys throughout the universe. The vastly distant and, as of now, almost totally mysterious phenomena of gamma-ray burst might act as the intergalactic network for information transfer—perhaps akin to a cosmic brain in which the bursts approximate the firing of neural synapses. If such keys exist and have been long ago transmitted in our direction, could we, perhaps, intercept them and use them to read the cosmic mind?

Conclusion

If humans can calm their ethnic passions and lessen their parochial identities they may have a glorious future in the universal order of things. If not, we may well be just another failed experiment, another dead civilization on a small planet orbiting a very ordinary star. It would be truly tragic to see such a promising species torn apart and destroyed by what it now believes are irreconcilable differences. You will remember that I began this chapter with the hope that was created by the dawn of the space age. This hope was that our movement into space might help us outgrow our provincialisms. Perhaps we would begin to define humankind in terms of a broader and more inclusive identity. Our initial adjustments to the new realities that space technology has brought us were insufficient to completely free us from our national hostilities and disputes.

We may soon enter the second phase of the space age: detection and attempts at communication with intelligent beings on other worlds. Perhaps if successful, this second phase of the space age can fulfill the value agenda of cultural anthropology. Since the early inception of cultural anthropology as a discipline here on Earth, its agenda has been to find and catalogue new and unknown cultures on Earth, then understand and appreciate the richness of this cultural diversity. This is very similar to the ultimate goal of SETI: find new civilizations in space, catalog new and unknown cultures in space, then understand and appreciate the increased richness of our cosmic diversity. In so doing SETI could contribute to the greater spirit of human unity and identity. We have much to learn and do. Let's get on with it.

Bibliography

Billingham, John, et al. 1999. *Societal Implications of the Detection of an Extraterrestrial Civilization*. Mountain View, CA: SETI Press.

Bova, Ben, and Byron Preiss, eds. 1990. *First Contact*. New York: NAL Books.

Cohen, Nathan. 1988. *Gravity's Lens*. New York: John Wiley.

Drake, Frank, and Dava Sobel. 1992. *Is Anyone Out There?* New York: Delacorte Press.

Einstein, Albert, Boris Podolsky, and Nathan Rosen. 1935. "Can the Quantum Mechanical Description of Physical Reality Be Considered Complete?" *Physical Review* 47: 777–780.

Finney, Ben. 1990. "The Impact of Contact." *Acta Astronautica* 21, no. 2: 117–127.

Harrison, Albert A. 1997. *After Contact: The Human Response to Extraterrestrial Life*. New York: Plenum Trade.

Maccone, Claudio. 1992. "SETISAIL: The New Space Mission by a Solar Sail/Antenna to Exploit the Sun's Gravitational Lens." Engineering School of Turin, Turin, Italy.

———. 2011. "Interstellar Radio Links Enabled by Gravitational Lenses of the Sun and Stars." In *Communication with Extraterrestrial Intelligence*, ed. Douglas A. Vakoch, 177–213. Albany, NY: State University of New York Press.

Sagan, Carl. 1985. *Contact*. New York: Simon and Schuster.

———. 1994. *Pale Blue Dot*. New York: Random House.

Saud, Prince Sultan bin Salman bin Abdulaziz Al. 1985. Interview with Bob McDonald, *Christian Science Monitor Broadcasting*, Program of September 9.

Tarter, Donald E. 1996. "Alternative Models for Detecting Very Advanced Extraterrestrial Civilizations." *Journal of the British Interplanetary Society* 49: 291–295.

———. 1997. "Is Real-Time Communication Between Distant Civilizations in Space Possible? A Call for Research." *Journal of the British Interplanetary Society* 50: 249–252.

———. 2000. "Security Considerations in Signal Detection." *Acta Astronautica* 46, no. 10–12, 725–728.

Chapter 6

AMERICAN ATTITUDES ABOUT LIFE BEYOND EARTH
Beliefs, Concerns, and the Role of Education and Religion in Shaping Public Perceptions

George Pettinico

In the spring of 2005, the National Geographic Channel, the SETI Institute, and the University of Connecticut partnered to conduct a nationally representative survey of public attitudes regarding extraterrestrial life. The telephone survey of one thousand Americans was among the largest and most extensive to date on this topic, measuring public beliefs on various aspects of life beyond Earth never before gauged in such a systematic fashion. This chapter will explore the survey findings regarding basic beliefs about life on other planets, the degree of excitement/nervousness if contact with extraterrestrial life were to be made, expected prevalence of life in the universe, types of extraterrestrial life expected, assumed likelihood of success regarding contact, and reasons for non-belief among those who do not accept the possibility of life on other planets.

Survey Methodology

The national telephone survey of adults aged eighteen and older was conducted by the Center for Survey Research and Analysis (CSRA) at the University of Connecticut from 18 April through 3 May 2005. The sample was generated using a Random Digit Dial (RDD) methodology.[1] This approach assures a sample that is representative of the national adult population, with a sampling error of +3.2 percent at the 95 percent confidence level. Numerous additional steps were taken by the CSRA staff to reduce other potential sources of error in this study.[2]

Impact of Educational Attainment and Religiosity

Survey results were analyzed among an extensive array of demographic and social characteristics. This analysis uncovered two key demographic drivers that account for the greatest differences in beliefs and attitudes regarding extraterrestrial life, namely an individual's educational attainment and his/her religiosity, measured in our study by frequency of religious service attendance. This chapter will explore the intersection of these two demographic traits with beliefs and attitudes about extraterrestrial life. By "beliefs" we mean whether or not an individual believes in extraterrestrial life and what types of life he/she deems likely. By "attitudes" we mean how the individual *feels* about the possibility of life beyond Earth; does it make him/her nervous, hopeful, etc.

The impact of educational attainment on attitudes and beliefs in this area may not be all that surprising to most readers, since education often has a significant impact on one's views of scientific topics. However, the role of religion in this area deserves some attention upfront. As any social observer knows, America is a deeply religious country, particularly when compared to other western advanced democracies. According to recent national surveys conducted by the Gallup Organization, fully 90 percent of Americans believe in God, and just about three-quarters (74 percent) describe themselves as a "religious person."[3] For generations, American religiosity has far surpassed the much weaker levels that have existed in European nations or Canada, countries that are very much like the United States on other social and economic measures (Ladd 1994).

In America, religious beliefs have long had a significant impact on the attitudes and behaviors of members of society. Social science research has shown how an individual's religious views impact his/her political and social preferences, and even his/her attitudes toward the environment (Guth et al. 1995; Leege and Kellstadt 1993). In this study, we uncovered very significant differences regarding beliefs and attitudes about life on other planets based on one's level of religiosity. The most pronounced difference is on the most fundamental issue on this topic—the belief in extraterrestrial life itself.

Belief in Life on Other Planets

The sense that we are not alone in the universe is the majority belief in America today. Six in ten Americans (60 percent) believe that "there is life on other planets in the universe besides Earth." Only 32 percent disagree that there is extraterrestrial life, while 8 percent don't have a clear belief either way.

On this fundamental question there are significant differences by religiosity. More religious Americans (as measured by frequency of religious service attendance) are twice as likely to *reject* the notion of life on other planets. Simply put, the more religious a person is in America today, the less likely he/she is to believe in life beyond Earth. Only 45 percent of Americans who regularly attend religious services believe in extraterrestrial life, versus 70 percent of those who rarely or never attend services (see table 6.1).

Why would religious Americans be less likely to believe in life on other planets? Despite our growing national diversity, the overwhelming majority of Americans are Christians (at least nominally). Devout Christians in America are more likely than other Americans to hold very traditional views of humanity as the single culmination of God's creation and the Earth as the one divinely chosen place for this culmination of creation to live and prosper. For many conservative Christians, the universe—despite its size and scope—exists for the benefit of humanity alone. In their belief system, humans are not simply one group among many in a crowded universe; this would take away much of the divine attention from humanity.

Table 6.1. Belief in life on other planets, by religiosity

Q. *"Do you believe that there is life on other planets in the universe besides Earth?"*

Note: asked of full sample			Attend religious services		
	All Americans		Weekly	About once a month	Rarely/never
	%		%	%	%
Yes—do believe	60		45	57	70
No—do not believe	32		48	34	21
Not sure	8		7	8	9
Refused	*		1	1	0
Count	(1,000)		(328)	(175)	(480)

* = less than 1%

	Value	Df	Significance (2-sided)
Pearson chi-square	66.321	6	0

Although most religious Americans accept the notion that the Earth is not at the physical center of the universe, for many of them the Earth is at the center of the universe in every other way—it is the single spot of divine focus where God placed life. The following is an excerpt from an essay addressing the topic of extraterrestrial life on ChristianAnswers.net, a popular fundamentalist Christian website that describes itself as a "mega-site providing biblical answers to contemporary questions": "Although the subject is not addressed explicitly, the Bible teaches implicitly that the only thing He [God] created with intelligence are the angels, man and the animals. ... Earth is unique and holds center stage in God's creation. ... Although our all-powerful God could have created such [extraterrestrial] life had He desired, it seems rather obvious from Scripture that He did not. ... It is our privilege to be the center of attention in our vast and wonder-filled universe" (Van Bebber 2011).

Importantly, as our survey shows, not *all* religious Americans today reject the possibility of extraterrestrial life. In fact, just about half (45 percent) of religious Americans believe in life on other planets. So, even among this group there is significant belief in extraterrestrial life. Yet, 48 percent of devout Americans reject the notion of life beyond Earth. This is a higher level of disbelief than is evident among any other subgroup. There is greater difference regarding belief in extraterrestrial life by religion than there is by education, age, income, race, gender or other sociodemographic variables tested (see table 6.2).

A Brief Historical Review of Extraterrestrials in Christian Thought

The debate within the Christian community regarding extraterrestrial life has been going on for centuries—with Christian leaders and scholars represented on both sides. The dispute is evident as far back as the Middle Ages. While many leading medieval church philosophers such as Thomas Aquinas (1224–1274) were against the idea of extraterrestrial life because they felt the Earth was the center of the universe and the only planet to harbor life in God's divine plan, other contemporary church leaders strongly supported the idea (Crowe 1997). For example, in 1277 the bishop of Paris, Etienne Tempier, issued a disapproval of any doctrines that set limits on God's power, including condemning the idea that God "cannot make many worlds" (Crowe 1997). Nikolaus of Cusa (1401–1464), Catholic priest (later cardinal), argued for the existence of life on other worlds and even on the Moon and Sun in his influential 1440 book *Of Learned Ignorance* (Crowe 1997).

Table 6.2. Belief in life on other planets, by demographic variables

Q. *"Do you believe that there is life on other planets in the universe besides Earth?"*

Rank order by % believe	Yes—believe in life on other planets	No—do not believe
	%	%
Attend religious services rarely/never	70 (Highest)	21 (Lowest)
Men	69	25
Aged 45 to 59	66	28
Nonwhite	65	27
Household income $75,000+	64	30
Some college education	63	28
College degree or more	63	28
All Americans (national average)	*60*	*32*
Household income under $40,000	60	33
Aged 18 to 44	59	34
White	59	33
Attend religious services about monthly	57	34
Household income $40,000 to under $75,000	57	33
High school education or less	56	37
Aged 60+	53	32
Women	51	39
Attend religious services weekly	45 (Lowest)	48 (Highest)

Notes: asked of full sample. Also tested (but not shown) by geographical region, marital status and political party identification. Religiosity proved to be a more important factor than these.

The Protestant Reformation, with its emphasis on a direct reading of the Bible, is associated with many Christian theologians who were generally against the view of life on other planets for two reasons: there is no mention of extraterrestrial life in the Bible and Christ's incarnation and redemption could not have occurred on multiple worlds. As Lutheran theologian Philip Melanchthon wrote in the mid 1500s, "We should not imagine many worlds because we ought not imagine that Christ died and was risen often" (O'Meara 1999).

By the 1700s and 1800s, after detailed observations of numerous planets and moons, a great number of secular western intellectuals came to believe in life on other planets (Crowe 1997). In turn, many Christian scholars began to incorporate the existence of extraterrestrial life into their theologies. For example, Timothy Dwight, a Congregational reverend and president of Yale University from 1795 to 1817, argued in support of life on other planets. Dwight dealt with criticisms that Christ could not have lived, died, and been resurrected on countless worlds by asserting that it was only on Earth where humans fell from grace and required saving (Crowe 1997). New Christian sects such as Mormonism and Seventh Day Adventists were founded in the 1800s with a clear acceptance (even celebration) of extraterrestrial life in their belief systems (Crowe 1997)

The debate within the Christian community continues today. Our survey found religious Americans are far more skeptical than their non-religious counterparts about life on other planets. Research published in 1980 among the clergy of various Christian sects found that fundamentalist priests and ministers were also more likely to reject the idea of extraterrestrial life than their less fundamentalist colleagues (Rosenbaum et al. 1980). On the other hand, the current official position of the Catholic Church is at least open to the possibility of life on other planets and willing to work this possibility into its theology. As Father Augustine Di Noia, Vatican undersecretary of the congregation for the doctrine of the faith, put it, "If there are other persons in the universe, we can at least say that they too are involved in the same divine plan" (Allen 2004).

When Will We Make Contact?

Returning to the survey results, Americans who are open to the possibility of life on other planets (68 percent of the total) are not quite sure *when* we will confirm the presence of extraterrestrial life. There is no majority agreement on an expected timeline for this. However, clearly the vast majority (79 percent) of Americans who are open to the possibility of life on other planets believe that we will eventually confirm the existence of life beyond our planet. Forty-five percent of Americans who are open to the possibility of extraterrestrial life actually think it will happen within the next few decades or less (see table 6.3). That seems to be a fairly optimistic outlook, perhaps due to the rapidly improving technology utilized to locate and observe new planets in the galaxy that has been getting a good amount of press over the past few years.

Degree of Concern

Most Americans who are open to the possibility of extraterrestrial life are not worried about it—this despite the onslaught of movies that try to convince the public that there is much to be frightened about from outer space (*Independence Day*, *War of The Worlds*, the *Alien* franchise, to name just a few). Seventy-two percent of Americans who are open to

Table 6.3. Estimates of when life on other planets will be confirmed

Q. *"When do you think we will confirm, without a doubt, that there is life on other planets?"*

	Among Americans who are open to the possibility of life on other planets
	%
In a few years	7
In the next few decades	38
In another century or more	34
Never	14
Not sure	7
Refused	0
Count	(678)

Note: asked of those who are open to the possibility of life on other planets (68% of all Americans—60% who believe and 8% who are not sure)

the possibility of life beyond our planet say that they would feel "excited and hopeful" if we were to confirm that there is life on other planets, while only 20 percent say they would feel "anxious and nervous." It may be that movies showcasing friendlier aliens (e.g., *E.T.*) have had a more lasting impact on people's thinking than those that portray more vicious and brutal aliens. Or, more likely, it may be that Americans who are open to the idea of life beyond Earth simply do not let Hollywood impact their views on this issue, keeping fantasy (however entertaining) separate from their own speculations regarding what is really out there.

Regarding one's fear versus excitement about eventual confirmation of extraterrestrial life, educational attainment has a significant impact. College-educated Americans are less fearful of the discovery of extraterrestrial life than are their less educated counterparts. Among believers in extraterrestrial life, only 10 percent of college educated individuals say they would be "afraid and nervous" if and when this is confirmed beyond a doubt, versus 26 percent (who say they would be "afraid and nervous") among those with only a high school degree or less (see table 6.4).

Prevalence of Life on Other Planets

When it comes to the prevalence of life on other planets, Americans who are open to the possibility of extraterrestrials are more likely to expect that life is fairly uncommon or sporadic at best. It seems that although they

Table 6.4. Degree of concern, by educational attainment

Q. *"If we were to discover, for certain, that there is life on other planets, which of the following best describes how you would most feel: afraid and nervous or excited and hopeful?"*

Note: asked of those who are open to the possibility of extraterrestrial life (68% of total)	Total	Educational Attainment		
		High school or less	Some college	College degree
	%	%	%	%
Afraid and nervous	20	26	18	10
Excited and hopeful	72	65	74	82
Not sure	8	9	8	6
Refused	*	0	0	2
Count	(678)	(176)	(190)	(306)

	Value	Df	Significance (2-sided)
Pearson chi-square	30.912	12	0.002

accept the idea of life beyond Earth, most find it hard to believe that the universe is teeming with it. When asked to think of the "entire universe" and to speculate how many planets currently have some form of life:

- only 15 percent say there is life on "millions of planets";
- 12 percent say there is life on "thousands of planets";
- 16 percent say there is life on "hundreds of planets";
- a plurality, 45 percent, say there is life on "only a few planets";
- and the remaining 11 percent cannot even fathom a guess.

(Note: Asked of those who are open to the possibility of life beyond Earth—68 percent of the public.)

It seems that when conceiving of life in the universe, believers are more likely to picture a density more akin to Northern Canada than Manhattan. Part of the issue here, likely, is that it is difficult for most people to conceive of the size of the universe. Despite Carl Sagan's excellent efforts to teach the general public about the immense scope of the universe ("billions and billions"), the sheer vastness of it is a difficult concept to grasp. Also, news reports about the discovery of new planets—or planet-like objects—beyond our solar system tend to emphasize smaller numbers. We simply have not discovered that many planets so far. This, of course, is because we can only look at a relatively small part of our galaxy, in a still very limited fashion (only spotting the biggest of the "planets"). But most of the public at this point appears to be thinking in smaller rather than larger numbers.

Criteria for Life

Can life develop without the presence of liquid water and sunlight? Americans who are open to the possibility of life beyond Earth are evenly divided on this, with 45 percent saying Yes and 47 percent saying No (see table 6.5). Interestingly, college-educated Americans are much more open minded about this and are thus more likely to believe that life can develop in the absence of the two key ingredients for life here on Earth.

Types of Extraterrestrial Life

When Americans who accept the possibility of extraterrestrial life are asked to speculate as to what type of life that might be, a strange dichotomy is evident. They are most likely to think that extraterrestrial life forms will either be very simple, such as single cell microbes, or very advanced, such as intelligent life forms more advanced than humans. They are less likely to believe that life forms will be more midrange—similar to plants and non-human animals (see table 6.6).

Table 6.5. Criteria for life, by educational attainment

Q. *"Do you think life can develop on a planet if there is no liquid water and no sunlight?"*

Note: asked of those who are open to the possibility of extraterrestrial life (68% of total)			Educational Attainment		
	Total		High school or less	Some college	College degree
	%		%	%	%
Yes	45		39	48	51
No	47		53	46	39
Not sure	8		8	6	10
Refused	0		0	0	0
Count	(678)		(176)	(190)	(306)

	Value	Df	Significance (2-sided)
Pearson chi-square	18.87	12	0.092

Table 6.6. Types of extraterrestrial life

Q. *"In your opinion, how likely is it that some of these life forms on other planets would be _____? Would you say it is very likely, somewhat likely, or not at all likely?"*

Among Americans who believe in life on other planets

		% saying *very* likely	% saying *somewhat* likely	% saying *not* likely at all
Less complex	Similar to single cell or few cell organisms like microbes or bacteria	45 (highest)	42	8
	Similar to plants like trees and flowers	25 (2nd lowest)	54	17
	Similar to animals, like birds, lizards or mammals	21 (lowest)	48	25
	Similar to humans	30	46	21
More complex	Intelligent life forms more advanced than humans	39 (2nd highest)	41	16
Count		(678)		

Note: asked of those who accept the possibility of life on other planets (68% of all Americans)

It is hard to know how to interpret these findings. It makes sense that the public feels very simple life forms such as microbes are the most probable extraterrestrial life forms, since most space scientists would generally agree—at least that extraterrestrial microbes would probably be more common than more advanced life forms. However, the public is more likely to believe in the probability of advanced life forms (more advanced than humans), or even life forms "similar to humans," than they are to believe in the probability of plant-like or animal-like life forms. This may be, in part, due to the impact of the media, which tends to emphasize human-like or advanced extraterrestrial life forms. When average Americans think about aliens, they may more easily envision *Star Trek's* Klingons than they do some sort of lower-level animal.

Do Americans believe in the notion of space-faring extraterrestrials? To a moderate degree, yes. A third of Americans who are open to the possibility of extraterrestrial life (34 percent) feel it is very likely that "there are life forms on other planets that have technology to travel through space and visit different solar systems." An additional 38 percent feel this is somewhat likely.

Communication with Extraterrestrial Civilizations

Americans who accept the possibility of life beyond Earth are hesitant to say whether or not these life forms will have the ability to communicate across deep space. Only 29 percent say it is very likely that extraterrestrials will be able to do this, while 44 percent say it is somewhat likely, and 22 percent say it is not likely at all.

However, there is a clear consensus on whether or not we should respond if we receive communications from another planet. A whopping 90 percent of Americans who are open to the possibility of extraterrestrial life say that if we do hear communications from another planet, we should respond to it. Only 7 percent say we should not, while 3 percent are undecided. This is the strongest response, meaning closest to unanimous, that we encountered in the entire survey. Without a doubt, if humanity one day receives a long distance call from deep space, Americans want us to pick up and say hello in return.

However, whether or not we would even know what we hear is a different story. Only 50 percent of Americans who are open to the possibility of life beyond Earth say Yes when asked "If beings from another planet sent a message to us through deep space, do you think we would be able to figure out what they were saying?" Thirty-eight percent say we would not be able to figure the message out, while 11 percent say they are not sure how successful humanity would be in this endeavor.

Reasons for Disbelief Among Nonbelievers

We will now turn our attention to the nonbelievers—Americans who reject the possibility of extraterrestrial life. Among the third of Americans (32 percent) who do not believe in life on other planets, we tested four possible rationales and, for each, asked if it is a major reason, minor reason, or not a reason at all as to why they do not believe in extraterrestrial life. The rationales tested were:

- "If there were life on other planets, they would have visited us or contacted us in some way by now";

- "Only the Earth has all the necessary ingredients for life";
- "We have sent probes into space and have telescopes examining space and we have not found any evidence of it yet";
- and "According to my religious beliefs, the only planet with life is Earth."

Three of these possible explanations rise to the top in prevalence, with slightly over half of nonbelievers saying it is a major reason why they reject the possibility of extraterrestrial life:

- 56 percent cite religious beliefs as a major reason;
- 53 percent say their perception of the Earth as the only life-sustaining planet is a major reason;
- 52 percent cite the fact that our space probes and telescopes have found no evidence so far as a major reason.

Clearly, the first two reasons are matters of faith—religious beliefs and the perception of Earth as the one and only life-bearing planet pertain to one's belief system. However, the third reason, lack of evidence so far, reflects a more "scientific" approach—based on evidence gathered to date. However, this rationale suggests a significant overestimate among these individuals of the current state of the technology—not taking into account that our space probes have barely gotten out of the solar system, that our deep-space listening abilities are still limited, and that we have only been listening for a few decades, and then only intermittently. Of course, it also may very well be an example of people using available "evidence" to fit a preconceived belief. These individuals do not believe in life on other planets and the fact that we haven't heard any interstellar messages yet or that Voyager 2 has not yet bumped into a star cruiser from another galaxy fits nicely into their preexisting belief system. Only 36 percent cite the lack of documented alien visitation to Earth as a major reason for their disbelief.

As one might expect, among strongly religious Americans, the religious belief argument as to why they cannot accept the possibility of extraterrestrial life is far more widespread than it is among less religious nonbelievers. Among less religious Americans, the argument of not having been contacted yet is a more persuasive rationale for disbelief (see table 6.7).

Looking at Americans who do not believe in extraterrestrial life by educational attainment, one difference is clear. Less-educated Americans are more likely to stand behind the argument that there have yet been no documented alien visitations (see table 6.8).

Those who do not believe in life beyond Earth were asked the same question that we also asked of believers, namely, how they would feel if extraterrestrial life was discovered and proven. Nonbelievers are twice as

Table 6.7. Reasons for disbelief in life on other planets, by religiosity

Q. *"For each of the following, please say if it is a major reason, a minor reason, or not a reason at all as to why you do not believe in life on other planets?"*

Shown: % who cite the following as a "major reason"

Note: Asked of those who do not believe in life on other planets (32% of all Americans)			By attendance at religious services		
	Total		Weekly	About once a month	Rarely/never
	%		%	%	%
According to my religious beliefs, the only planet with life is Earth	56		72	60	31
If there were life on other planets, they would have visited or contacted us in some way by now	36		30	32	48
Count	(321)		(156)	(59)	(102)

(Row 1)	Value	Df	Significance (2-sided)
Pearson chi-square	50.244	8	0

(Row 2)	Value	Df	Significance (2-sided)
Pearson chi-square	25.222	8	0.001

likely to express apprehension than are believers (42 percent compared to 20 percent; see table 6.9). It may be that because nonbelievers do not currently accept extraterrestrial life, the discovery of it would make them more fearful than their believing counterparts. Or, cause and effect may be the reverse. For some nonbelievers, it may be that they are so fearful of the thought of extraterrestrial life that they choose not to believe in it in the first place.

Conclusion

In America today, most people (six in ten) believe in life on other planets. If the additional 8 percent who are "not sure" are factored in, that makes almost seven in ten open to the possibility of life beyond Earth. Among the remaining (roughly) three in ten who are nonbelievers, re-

Table 6.8. Reasons for disbelief in life on other planets, by educational attainment

Q. *"For each of the following, please say if it is a major reason, a minor reason, or not a reason at all as to why you do not believe in life on other planets?"*

Shown: % who cite it as a "major reason"

Note: asked of those who do not believe in life on other planets (32% of all Americans)			By educational attainment		
	Total		High school or less	Some college	College degree
	%		%	%	%
If there were life on other planets, they would have visited or contacted us in some way by now	36		41	32	26
Count	(321)		(156)	(59)	(102)

	Value	Df	Significance (2-sided)
Pearson chi-square	28.037	12	0.005

ligious convictions are clearly a major force causing them to reject the possibility of extraterrestrial life.

It will be useful to keep an eye on public opinion over the next few years and decades, as more planets are discovered and more time is spent listening to various corners of our galaxy. Will the discovery of more planets increase public belief in extraterrestrial life, or will more years of listening for extraterrestrial communications without hearing anything definitive reduce public belief? Only time will tell. Of course, if and when

Table 6.9. Degree of concern, by belief or disbelief in life on other planets

Q. *"Just imagine for a moment that we were to discover, for certain, that there was intelligent life on other planets. If that were to occur, which of the following best describes how you would feel: afraid and nervous or excited and hopeful?"*

	Among Americans who do NOT believe in extraterrestrial life (32% of total)	Among Americans who DO believe in extraterrestrial life (60% of total)
	%	%
Afraid and nervous	42	20
Excited and hopeful	44	72
Not sure/refused	14	8

definitive contact with extraterrestrial life is finally made, the more religious members of society will have to factor this reality into their belief system, just as they were forced a few hundred years ago to acknowledge that the Earth is not at the physical center of the universe.

Notes

1. The survey utilized a Random Digit Dial (RDD) methodology to generate a random sample of telephone households in the contiguous forty-eight states. Within each telephone household, one adult individual was randomly selected to complete the survey. The RDD sample was drawn using the GENESYS Sampling System, which is licensed by CSRA. RDD methodologies generate telephone numbers from banks of one hundred telephone numbers. For example: 860-486-33XX is the telephone bank which contains one hundred telephone numbers from 860-486-3300 to 860-486-3399. By generating phone numbers in this way, we are able to include both directory-listed and -unlisted telephones (for more information on RDD methodology for telephone surveys, see Lepkowski 1988). Phone banks are generated proportionally, based on the population in each area code and phone exchange (according to the latest US Census data).
2. Several steps were taken by CSRA to insure representativeness, such as: multiple attempts to each household over the course of several days and at different times of the day to include even the busiest respondents; refusal conversions (a refusal conversion occurs when a person who initially refuses to participate in a survey is called back a few days later by a more experienced interviewer who attempts to re-engage the individual in the study); and bilingual interviewing (English and Spanish). All CSRA interviewers undergo an extensive training process and all interviewing sessions are monitored by supervisors. Following standard survey procedures, survey results were weighted to match the latest Census population figures on key demographic variables.
3. Gallup telephone survey conducted 2 to 4 May 2004 among a national sample of 1,000 American adults were asked: "For each of the following items I am going to read you, please tell me whether it is something you believe in, something you're not sure about, or something you don't believe in: God": 90 percent Believe in; 5 percent Not sure about; 4 percent Don't believe in; and 1 percent No opinion. Gallup telephone survey conducted 29 June to 3 July 2005 among a national sample of 504 American adults were asked: "Irrespective of whether you attend a place of worship or not, would you say you are a religious person, not a religious person, or a convinced atheist?": 74 percent A religious person; 24 percent Not a religious person; 1 percent Convinced atheist; and 1 percent Don't know / refused.

Bibliography

Allen, John L., Jr. 2004. "This Time, Catholic Church Is Ready." *National Catholic Reporter*, 27 February: 5–6.

Crowe, Michael J. 1997. "A History of the Extraterrestrial Life Debate." *Zygon* 32, no. 2: 147–162.

Guth, James L., et al. 1995. "Faith and the Environment: Religious Beliefs and Attitudes on Environmental Policy." *American Journal of Political Science* 39, no. 2: 364–382.

Ladd, Everett C., Jr. 1994. *American Ideology: An Exploration of The Origins, Meaning and Roles of American Political Ideology*. Storrs, CT: Roper Center for Public Opinion Research.

Leege, David C., and Lyman A. Kellstedt, eds. 1993. *Rediscovering the Religious Factor in American Politics*. Armonk, NY: M. E. Sharpe.

Lepkowski, James M. 1988. "Telephone Sampling Methods in the United States." In *Telephone Survey Methodology*, eds. Robert M. Groves, et al., 73–98. New York: John Wiley and Sons.

O'Meara, Thomas F. 1999. "Christian Theology and Extraterrestrial Life." *Theological Studies* 60, no. 1: 3–30.

Rosenbaum, Dennis P., Richard A. Maier, and Paul J. Lavrakis 1980. "Belief in Extraterrestrial Life: A Challenge to Christian Doctrine and Fundamentalists?" *Journal of UFO Studies* 2: 47–57.

Van Bebber, Mark. 2011. "What Does the Bible Say about Intelligent Life on Other Planets." http://www.christiananswers.net/q-eden/edn-c012.html. Accessed on 18 April 2011.

Chapter 7

Cultural Beliefs about Extraterrestrials
A Questionnaire Study

William Sims Bainbridge

Since European explorers first reached all regions of the Earth, there have been no real "aliens" or "outsiders," and all of humanity is currently linked into a single, global community. However, it is possible that contact will soon be made with a very different kind of alien—namely, non-human inhabitants of other worlds—and it is worth understanding our own degree of preparation for this event. The concept of extraterrestrial intelligence has become part of modern culture, but it holds different meanings for various groups that can be uncovered through social-scientific research. With that goal in mind, this questionnaire study replicates and extends one that was carried out in 1981 and reported in the 1983 pages of the *Journal of the British Interplanetary Society* (Bainbridge 1983, 1991). As the earlier report asserted, communication with extraterrestrial intelligence depends as much upon social support for the project as upon appropriate engineering design and upon the actual existence of a nearby extrasolar civilization. Furthermore, it would be wise to understand the culturally based assumptions that would shape world reaction to the discovery of extraterrestrial intelligence, a momentous event that could come at any time.

The 1981 study administered its questionnaire to 1,465 students at the University of Washington in Seattle, and it made no pretense of having a random sample of the general population. However, given the large number of respondents, statistical analysis could focus on the complex relationships between variables and uncover regularities that might be expected to apply to other groups as well. For example, a major factor discouraging people from supporting attempts to communicate with extraterrestrial intelligence was their religion—in this case evangelical Protestants, exemplified by the "Born Again" movement that was prominent on campus at the time the data were collected. The present study seeks to replicate such findings, but also looks for new discoveries, primarily using data from 3,909 adults who responded to the English-language version of *Survey2001*, an online questionnaire sponsored by the National Geographic Society and the National Science Foundation (Witte et al. 2000; Witte 2004).

Administering a questionnaire online offers a mixture of advantages and disadvantages. In general, it is far less costly to obtain responses from a large number of people, which can translate into the capability of including far more questions and thus examining topics either in greater depth or of wider range. The cost is a reduced ability to extrapolate to the population as a whole because one does not get a random sample. There is good reason to believe that non-sample online questionnaires are pretty good at measuring the relationships between variables and at comparing subgroups of respondents, but not good for estimating the population parameters (Bainbridge 2002c). For topics that have not already been studied extensively by social scientists, as is the case for beliefs about extraterrestrials, the advantages predominate. Later, once we have used data like those from the present study to develop clear, theory-based predictions, we can consider investing the great cost required to administer key questionnaire items in random-sample replication research. Alternately, we may find it is more scientifically profitable to carry out a variety of studies, for the aggregate cost of doing one random-sample survey, administering questionnaires to selected groups that may reveal deeper insights than those reflected in the general population.

An International Questionnaire

Survey2001 contained three items related to extraterrestrial intelligence. Two were part of a battery of thirty statements about science, technology, and pseudoscience, with which the respondent was asked to agree or disagree. One agree/disagree item was taken verbatim from the 1981 study: "Intelligent life probably does not exist on any planet but our own."

Available responses were: Strongly agree, Agree, Do not know, Disagree, and Strongly disagree. People who disagree with this statement thereby express some willingness to believe that extraterrestrial intelligence does exist, but they do not necessarily believe that extraterrestrials (ETs) dwell near the Earth or have traveled here. Another agree/disagree item concerns this possibility: "Some UFOs (Unidentified Flying Objects) are probably spaceships from other worlds." The third item, which will be analyzed near the end of this chapter, repeated the two statements and asked respondents to write comments about the topic.

The questionnaire was administered in four languages. A total of 4,577 respondents answered the item about the existence of ETs in English, 215 in Spanish, 349 in German, and 142 in Italian. The National Geographic Society publishes its magazine in all four of these languages, and many respondents were recruited from its international print publications and websites. In addition, respondents were recruited by the research team through their educational institutions, and the team included social scientists in countries speaking all four languages. An earlier project, *Survey2000*, had been administered only in English, with research partners in each US state and province of Canada, so it is to be expected that most of the *Survey2001* respondents used the English language.

Altogether, only 10.8 percent of respondents agreed that ETs do not exist, combining "Agree" with "Strongly Agree": 11.0 percent of those responding in English, 9.8 percent of those using Spanish, 11.7 percent of German speakers, and 4.9 percent of Italian speakers. Perhaps it is more interesting to see the percentages who disagreed with this item, thereby expressing a willingness to believe that ETs could exist: English 64.3 percent, Spanish 70.2 percent, German 61.6 percent, and Italian 72.7 percent. The percentages agreeing with the UFO item vary much more widely: English 22.4 percent, Spanish 46.2 percent, German 8.9 percent, and Italian 26.8 percent. Despite the fact that the UFO craze originated in the English-speaking United States, it appears to have taken hold more strongly among Spanish speakers, and German speakers appear relatively immune to it.

Another way of analyzing the international data, naturally, is in terms of the nations in which respondents live, but only six nations contributed at least one hundred responses to the ET and UFO questions, thereby offering a minimally sufficient number for statistical analysis. The percentages disagreeing that ETs do not exist are: 68.4 percent for Australia, 62.7 percent for Canada, 62.1 percent for Germany, 70.7 percent for Italy, 71.7 percent for the United Kingdom, and 64.8 percent for the United States. Unfortunately, responses from Spanish-speaking nations with a fair number of respondents—notably Argentina, Mexico, and Spain—were substantially fewer than one hundred. Belief that some UFOs are spaceships showed these percentages: 27.2 percent for Australia, 25.7 percent for Canada, 10.2 percent for Germany, 26.7 percent for Italy, 22.1 percent for the United Kingdom, and 21.7 percent for the United States.

Despite German skepticism about UFOs, ideas about ETs are widely held and clearly play a role in global culture. Future studies with larger numbers of Hispanic and German respondents will be needed to understand why these cultures are unusually favorable or unfavorable to notions about UFOs. Belief in the possibility of extraterrestrial intelligence seems about equally prevalent across the languages and nations studied, however. One might be concerned that National Geographic magazine is so much less well-established outside the English-speaking world that National Geographic respondents using Spanish, German, and Italian are significantly different from English-speaking National Geographic respondents. Thus, for deeper examination of the data it will be wise to focus on the numerous respondents who used English. It is important to note that cross-cultural research in the modern world need not be limited to studies in which the unit of analysis is the nation or the language area, but it can also look for evidence of competing subcultures with data where the unit of analysis is the individual respondent.

Correlated Variables

The following analysis focuses on 3,909 English-language respondents who answered all thirty of the items in the battery of agree/disagree items that contained the two ET statements. Of these, 3,898 reported their genders: 1,787 males and 2,111 females. Table 7.1 shows the patterns of agreement and disagreement. Keeping in mind that the respondents are not a random sample of the general population, it is interesting to note that more people disagree with these two statements than agree with them. Fully 64.3 percent are prepared to believe that ETs exist (the 34.0 percent plus 30.3 percent who disagree or strongly disagree with the first statement), but only 22.2 percent agree or strongly agree that some UFOs are probably spaceships. It is also worth noting that women are more likely than men to say they do not know, replicating a finding from the study done two decades earlier.

There are also weak but statistically significant tendencies for women to agree with both statements more often than men, as measured by both gamma and r correlation coefficients (gamma = 0.14, 0.16; r = 0.07, 0.11). To the extent that this is a logical contradiction, it may represent an acquiescence bias or "yea-saying" bias among females, or the opposite

Table 7.1. Responses to two statements about extraterrestrials, by gender (percent)

Response	Intelligent life probably does not exist on any planet but our own.		Some UFOs (Unidentified Flying Objects) are probably spaceships from other worlds.		
	%		%		
	Male	Female	Male	Female	All
Strongly agree	4.4	3.5	3.7	5	4.4
Agree	6.3	6.8	16.5	18.9	17.8
Do not know	21.2	28.5	36.5	43.5	40.3
Disagree	32.3	35.5	20.5	18	19.1
Strongly disagree	35.8	25.8	22.8	14.5	18.3
Total	100	100	100	100	100
Count	(1,787)	(2,111)	(1,787)	(2,111)	(3,898)

bias among males (Couch and Keniston 1960). For readers who do not often work with correlation measures, it is worth mentioning that these numbers range from +1.00 down through 0.00 to –1.00. A positive correlation means that people who agree with one item tend to agree with the other. A negative correlation indicates that respondents who agree with one tend to disagree with the other. Numbers near zero are not "statistically significant" and thus suggest no relationship between the two variables. The correlation between the ET and UFO items, as measured by the Pearson's r statistic, is –0.35 for all 3,909 respondents. This is quite strong, as questionnaire data go, and it confirms the intuition that people who believe ETs do not exist have a strong tendency to reject the idea that UFOs are spaceships. Later, however, we shall see that the relationships between these two variables is actually quite complex.

Because respondents were college students, the 1981 study was able to look at the influence of various academic subjects. It found the expected negative correlations between rejecting the existence of ETs and liking astronomy (tau = –0.23) and "the sciences, in general" (tau = –0.14). However, because the respondents were students in a single large university, it was not possible to compare people of very different educational backgrounds. The new data do permit such a comparison, as shown in table 7.2, with a subset of respondents who provided information about whether they had graduated from college. We see no real difference between college-educated respondents and those who have not graduated with respect to rejection of the existence of ETs (gamma = –0.01; r = –0.01 between having graduated and agreeing). However, the difference is quite substantial for the item about some UFOs being spaceships, with college-educated people being significantly less likely to believe this (gamma = –0.21, r = –0.14).

Table 7.2. The effect of having a college degree (percent)

Response	Intelligent life probably does not exist on any planet but our own.		Some UFOs (Unidentified Flying Objects) are probably spaceships from other worlds.	
	College Degree	No Degree	College Degree	No Degree
	%		%	
Strongly agree	3.8	4.2	3.7	6.1
Agree	6.1	7.4	13.5	21.9
Do not know	25.2	24	40.4	40
Disagree	34.3	33.8	20.6	17.9
Strongly disagre	30.6	30.5	21.8	14.2
Total	100	100	100	100
Count	(1,775)	(1,186)	(1,775)	(1,186)

The 1981 study found a strong connection between enthusiasm for communication with extraterrestrial intelligence and support for the space program. Two of the agree/disagree items used back then were: "Funding for the space exploration program should be increased" and "Space exploration should be delayed until we have solved more of our problems here on earth." These items were also used in the 2001 study, with slight editing by the *National Geographic* team, removing the words "exploration" from the first, and "here" from the second. In the 1981 data, the item denying the existence of ETs correlated negatively with increasing funding for the space program, as measured by Kendal's tau (tau = −0.29) and positively with delaying space exploration (tau = 0.24). In the 2001 data, the correlations are comparable but somewhat weaker (tau = −0.22, 0.17). One might speculate that the failure of planetary probes to detect signs of life, and the invisibility of SETI efforts within the space program, have to some extent weakened the perceived connection between ETs and the space program over the two decades. However, the two sets of respondents are sufficiently different that one cannot have confidence in this interpretation. Interestingly, the UFO item in the 2001 study does not correlate significantly with either space program item (tau = 0.02, 0.05).

The thirty agree/disagree items in the recent dataset include three pairs having to do with controversies in science-based technologies: nanotechnology, nuclear power, and psychoanalysis. Table 7.3 shows the correlations between agreeing with these six items and the two about ETs, as measured by Pearson's r. The largest correlations are not very strong, and some are not significantly different from zero. With fully 3,909 respondents, it does not take much of an association to achieve statistical significance, here measured as having less than one chance in a thousand that the number is different from zero only by luck. Belief that ETs do not

Table 7.3. Correlations (Pearson's r) with statements about science-based technologies

Statement	Intelligent life probably does not exist on any planet but our own.	Some UFOs (Unidentified Flying Objects) are probably spaceships from other worlds.
Human beings will benefit greatly from nanotechnology, which works at the molecular level atom by atom to build new structures, materials, and machines.	-0.18*	0
Our most powerful 21st-century technologies—robotics, genetic engineering, and nanotechnology—are threatening to make humans an endangered species.	0.08*	0.14*
Development of nuclear power should continue, because the benefits strongly outweigh the harmful results.	-0.01	-0.09*
All nuclear power plants should be shut down or converted to safer fuels.	0.02	0.10*
Forgotten childhood experiences and subconscious conflicts have a great effect on people.	-0.11*	0.16*
Psychoanalysis and most varieties of psychotherapy are useless techniques based on false conceptions of the mind.	0.12*	-0.10*

*Statistically significant beyond the 0.001 level.

exist correlates with rejecting both nanotechnology and psychoanalysis, two forms of science-based technology that could hardly be more different but that have the common property that they were not involved in political controversies when the questionnaire was administered. There is no association with attitudes toward nuclear power, which is a politically salient topic. The pro-UFO item, however, shows a weak connection to rejection of nuclear power.

Eighteen of the other agree/disagree items are about pseudoscience or so-called New Age beliefs, and one would think they might connect to beliefs about UFOs. There are several historical connections. The intellectual basis of ancient Babylonian astrology was the belief that the planets actually were the gods, or that the gods dwelled in them (Toulmin and Goodfield 1961). In 1758, the Swedish mystic, Emanuel Swedenborg, claimed to have communicated with angels living on other planets (Swedenborg 1950). A number of twentieth-century cults were oriented toward extraterrestrials, including Aetherius, Unarius, Raelians, and Heaven's Gate (Lewis 1995; Palmer 1995; Partridge 2003). In any case, table 7.4 shows very strong correlations between the UFO item and the New Age items, showing that people who think UFOs might be spaceships also accept the possibility of astrology, communication with the dead, telepathy, telekinesis, and Atlantis.

Table 7.4 shows much weaker associations between belief in the New Age and rejection of the possibility that ETs exist. Consider the –0.06 correlation between rejecting the idea of intelligent life on other planets and acceptance of astrology. This means there is a very slight tendency for people who believe in astrology to believe in ETs. But the correlation between UFOs and astrology is 0.40. The ratio of 0.06/0.40 is 6.6, suggesting that the UFO connection is six times stronger. But statisticians like to square correlation coefficients before comparing them, transforming them into the proportion of variance explained by the correlation. By that standard, the association between belief UFOs are spaceships and belief in astrology is more than forty-four times greater than the association between belief ETs might exist and belief in astrology. Another way of putting this is to say that the correlation between belief in ETs and in astrology is spurious. There really is no direct relationship at all between belief in the possibility of life on other planets and acceptance of New Age beliefs. Rather, some people believe in ETs only because they already believe in UFOs, thereby connecting ETs to New Age ideas in their own minds, whereas most people with opinions about the existence of ETs make no such connection. This hypothesis suggests it is worth looking more closely at the differences between people who hold different combinations of opinions about the ET and UFO items.

Three Logically Consistent Viewpoints

If we set aside the people who replied "Do not know" to either of the two questions, there are four possible viewpoints, only three of which are logical. The illogical viewpoint is to deny that ETs exist but to assert that UFOs could be spaceships. Less than 1 percent of respondents are in this category, and we will ignore this tiny minority because they apparently made an error in reading the statements or in responding. That leaves three groups that deserve analysis.

Table 7.4. Correlations (Pearson's r) with pseudoscientific or New Age statements

Statement	Intelligent life probably does not exist on any planet but our own.	Some UFOs (Unidentified Flying Objects) are probably spaceships from other worlds.
There is much truth in astrology - the theory that the stars, the planets, and our birthdays have a lot to do with our destiny in life.	-0.06*	0.40*
Astrologers, palm readers, tarot card readers, fortune tellers, and psychics can't really foresee the future.	0.09*	-0.60*
Every person's life is shaped by three precise biological rhythms - physical, emotional, and intellectual - that begin at birth and extend unaltered until death.	0.00	0.28*
Numerology, biorhythms, and similar attempts to chart a person's life with numbers are worthless.	0.11*	-0.33*
Some people can hear from or communicate mentally with someone who has died.	-0.15*	0.47*
Psychic mediums who claim they can communicate with the dead are either frauds or mentally ill.	0.14*	-0.42*
Some people really experience telepathy, communication between minds without using the traditional five senses.	-0.17*	0.48*
Extra-sensory perception (E.S.P.) probably does not exist.	0.23*	-0.48*
Some people can move or bend objects with their mental powers.	-0.18*	0.47*
It's not possible to influence the physical world through the mind alone.	0.18*	-0.32*
Some techniques can increase an individual's spiritual awareness and power.	-0.14*	0.27*
Yoga, meditation, mind control, and similar methods are really of no value for achieving mental or spiritual development.	0.23*	-0.23*
Dreams sometimes foretell the future or reveal hidden truths.	-0.11*	0.31*
Analyzing dreams is a waste of time because they are random fragments of thought and memory.	0.13*	-0.21*
Some scientific instruments (e.g., e-meters, psionic machines, and aura cameras) can measure the human spirit.	-0.11*	0.39*
Perpetual motion machines, anti-gravity devices, and time travel machines are physically impossible.	0.24*	-0.32*
Scientifically advanced civilizations, such as Atlantis, probably existed on Earth thousands of years ago.	-0.13*	0.44*
All ancient people were less advanced than modern civilization in science and technology.	0.10*	-0.30*

First, some respondents believe ETs do not exist and perhaps therefore believe that UFOs are never spaceships from other worlds. In fact, just three hundred respondents hold this position. This figure was calculated by combining "Strongly agree" responses with "Agree," and "Strongly disagree" with "Disagree," then counting the people who agree with the negatively phrased ET statement and disagree with the positively phrased UFO statement. We can call these three hundred people "geocentrists," because they believe the Earth is unique in being the only planet that harbors intelligent beings.

Second, 754 respondents accept the possibility of intelligence on other planets but reject the claim that some UFOs are spaceships. Many who hold this opinion are probably aware of the great distances between the stars, suspect that life is rare in the galaxy, and therefore conclude that other intelligent species live too far away to visit us in person. Common words like *isolationist, segregationist,* or *separatist* come to mind, but they imply the person wants to be separated rather than merely recognizing that separation exists. The technical term *allopatric* from population biology is appropriate if unfamiliar, referring to a geographic separation between two gene pools, so I will call this group "allopatrists."

Third, 806 respondents believe some UFOs could be spaceships, and they logically accept the possibility of extraterrestrial intelligence. The words *saucerite* and *saucerian* sometimes describe beings associated with flying saucers, but usually extraterrestrials themselves. People who actively study UFOs call themselves *ufologists,* so this term cannot properly be extended to people who merely believe in them. The word *ufophile* is very rarely used, but for present purposes perhaps its meaning is clear enough.

Some variables are especially good at distinguishing allopatrists from ufophiles. For example, 59.0 percent of ufophiles are female, compared with only 40.1 percent of allopatrists. Geocentrists fall between these extremes, with 54.3 percent being female. Education is another powerful variable. Fully 69.6 percent of allopatric respondents to *Survey2001* have graduated from college, compared with only 48.0 percent of ufophiles and 56.5 percent of geocentrists. The mean age for allopatrists is 37.54 years, compared with 36.93 for ufophiles and 35.85 for geocentrists. These age differences are not huge, and it would be hazardous to conclude that allopatrists tend to be older because they have had more time to inform themselves about relevant subjects like astronomy.

Support for the space program differs across the three groups. Among allopatrists, fully 60.5 percent want funding increased, compared with 52.7 percent of ufophiles and only 29.3 percent of geocentrists. This lack of enthusiasm for space travel among geocentrists provides an additional justification for the name I have given them. The well-educated and disproportionately male respondents who accept the possibility of ETs but reject UFOs are somewhat more enthusiastic about two other kinds of advanced technology as well. Fully 70.6 percent of allopatrists agree that nanotechnology will benefit human beings, compared with 60.3 percent of ufophiles and 43.0 percent of geocentrists. Continuation of nuclear power development is favored by 43.5 percent of allopatrists, 31.5 percent of ufophiles, and 35.0 percent of geocentrists.

In the 1981 study, religion proved to be a very powerful variable affecting attitudes and beliefs concerning extraterrestrials, with highly religious people being especially likely to reject the idea. The new dataset contains several religion variables, including a question about how frequently the respondent attends religious services. Of the total of 1,837 respondents who answered this question plus the ET and UFO items, 46.4 percent attend religious services less than once a year, which must be described as very rarely. Another 35.3 percent attend more frequently but not often. The remaining 18.3 percent attend nearly every week or even more frequently, which is often. Geocentrists are more religious than average, only 26.8 percent attending less than once a year, versus 45.3 percent attending often. Among allopatrists, the pattern is reversed, 50.4 percent attending essentially never and 15.6 percent often, and the comparable figures for ufophiles are 50.1 and 10.7. Thus, geocentrists, who reject the possibility of extraterrestrial intelligence, tend to be much more involved in traditional religious organizations and activities.

Of course, some people attend church simply because their families want them to, and others are unable to attend for practical reasons such as ill health. Table 7.5 compares the three groups in terms of a variable more closely related to the individual's religious orientation, the respondents' own judgments of how religious they are. The plurality of each group proclaims some degree of religiousness. But in analysis of social data it is important to look at relative tendencies, in the awareness that our data are always noisy and many factors shape an individual's beliefs. A larger fraction of allopatrists are non-religious, and a larger fraction of geocentrists are religious. The really interesting thing in table 7.5 is the fact that a significant majority of ufophiles, 60.6 percent, are in the moderate "Somewhat religious" or "Neither religious nor non-religious" categories.

The semi-religiousness of ufophile exactly fits recent discoveries in the sociology of religion. A considerable variety of earlier research studies have shown that New Age and cultic phenomena tend to arise in communities where traditional religious organizations are weak, and among people who retain a positive orientation toward the supernatural but are not deeply involved in conventional religious congregations (Stark and Bainbridge 1985; Bainbridge 1997, 2004a). Unlike fully secular people, they have religious urges. Unlike traditionally religious people, these urges are unsatisfied. Therefore, they are open to novel religious and quasi-

Table 7.5. Religiousness of respondents (percent)

Self-Description	Allopatrists	Ufophiles	Geocentrists
	%	%	%
Extremely non-religious	14	7.5	9.3
Very non-religious	14.4	9.1	3.9
Somewhat non-religious	11.6	8.5	4.6
Neither religious nor non-religious	21.4	23.9	12.5
Somewhat religious	25.3	36.7	30.2
Very religious	10.2	12.3	30.2
Extremely religious	3	2	9.3
Total	100	100	100
Count	(723)	(757)	(281)

religious appeals, like the UFO mythology. Earlier, we saw a strong connection between belief in UFOs and various other New Age beliefs. Now we see how that connection arises from the religious context. For many people, belief in UFOs is an analog to religion, but one that lets them feel they are modern people in tune with the scientific culture. Thus, a tendency to believe that some UFOs are spaceships is a natural result of the process of secularization, which has weakened traditional faith without removing many people's need for transcendent hopes.

Table 7.6 verifies that ufophiles strongly tend to be members of the New Age movement. To be sure, less than a third of ufophiles believe in astrology, but this is more than five times the miniscule fraction of

Table 7.6. New Age beliefs of respondents (percent)

Statement	Allopatrists	Ufophiles	Geocentrists
	%	%	%
There is much truth in astrology, the theory that the stars, the planets, and our birthdays have a lot to do with our destiny in life.	5.2	29	7.3
Scientifically advanced civilizations, such as Atlantis, probably existed on Earth thousands of years ago.	19.8	62.5	22.7
Some people can hear from or communicate mentally with someone who has died.	10.3	48	10.3
Some people really experience telepathy, communication between minds without using the traditional five senses.	28.8	77.3	27.7
Some people can move or bend objects with their mental powers.	9.7	39	5.7

allopatrists, and nearly four times the fraction of geocentrists. A majority of ufophiles believe in Atlantis and telepathy, and large fractions believe in communication with the dead and mental movement of physical objects, often called "telekinesis" or "psychokinesis" by self-professed "parapsychologists." The allopatrists and geocentrists, for all their other differences, hardly differ in their lack of interest in the New Age. We shall return to this comparison after considering the qualitative data from *Survey2001*.

The Open-Ended Questionnaire Item

A randomly selected subset of about eight hundred respondents commented on the pair of items, writing whatever they chose to express in a text area of the online questionnaire. Following methods that had been developed in earlier projects (Bainbridge 1991), a large number of distinct statements about extraterrestrials were culled from these open-ended responses and edited into statements that would be suitable as agree/disagree items for future questionnaires. Table 7.7 lists ninety-eight of these statements, along with the two stimulus statements, for a total of one hundred distinct ideas about extraterrestrials. The numbers in the table are data from a single individual.

The one hundred statements about extraterrestrials are a small part of a major research project on personality capture, the science and technology of entering measurements of a human personality into a computer or information system. There are many methods for doing personality capture, and some visionaries imagine it will some day be possible to scan the neural connections in the person's brain (Kurzweil 1999). This project explores a different and more conservative approach, building upon conventional questionnaire research in psychology, sociology, and political science. The immediate goal is to collect or create 100,000 questionnaire items, incorporate them in software modules for convenient administration, and obtain responses to all 100,000 items from a single individual. As a research project, this work has already resulted in many scientific publications (Bainbridge 2002a, 2003, 2004b, 2004c, 2004d).

There is also a very long-term goal related to communication with extraterrestrial intelligence, as was explained in a NASA publication (Bainbridge 2002b) and in chapter 11 of this volume (Bainbridge, 2011). If human beings are ever going to travel to the stars, they may do so not as biological organisms but as dynamic patterns of information either contained in databases on long-duration space probes or transmitted by radio. Indeed, it is conceivable that advanced civilizations exchange ambassa-

Table 7.7. One respondent's ratings of one hundred ET statements

Item	Order Answered	Statement	"True" Rating	"Important" Rating
1	14	If one out of a million planets contains an atmosphere capable of sustaining life, then in the galaxy there could be a million planets with life.	7	7
2	15	The universe is a huge waste of space if we are the only intelligent life.	7	6
3	23	Aliens would be welcomed as saviors if they had the technology to solve any of our problems.	7	7
4	25	After many years of supposed sightings, if UFOs were real the secret would have come out by now.	7	6
5	27	UFOs are the figments of people's imagination.	7	6
6	28	There is some hope that we might be able to detect radio messages from distant extraterrestrial civilizations.	7	7
7	29	It is nice to think that there may be intelligent life elsewhere.	7	7
8	30	Extraterrestrials would adhere to the same physical laws discovered by Earth science, so they could not travel faster than light.	7	7
9	33	Most UFOs are human interpretations imposed on other types of phenomena.	7	7
10	48	People believe in UFOs because they want to believe in them.	7	6
11	49	If extraterrestrials came to Earth they would not sneak around abducting the residents.	7	6
12	54	An encounter with an extraterrestrial would be a fulfillment of our wildest dream.	7	7
13	61	An extraterrestrial civilization smart enough to visit us would be able to keep their presence a complete secret.	7	7
14	64	Bacteria can live in hot sulfur vents at the bottom of the ocean, so there is a chance we can find life on other planets.	7	7
15	65	Given the number of stars in the universe, it is highly unlikely that we are the only intelligent form of life.	7	7
16	75	Intelligent beings from another planet could teach us something about our own planet.	7	6
17	76	If intelligent life happened here on Earth, it certainly could happen elsewhere.	7	6
18	81	It would be unwise to bet on any aliens showing up shortly.	7	6
19	89	UFOs are not spaceships from other planets.	7	7
20	92	Scientists have recently confirmed that other stars have accompanying planets.	7	7

Table 7.7. Continued

Item	Order Answered	Statement	"True" Rating	"Important" Rating
21	98	We have not explored space enough to know if we are or are not alone in the universe.	7	7
22	100	Many UFO sightings are just balloons, planes, or satellites.	7	6
23	3	Earth is most likely too far from any planet that could have intelligent life to have direct contact with it.	6	6
24	7	Some people are scared of what they do not understand, so they dismiss the idea of intelligent aliens.	6	6
25	8	The so-called UFO evidence in photos and videos was engineered in a photo lab.	6	5
26	18	If we were visited by aliens, they would not pick some yahoo from the country to reveal themselves to but go to someone credible.	6	6
27	19	It is possible that life or its building blocks arrived here from space via asteroids or comets.	6	6
28	31	No race of extraterrestrials is spying and studying us.	6	6
29	35	If extraterrestrials had the technology to travel between the stars, they would have taken over the universe by now.	6	7
30	36	It would be a sad thing if we were the only intelligent beings in the universe.	6	6
31	47	UFOs are weather phenomena and freak clouds.	6	6
32	53	Information on UFOs in the media is too questionable to conclude they are spacecraft from other planets.	6	6
33	56	The whole fuss about UFOs is merely a projection of people's hopes onto unusual natural and weather appearances.	6	7
34	60	There is no credible evidence to support claims of UFO encounters.	6	6
35	70	UFO sightings are wishful thinking.	6	6
36	71	It is equally amazing if intelligent life exists on another planet or if it does not.	6	6
37	74	UFOs as portrayed in popular media are pure fantasy.	6	6
38	77	It is unlikely that an alien craft has entered Earth's atmosphere within the span of recorded history.	6	6
39	85	If intelligent life exists on other worlds, they are probably as dumb as we Earth people and involved with their own local concerns.	6	6
40	87	Intelligent extraterrestrials exist but have not yet visited Earth.	6	6

Table 7.7. Continued

Item	Order Answered	Statement	"True" Rating	"Important" Rating
41	90	Intelligent beings from another planet could be more advanced than we are and have the means for interstellar space travel.	6	6
42	4	UFOs are generally natural events that people see without understanding.	5	5
43	11	UFOs are nonsense.	5	5
44	20	Intelligent beings on other planets are too far away to visit the Earth.	5	6
45	26	If we should find aliens less advanced than ourselves, it would be our duty to enlighten them	5	5
46	38	Most UFOs are optical illusions.	5	6
47	41	The odds of intelligent life finding our planet by random space travel is remote.	5	5
48	43	The diversity of life on this planet with all of its extremes helps to demonstrate that life is probably common.	5	6
49	44	Intelligent life on other planets does not resemble our culture's images of it.	5	5
50	51	Belief in UFOs illustrates the fact that people are willing to believe almost anything at times.	5	5
51	58	UFOs are physical phenomena and can be explained by physics.	5	5
52	59	It is incredibly self-centered and egotistical for humans to believe they are the only form of intelligent life.	5	6
53	67	An advanced civilization that has interstellar travel does not need to hide from people.	5	6
54	69	UFOs are only in the realm of science fiction.	5	5
55	80	Given the age of the universe, many aliens are more intelligent than we are	5	5
56	83	It is illogical to think intelligent life would send spacecraft to visit before first trying to communicate with us by radio.	5	6
57	86	UFOs are not from other worlds, because it makes no sense for them to spend years flying here, enter our atmosphere, and not land.	5	5
58	91	UFOs are probably space junk falling into the atmosphere and burning up.	5	5
59	97	Intelligent beings on another planet would feel curiosity and travel through space to learn about other worlds.	5	6
60	5	Life on other planets must be very different, since conditions of climate and terrain are so different.	4	6
61	21	It is doubtful that beings from another star are able to survive such a long flight, in zero gravity, to our planet.	4	7

Table 7.7. Continued

Item	Order Answered	Statement	"True" Rating	"Important" Rating
62	24	We should just leave what is out there in space alone as it may be very dangerous to our civilization.	4	6
63	39	Some planets may have life based on other chemical elements than carbon.	4	5
64	40	In comparison with the intelligence that may exist on other worlds, we are stupid.	4	6
65	45	Intelligent life on other planets is unlikely to take a bipedal, humanoid form.	4	5
66	52	The Earth probably was visited by intelligent extraterrestrials many millions of years ago.	4	6
67	57	The lunatic fringe with wild stories about UFOs have prevented us from doing sound research on such phenomena.	4	6
68	62	An extraterrestrial civilization capable of receiving our television images of wars and soap operas will probably take steps to avoid us.	4	6
69	63	We face a lonely existence if life does not exist beyond Earth.	4	6
70	68	Other planets are not naturally able to support life, because of extreme temperatures and weather conditions.	4	5
71	73	It is unlikely that spaceships could travel into our atmosphere undetected by radar or satellites.	4	6
72	82	If UFOs were built by extraterrestrials, they must be far more intelligent than humans.	4	6
73	88	Most claimed UFO sightings are just blatant lies by people seeking fame.	4	5
74	94	UFOs certainly exist but are of terrestrial origin.	4	5
75	95	Almost all sightings of UFOs have been hoaxes.	4	5
76	96	UFOs are just that: unidentified flying objects.	4	3
77	1	Some UFOs (Unidentified Flying Objects) are probably spaceships from other worlds.	3	6
78	6	Possibly life existed at another time in history, but there are no aliens on other planets at this time.	3	5
79	10	People whose claims are worthy of respect say they have experienced UFOs.	3	5
80	13	UFOs are probably secret experiments of governments here on Earth.	3	6
81	16	It does not matter if extraterrestrials exist, because we inhabitants of this Earth have enough of our own problems to solve.	3	6

Table 7.7. Continued

Item	Order Answered	Statement	"True" Rating	"Important" Rating
82	17	Scientists already found that micro-life exists on Mars.	3	7
83	22	The government explains UFOs away with ridiculous explanations, because it believes the public is not ready for the truth.	3	4
84	32	Proof about the existence or nonexistence of extraterrestrial visitors will come within a decade.	3	5
85	34	UFO are probably American spy planes.	3	5
86	37	Extraterrestrials visit the Earth without making overt contact because they have a policy of non-interference.	3	7
87	46	Some selected groups of humans built UFOs with advanced technology.	3	6
88	50	Speculation about intelligent life from other planets is of little value.	3	6
89	55	If there were other intelligent life, we would have found each other by now.	3	6
90	66	Visitors from other worlds have assisted the development of our civilization.	3	6
91	79	Intelligent beings from somewhere else are already here, living among us.	3	7
92	93	If advanced civilizations exist in other galaxies, they would have no reason to come here.	3	6
93	99	A lot of strange UFO-related occurrences have happened to people.	3	5
94	2	Intelligent life probably does not exist on any planet but our own.	2	7
95	9	The distances between solar systems are so great that the laws of physics preclude travel from one to another.	2	7
96	12	Evidence of extraterrestrial visits have been found in hieroglyphics in Egypt as well as other locations across the Earth.	2	6
97	42	UFOs are our own ships from the future that can travel back in time.	2	7
98	72	There has been enough documented evidence from credible sources to indicate that some UFOs are spacecraft.	2	6
99	78	Extraterrestrials, endowed with an immortal soul, would have somehow been redeemed by the redemptive mission of Jesus Christ.	2	4
100	84	Some people have actually been abducted by UFOs.	2	6

dors in this manner, and colonists for uninhabited star systems could be transmitted after robots had established a base for them.

The one hundred ET-related items were incorporated in a Windows-based software module called *Beliefs II*, the second of three modules, each of which was based on two thousand statements of belief. The chief goals of *Beliefs II* are:

1. to be an interactive tool for private exploration of a person's own beliefs, thus a map of his or her mind and tool for making decisions;

2. to be a system for recording a person's beliefs and values, thus a time capsule to preserve an important aspect of that individual;

3. to be an educational system for preparing essays in courses such as the psychology of personality, philosophy, and social science.

The user reads each statement, and then evaluates it on two 8-point scales, in terms of how true versus false and important versus unimportant he or she feels it is. Table 7.7 arranges the one hundred statements from the most true to least true, as judged by the research subject. Within each truth grouping, the statements are arranged in the order in which they were presented to the research subject. This particular respondent judged none of the statements to be absolutely true, but rated fully twenty-two of the one hundred statements "7," which is high on the 1–8 truth scale. At the opposite extreme, this respondent did not rate any statements absolutely false, but did give "2" ratings to seven statements, indicating that the respondent feels these are very false. On average, the respondent rated the statements 4.91 on the false–true scale, and 5.92 on the unimportant–important scale, indicating that on balance they are somewhat true and rather important.

The data analysis tools of the *Beliefs II* software offer many options. A key quantitative statistic measures the veracity of the statements, defined as the correlation between how true the respondent rated the beliefs and how important he or she considered them to be. Thus, *veracity* is defined straightforwardly as the amount of significant truth in the statements. It is measured relative to the respondent's own personal standards of truth and importance, rather than imposing other people's standards on him or her. A positive number (between 0 and +1) means the respondent judges that the statements about important things are true. A negative number (between −1 and 0) means the important statements are false. The correlation between the numbers in the last two columns of table 7.7 is 0.31—positive but rather weaker than the 0.45 veracity of the other nineteen hundred statements in the set, as rated by the research subject.

In the present context, the chief value of table 7.7 is the texts of the one hundred items themselves. They express a wide range of ideas relevant to extraterrestrials, and they are suitable for use in future research studies seeking to determine the social, cultural, and personality factors that shape beliefs. This particular respondent is clearly an allopatrist, believing that ETs exist but UFOs are not spaceships from their worlds. In an interview, the respondent reported having met two people who claimed to have been abducted by UFOs, one of them being Wayne Aho who created the New Age Foundation, but the respondent rates very false the statement "Some people have actually been abducted by UFOs." This illustrates how a general viewpoint may be somewhat resistant to input from people with a different viewpoint.

Conclusion

The three distinct categories of respondents—allopatrists, ufophiles, and geocentrists—by no means capture all the complexity of the dataset or all the interesting associations between variables. However, they do offer a valid and useful way of thinking about three competing cultural orientations toward the subject of extraterrestrial intelligence.

Although geocentrists were somewhat rare in the *Survey2001* dataset, they are probably more common in the general population. Respondents to online surveys tend to be richer, better educated, and somewhat more secular than the population as a whole, and this particular dataset contains about double the proportion of atheists in the general population (Bainbridge 2005). Thus, rejection of the existence of extraterrestrials may be common in society. In a questionnaire study carried out in both the United States and China, Douglas Vakoch and Yuh-Shiow Lee (2000) found that anthropocentric and religious individuals were less likely to believe in the existence of extraterrestrial intelligence, and this is essentially the geocentric group identified in this study. In the history of western civilization, the geocentric viewpoint reflected the religious belief that human beings were central to God's plan for the universe, and this prejudice retarded the development of science (Russell 1935; Kuhn 1957). Modern societies contain a wide range of religious views, and many religious people will be comfortable with the idea that God created abundant life through the galaxy. However, both the 1981 study and the recent study suggest that highly religious fundamentalists or evangelicals may be hostile to the idea.

Ufophiles are very much involved in the New Age movement, which is an alternative to traditional religion among people who might be described as half-secularized (Bainbridge 1997, 2004a). Many New Age beliefs have the gloss of science but are supernatural in substance. People who are heavily involved in the New Age subculture are detached from conventional churches or congregations, but they possess spiritual or religious needs. These could be described as unmet desires for a more meaningful life, for more satisfying social relationships, or for hope that transcends the material world (Stark and Bainbridge 1987). In a sense, the ufophile beliefs are reasonable, because nothing in science contradicts the possibility of travel between the stars. Perhaps also reasonably, they believe extraterrestrial visitors would be spiritually and technologically superior beings, because our own current level of historical development has not yet given us interstellar flight. However, many ufophiles imagine extraterrestrials are demigods who can offer humans some kind of salvation (Festinger et al. 1956; Saler et al. 1997). Clearly, the ufophile subculture is quasi-religious in nature.

Allopatrists are not members of a religious or quasi-religious movement. Rather, they reflect the views of scientists, as these views have been communicated to the public for decades (e.g., Jones 1951; Cameron 1963; Shklovskiĭ and Sagan 1966). Life evolved naturally on Earth, so it could do so elsewhere as well. If allopatrists pay attention to the science news, they will be aware that astronomers have discovered more than a hundred large planets outside the solar system, and that the universe contains a vast number of galaxies of stars that may possess Earth-like planets. While many allopatrists may be personally religious, they are unencumbered by the kind of faith that requires them to view extraterrestrials in religious terms. Thus, allopatrists are part of the secular, science-oriented subculture, open-minded without being empty-headed, possessing at least some information that lets them evaluate the potential reality of extraterrestrials in a rational manner.

The fact that many people react to the idea of extraterrestrials in religious terms could impede scientific attempts to seek or to communicate with extraterrestrial civilizations. There is an unfortunate potentiality for allopatrists to be mistaken for ufophiles by other members of the general public, by all those people who responded "Do not know" to our two ET and UFO questions. Furthermore, geocentrists have considerable political influence, especially in the United States. Research like the present study can play a useful role is disabusing people of prejudices, for example by clearly demonstrating that many people who accept the possibility of extraterrestrial intelligence are very different from the stereotypical ufophile. A new questionnaire study, employing all one hundred ideas relating to extraterrestrials, could clarify the situation further and potentially give policymakers greater confidence that the search for extraterrestrial civilizations was far more than a mere New Age fantasy.

Author's Note

The views expressed in this essay do not necessarily represent the views of the National Science Foundation or the United States.

Bibliography

Bainbridge, William Sims. 1983. "Attitudes Toward Interstellar Communication: An Empirical Study." *Journal of the British Interplanetary Society* 36: 298–304.
———. 1991. "Communication with Extraterrestrial Intelligence." In *Goals in Space*, 193–218. Albany, NY: State University of New York Press.
———. 1997. "The New Age." In *The Sociology of Religious Movements*, 363–391. New York: Routledge.
———. 2002a. "Public Attitudes toward Nanotechnology." *Journal of Nanoparticle Research* 4: 561–570.
———. 2002b. "The Spaceflight Revolution Revisited." In *Looking Backward, Looking Forward*, ed. Stephen J. Garber, 39–64. Washington, DC: National Aeronautics and Space Administration.
———. 2002c. "Validity of Web-Based Surveys." In *Computing in the Social Sciences and Humanities*, ed. Orville Vernon Burton, 51–66. University of Illinois Press.
———. 2003. "Massive Questionnaires for Personality Capture." *Social Science Computer Review* 21, no. 3: 267–280.
———. 2004a. "After the New Age." *Journal for the Scientific Study of Religion* 43: 381–394.
———. 2004b. "The Future of the Internet: Cultural and Individual Conceptions." In *Society Online: The Internet in Context*, ed. Philip N. Howard and Steve Jones, 307–324. Thousand Oaks, CA: Sage.
———. 2004c. "Personality Capture." In *Berkshire Encyclopedia of Human Computer Interaction*, 546–551. Great Barrington, MA: Berkshire Publishing Group.
———. 2004d. "Sociocultural Meanings of Nanotechnology: Research Methodologies." *Journal of Nanoparticle Research* 6: 285–299.
———. 2005. "Atheism." *Interdisciplinary Journal of Research on Religion.* http://www.bepress.com/ijrr/vol1/iss1/art2/. Accessed on 18 April 2011.
———. 2011. "Direct Contact with Extraterrestrials via Computer Emulation." In *Civilizations Beyond Earth: Extraterrestrial Life and Society*, eds. Douglas A. Vakoch and Albert A. Harrison. New York: Berghahn Books.
Cameron, A. G. W., ed. 1963. *Interstellar Communication*. New York: Benjamin.
Couch, Arthur, and Kenneth Keniston. 1960. "Yeasayers and Naysayers: Agreeing Response Set as a Personality Variable." *Journal of Abnormal and Social Psychology* 60: 151–174.

Festinger, Leon, Henry W. Riecken, and Stanley Schachter. 1956. *When Prophecy Fails*. New York: Harper and Row.

Jones, H. Spencer. 1951. *Life on Other Worlds*. New York: Mentor.

Kuhn, Thomas S. 1957. *The Copernican Revolution: Planetary Astronomy in the Development of Western Thought*. Cambridge, MA: Harvard University Press.

Kurzweil, Ray. 1999. *The Age of Spiritual Machines*. New York: Viking.

Lewis, James R., ed. 1995. *The Gods Have Landed: New Religions from Other Worlds*. Albany, NY: State University of New York Press.

Palmer, Susan J. 1995. "The Raëlian Movement International." In *New Religions in the New Europe*, ed. Robert Towler, 194–210. Aarhus, Denmark: Aarhus University Press.

Partridge, Christopher, ed. 2003. *UFO Religions*. London: Routledge.

Russell, Bertrand. 1935. *Religion and Science*. London: Butterworth.

Saler, Benson, Charles A. Ziegler, and Charles B. Moore. 1997. *UFO Crash at Roswell: The Genesis of a Modern Myth*. Washington, DC: Smithsonian Institution Press.

Shklovski , Iosif S., and Carl Sagan. 1966. *Intelligent Life in the Universe*. New York: Dell.

Stark, Rodney, and William Sims Bainbridge. 1985. *The Future of Religion*. Berkeley, CA: University of California Press.

———. 1987. *A Theory of Religion*. New York: Toronto/Lang.

Swedenborg, Emanuel. 1950. *Earths In Our Solar System Which Are Called Planets, and Earths In The Starry Heaven Their Inhabitants, And The Spirits And Angels There*. Boston, MA: New Church Union.

Toulmin, Stephen Edelston, and June Goodfield. 1961. *The Fabric of the Heavens*. New York: Harper.

Vakoch, Douglas A., and Yuh-Shiow Lee. 2000. "Reactions to Receipt of a Message from Extraterrestrial Intelligence: A Cross-Cultural Empirical Study." *Acta Astronautica* 46: 737–744.

Witte, James C. 2004. "Prologue: The Case for Multimethod Research: Large Sample Design and the Study of Life Online." In *Society Online: The Internet in Context*, ed. Philip N. Howard and Steve Jones, xv–xxxiv. Thousand Oaks, CA: Sage.

Witte, James C., Lisa M. Amoroso, and Philip E. N. Howard. 2000. "Method and Representation in Internet-based Survey Tools: Mobility, Community, and Cultural Identity in *Survey2000*." *Social Science Computer Review* 18: 179–195.

Chapter 8

The Science and Politics of SETI
How to Succeed in an Era of Make-Believe History and Pseudoscience

Albert A. Harrison

Perceived prospects for life beyond Earth have waxed and waned over the centuries, but by the mid twentieth century the notion that we share the universe with other intelligent life made a pronounced shift from fantasy to science. This transition rested in part on a long accumulation of major discoveries including the Copernican model of the universe, which suggests that our Sun and planet are not privileged, and Darwin's theory of evolution, which contends that life and intelligence are the result of entirely natural processes that could occur anywhere (Dick 1996). Perhaps the defining moments came in 1959 when Giuseppe Cocconi and Philip Morrison demonstrated that interstellar radio communication is possible in theory, and in 1960 when Frank Drake conducted *Project Ozma*, the first systematic microwave search for extraterrestrial intelligence, or ETI (Drake and Sobel 1992).

While the idea of life on other worlds was gaining a toehold in modern science, it was already firmly entrenched in popular culture. By the 1920s, gods, angels, demons, and other spiritual beings that are typically associated with religion and myth were joined by incarnate counterparts in the form of "ancient astronauts" that purportedly came to observe Earth and occasionally intervene in our biological and cultural evolution (Colavito

2005). Their alleged meddling in our affairs provides a basis for make-believe or "alternative history" (e.g., visitors from another galaxy built the Egyptian pyramids), which plays counterpoint to make-believe or pseudoscience. By the late 1950s, flying saucers had become a major theme in American folklore (Peebles 1994; Jacobs 2000; Denzler 2001). The most prominent explanation of UFOs, the "extraterrestrial hypothesis," holds that at least some UFOs are interstellar spacecraft (Goode 2000). By 1959, reports of extraterrestrial spacecraft had been joined by claims that aliens walk among us and that government operatives keep the public from knowing the facts about UFOs (Peebles 1994).

It is not possible to prove that interstellar travelers have never set foot on Earth, and some accounts of UFOs are more engaging than others. But as claims of extraterrestrial visitation became increasingly incredible, interest on the part of physical scientists first diminished and then all but vanished. Critics charge that today, as in the early 1960s the field of UFOlogy is suffused with errors, frauds, and hoaxes (Hansen 2001) and even many investigators that are open to the extraterrestrial hypothesis of the origin of UFOs conclude that the physical evidence offered in support of this hypothesis does not withstand scrutiny (Sturrock 1999; Kelleher and Knapp 2005). An increasing number of findings from the behavioral sciences, including the results of experimental research, suggest most strongly that claims of alien abductions are fully understandable in terms of cultural and psychological phenomena (Randle, Estes, and McCone 1999; Clancy 2005; Harrison 2007).

When SETI burst forth as a fresh area of scientific inquiry, the standard challenges of establishing a new discipline—competing successfully for research funds, securing use of expensive equipment, recruiting talented graduate students, and finding journal space—were only part of the problem. SETI scientists also had to distinguish their views from those of people who "believed in" UFOs and other mythic and paranormal phenomena. Avoiding the UFO taint was important for SETI scientists to gain standing with peers, granting agencies, and the public. As an interviewee told historian James E. Strick, "because of the UFO craze that had been sweeping the country since 1947," looking for life elsewhere in the universe "walked a fine line between being perceived as at the cutting edge of futuristic science and seeming in the public eye to be a search for little green men" (2004: 140). Thus, SETI founders sought to establish that—methodologically and professionally—SETI falls squarely within science, to convince other scientists that SETI is a serious and potentially fruitful enterprise, and to build public support.

As Graham Howard points out, this was not the first time that astronomers fought to distance themselves from crank or dissident activity

(2004). Early on, they had to dissociate themselves from astrology, and in the 1950s, from fanciful but popular theories of planetary formation. Nor is astronomy the only discipline that has fought to distance itself from undisciplined ideas. As already noted, archaeology has sought to maintain distance from outright fraud (such as Piltdown Man) and from fanciful theories involving ancient astronauts or an attained but lost golden age of man (Atlantis). In the nineteenth century, anatomists disavowed phrenology, the purported science of relating protuberances and indentations on people's skulls to character, motivation, and interests. In Victorian times, too, scientists went out of their way to show that they offered more than mere mechanics that got results through trial and error and could not explain achievements. Today, many mainstream psychologists ignore or denigrate parapsychologists, even those who use reliable methods, employ robust statistical techniques, and show extreme care in their conclusions. Many professional groups are wary of "alternative medicine" such as acupuncture, homeopathy and other forms of alternative medicine that are based on unorthodox ideas and whose effectiveness is not proven, and of non-traditional forms of psychotherapy, which show promise and then disappear with the regularity of fad diets.

Distinguishing Science and Non-Science

The demarcation problem refers to deciding whether a field of inquiry is science or non-science. Although sometimes referred to as "borderland science" (Shermer 2000), by current criteria SETI falls squarely within science. It is compatible with widely accepted theories and findings in many scientific fields. It rests on a strong scientific rationale and good circumstantial evidence, even though the search itself has yet to confirm the existence of extraterrestrial life. Furthermore, the search itself is fruitful because it contributes to the development of science and technology even in the absence of a confirmed detection.

SETI is located firmly within the larger framework of astrobiology. Initially known as exobiology and later as bioastronomy, astrobiology is dedicated to understanding the origin and distribution of life in the universe. Astrobiology gained viability in the last decades of the twentieth century as it coalesced from many different disciplines including modern astronomy, chemistry, physics, planetary science, and evolutionary biology (Dick and Strick 2005). The context of astrobiology helps define SETI as scientific and provides the search with strong lateral support from non-astronomers. SETI also reaches out to social scientists, thereby gaining support from a larger community of scientists than it would if it were limited to the physical and biological sciences alone. As a general trend, building strength through combining different disciplines began in the 1930s, increased during World War II and the Manhattan Project, declined a bit in the late 1940s and early 1950s, then regained momentum and accelerated beginning in the 1960s (Palmer 1999).

Methodology plays a crucial but not necessarily all-defining role in demarcating science. Unlike many UFOlogists, who take extraterrestrial life as a foregone conclusion, SETI scientists treat it as hypothetical and then use careful procedures to test this hypothesis. Terms are defined operationally: in SETI, intelligent civilizations are characterized by their ability to communicate with microwave radios and lasers. And, despite occasional complaints to the contrary, SETI scientists do address a falsifiable hypothesis: specifically, the search can *disprove* the hypothesis that we are alone in the universe!

If we rely on methodology alone, we run the risk of lumping together both good and bad science. That is, scientific methods can be applied to all sorts of phenomena including those that many scientists consider unpromising or outright worthless. Consequently, sociological factors provide additional differentiation of SETI from pseudoscience (Gieryn 1983; Howard 2004; Martin 2005). The key is that astrobiologists function as a part of the larger community of scientists. Mark Moldwin points out that this means "having the appropriate educational credentials, discussing ideas at scientific meetings and conferences, and presenting results for peer review in respected journals" (2004: 40). He adds that SETI is professional science while UFOlogy is largely the province of amateurs, or of professional scientists who are operating outside of their fields. Professionals define what is and what is not science, and then defend the boundaries. Knowledgeable amateurs can pursue the same worthwhile goals as professional scientists (for example, members of the SETI League conduct legitimate microwave searches), but because they do this on a part-time basis with relatively inexpensive equipment their chances for success seem limited.

One of the greatest benefits of membership in the community of science is a set of checks and balances that help scientists converge upon the truth. Critics complain that these safeguards are not available, or at least not used, by UFOlogists and others who study the paranormal. As Moldwin points out, "Those who attempt to practice outside the scientific community [scientific hermits] attempt to avoid a critical assessment of their ideas. What they are attempting to avoid is [an important] characteristic of science ... the contesting of scientific ideas compared to previous understanding and observation" (2004: 40). Highly sensitive to the mistakes made by earlier scientists who thought that they had detected signs of life on Mars (as well as later investigators who misinterpreted re-entering satellites as extraterrestrial spacecraft), SETI searchers are rightly fanatic about verification and replication and steer clear of conclusions based on incomplete or potentially erroneous information.

As one of the founders of SETI, John Billingham, a physician who was hired by NASA to study physiological adaptation to space but who later became enthralled with the possibility of life beyond Earth, told sociologist David W. Swift:

> If you have a signal you believe is likely to be of extraterrestrial origin, the very first step is to bring all your scientific, technological knowledge—the knowledge of many people—to bear on confirming that it really is of extraterrestrial origin, because the vast majority of signals that we see are going to be something which is masquerading as a ... signal: all the way up from weather balloons to a new spacecraft which has just gone up, to reflections of the moon on radio signals, to new astrophysical objects not yet discovered, to glitches in one's electronics, to finally, at the extreme, a hoax. We think that the worst possible thing that anybody could do is to announce that they have discovered another civilization only to find out, as Barney Oliver says, that the Cal Tech students have chalked up another success. (Swift 1990: 268)

Thus, SETI searchers have elaborate protocols, including verification by other observatories, for confirming possible detections. No matter how intriguing or, for that matter, how compelling a possible detection, it is not considered definitive in the absence of verification.

Although it is possible to conduct scientific searches for extraterrestrial spacecraft or artifacts within our solar system, many scientists see the rationale for this as weaker than that for microwave and optical searches, simply because of the immense difficulties associated with interstellar travel. Astronomers in particular are sensitive to the enormity of the distances involved. Astronomers have looked for signs of construction undertaken in distant solar systems but without remarkable results; one twenty-five-year study of celestial objects within twenty thousand light-years found much of interest but nothing that could be interpreted as construction undertaken by an advanced extraterrestrial civilization (Grinspoon 2004). Perhaps few professional scientists are interested in using state-of-the art equipment to look for interstellar visitors because, in the past, too many searches of this type were poorly conducted. But I suspect that more importantly, for many professionals, scientific searches for extraterrestrial artifacts are simply too close to UFOlogy for comfort. Consequently, scientists who propose such searches find themselves in a situation not entirely unlike that which confronted astrobiology and

SETI fifty years ago. Unlike their predecessors, they lack the powerful advocates and institutional support that helped place SETI within mainstream science.

Institutional Support

Science is, in part, a set of assumptions about the nature of reality (materialistic) and paths to knowledge (empiricism). Science is also a social institution (Friedlander 1995; Harrison 2007). Although scientists understand this and find evidence of this in their daily activities, they may be reluctant to focus on how attitudes and emotions, social-influence processes, and other human qualities affect their work. There should be nothing embarrassing about this, because psychological and interpersonal forces influence all organized (and semi-organized) human activity. Indeed, "organization" implies a social hierarchy, specialization of labor, distribution of resources, and much more. Consequently, universities and research institutes, like military formations, churches, and businesses, have leaders, communication channels, conformity pressures, and the like. Discussions of science as an institution have tended to dwell on the potential downside: for example, bright young scientists whose ideas are so far ahead of their time that they cannot get a fair hearing by closed-minded superiors. These discussions—in some cases, diatribes—overlook the underlying reasons for social organization: coordination, quality control, and in many cases, facilitation. Balance is essential. The task confronting knowledge-generating institutions such as research institutes and universities is to impose some degree of coordination and conformity while leaving room for creativity and new discoveries.

Steven J. Dick (1996) and James Strick (Dick and Strick 2005) have reviewed how astrobiology and SETI gained strength within science, and their work—along with Graham Howard's doctoral thesis (2004)—provides the basis for my account. Contemporary astronomy, according to Howard, is "big business," not necessarily in terms of the numbers of people involved, but in terms of the complexity of the organization of the project and equipment requirements. The days when major discoveries came from ogling nearby planets through small optical telescopes are long gone. Astronomers, writes Howard, have long understood that the success of their field requires developing good relations with government and the public, and they are well organized to do this. He reports that astronomers have launched successful, large-scale letter-writing campaigns to prevent the cutoff of funding for major projects. Astronomers' professional organizations, in fact, offer useful instructions for lobbying (e.g., make the presentation as simple as possible, avoid side issues, be careful when criticizing competitors, and do not bore the audiences with nuances that you yourself find fascinating).

Philip Morrison, Frank Drake, and other SETI pioneers rapidly gained the interest and support of powerful, influential scientists (Dick 1996). MIT physicist Lloyd Berkner, who was involved in the development of the atomic bomb and many other great science projects as well as a member of the Space Sciences Board of the National Academy of Science, encouraged Frank Drake to undertake *Project Ozma*, his initial radio telescope search.

SETI was initiated shortly after the dawn of the space age and only a year or so after the creation of NASA. At that time, the Space Agency was liberally funded, and it took a broad view of its mandate. After all, proposed studies for evidence of life on Mars provided a natural entree to studies for signs of extraterrestrial intelligence in distant solar systems. Less conservative than other agencies such as the National Science Foundation or National Institutes of Health and more willing to support cutting-edge research, NASA dollars became available to the SETI pioneers. This funding was not an unmixed blessing—in some scientists' eyes NASA largesse was more heavily influenced by politics than is funding from other civilian agencies, and they suspect that compared to other funding agencies, NASA supports more speculative projects.

NASA support had several important consequences beyond sheer association with a powerful and popular government organization. NASA resources made it possible both to develop new technology for microwave searches and to transform SETI from an intellectual exercise into an ongoing search. It also enabled symposia and conferences to lay the groundwork and gain the interests and contributions of senior scientists from many different academic fields. These meetings were powerful forces for networking, and they established international, interdisciplinary, interinstitutional, and interpersonal connections that served SETI well. Many of these conferences were invitational, in order to attract "blue ribbon" participants and help assure both visibility and quality control, but some were open, to draw a broader base of support. The fact that these initial gatherings were interdisciplinary (and became even more so) also helped SETI gain acceptance within a broad scientific community.

Carl Sagan and others actively lobbied Congress to fund SETI. Howard Blum (1990) describes a 1983 meeting between Carl Sagan and Senator William Proxmire, who had awarded SETI a "Golden Fleece Award" for wasting taxpayer dollars. Both Sagan and Proxmire deplored nuclear war and Sagan began the discussion with this topic to establish rapport. At one point Sagan offhandedly mentioned Proxmire's opposition to SETI.

The senator replied that the whole idea was nonsense; if they exist, why had they not landed on the White House lawn? Keeping his composure, Sagan replied that whereas there may be thousands of civilizations out there, they could be many light-years away and difficult to find. He then reviewed a list of factors expected to influence the number of technologically advanced civilizations that overlap ours in time. The last independent variable is L, the civilization's longevity. The way for a civilization to achieve great age is to work through its period of technological adolescence, for example, by not undergoing self-destruction shortly after the advent of nuclear technology. The older the civilization, the more likely it is to co-exist with our own. As Blum recounts: "The senator was incredulous. 'So you mean' he asked Sagan, 'that if we find some evidence of extraterrestrial intelligence, somebody elsewhere has avoided self-destruction?' 'That's very much what many of us believe' said Sagan. 'Well,' considered the senator, 'if that's the case, if other worlds might be able to teach us how to survive, maybe SETI's worth the investment. I'd like to think about the problem'" (1990: 140).

Proxmire did think about it, and on 1 October 1982 Congress approved a budget line item for NASA's SETI Program. A setback occurred when, in 1992, Senator Richard Bryant led the effort to eliminate SETI from the NASA budget, but the broader field of astrobiology remained within NASA and continued to gain strength. Part of NASA's project was shifted to a private organization, the SETI Institute, which continued to receive government funding for many of its activities and found other support for the microwave search. In 2003, following a rigorous peer-review process, the SETI Institute was named a member of NASA's Astrobiology Institute.

Early on, SETI established itself within professional astronomy organizations. Perhaps the most important of these is the prestigious International Academy of Astronautics. In cooperation with the International Astronautical Federation and the International Institute of Space Law, the Academy sponsors the International Astronautical Congress (IAC) each fall. This gathering, which includes governmental representatives and industry executives as well as scientists and engineers, holds regular sessions on both the technical and cultural aspects of SETI. It also provides a framework for committees and subcommittees (the committee structure and names have varied somewhat over the years) that address SETI and issues related to SETI, as well as linkages with organizations such as the United Nations. Periodically, premiere papers from these sessions appear in a special issue of the Academy's journal, *Acta Astronautica*.

SETI could not have gained legitimacy without a core of forceful eminent spokespersons and influential scientists sought to recruit other high-profile, respected senior scientists to their cause. They surmised that, once these opinion leaders were on board, other scientists would follow. The pioneers had already established their scientific credentials at the time that they became engaged in SETI, and they continued their more traditional research to remain front-and-center in the scientific enterprise. SETI scientists are closely identified with the skeptic's cause, and some serve on Paul Kurtz's Committee for Skeptical Inquiry (formerly the Committee for the Scientific Investigation of Claims of the Paranormal) and write articles for the *Skeptical Inquirer*. Carl Sagan, who initially expressed some tolerance for UFOs, became an outspoken critic of everything paranormal, especially UFOs, as evidenced in one of his last books, *This Demon Haunted World* (1996). He was regarded as a gatekeeper who decided "which ideas about extraterrestrial life would be admitted to the annals of science, and which would be left outside, panting on the sidewalk" (Achenbach 1999: 174). Although Sagan was intrigued with the possibility of extraterrestrial visitation, from the early 1970s on, anything that smacked of UFOs was left outside.

Popularization

Science benefits from popular support and, according to Graham Howard, astronomers in particular are interested in winning the public's favor (2004). Unlike many other fields, he contends, astronomy offers little in the way of immediate practical benefits. Other fields of physics, along with chemistry and biology, offer clear utilitarian benefits in such areas as transportation, national defense, and medical treatment. Still, we might note that, over the past fifty years, astronomy has helped track satellites and contributed to global position systems and its ability to identify and track asteroids and comets will be extremely valuable if it aids in our planet's defense.

But to help market their discipline, many astronomers point to humanistic dividends. As Howard notes, "Astronomy appears to occupy an anomalous position between the big hard sciences such as physics and the popular culture. It is 'big' and 'hard' in the sense that it uses large, expensive equipment but 'soft' in that because of its tenuous utilitarian and defense links it must legitimate [explain and justify] itself in populist and non-pragmatic terms, much in the way that the humanities and arts must legitimate themselves" (2004: 83). Justifications in astronomy have been "oblique, esoteric, and often refer to the nature of societies, the nature of humans; they are sometimes philosophical and can even border on the spiritual and quasi-religious" (Howard 2004: 23). Astronomy's success campaigning on the basis of intellectual, educational, and cultural dividends is evident in a large number of television documentaries, popular books and magazines, and astronomy clubs.

Popularization is a double-edged sword, in that whereas it attracts benign and supportive audiences it also attracts cranks, dissidents, and hangers-on. Astronomy's appeal to human needs and motives complicates the task of distancing itself from UFOlogy, flying saucer cults, and the like. This can be particularly challenging in the case of SETI, since some scholars see SETI as bordering on a religious quest or propose expansive new theologies to encompass a plethora of intelligent civilizations (Harrison 2007).

SETI's efforts to distance itself from alternative history and pseudoscience is referred to as "border work," that is, ensuring that SETI is not confused with efforts that sound similar or appeal to similar values (Howard 2004; Martin 2005). Thomas F. Gieryn asserts that border work involves a mixture of ideology, rhetoric, and content intended to ensure that one's research falls on the correct side of the line demarcating science and nonscience (1983).

The basic tactic is to make positive attributions about one's research and its products while criticizing if not outright denigrating the work of pseudoscientists, who ignore or misapply the rules of science. The message is that real science is a good investment, while counterfeit science is a waste of time and money. Border work varies somewhat depending on the current state of knowledge and also specific objectives. For example, to encourage government funding scientists may underscore their work's importance for national defense, but later downplay its relevance in order to avoid government interference in such areas as dissemination of results. The basic goals of boundary work are monopolization of professional authority and resources, expansion of authority of expertise into domains claimed by other professions and occupations, and the protection of autonomy. Gieryn writes that even as philosophers and sociologists of science debate the defining characteristics of science the boundary work continues in practical, everyday settings: education administrators set up curricula that include chemistry but exclude alchemy; the National Science Foundation adopts standards to assure that some physicists but no psychics get money; journal editors reject some articles as unscientific (1983: 781). Librarians contribute to border work when they bypass a book on Bigfoot to purchase one on wildlife in Yosemite, or classify a book about ancient astronauts as fiction while classifying a book that debunks that thesis as science.

People who believe in Bigfoot, the magic of the pyramids, and reincarnation are not the only people who have strong, emotionally based attitudes. Most professional scientists do not suffer fools gladly and on occasion have been known for ham-handed treatment of the opposition. Halfway through the last century Immanuel Velikovsky published a controversial book entitled *Worlds in Collision* (1950). Although his book was entertaining and well written, Velikovsky was better versed in psychoanalysis than in physics and astronomy, and scientists then (as now) considered the work fanciful (Friedlander 1995). Scientists were outraged that this would be presented as a work of non-fiction. Harvard astronomer Cecilia Payne-Gaposchkin, who admitted that she had not actually read the book, wrote a scathing review. Not content with this, a group of astronomers went to Velikovsky's publisher and threatened to boycott its textbooks if the company persisted with *Worlds in Collision*.

Years later, in an effort to convince the public those scientists favored fair play, Carl Sagan arranged for Velikovsky to present his views at a prestigious scientific meeting. As planetary scientist David Morrison recounts, Sagan's comments following Velikovsky's talk were a little too long, a little too smug (2001). Sagan's put-down convinced Velikovsky and his followers that they had been "set up" for further ridicule. To his everlasting credit, Morrison tried to help Velikovsky frame his claims in ways that could be tested scientifically. By that time, Velikovsky and his followers lost all interest in cooperating with the scientific establishment and jeered Morrison.

Although going on the attack may bring a certain sense of satisfaction, there are also certain downsides, especially if the attack is based on ridicule and name calling. Whereas ridicule reassures us that outsiders' deviant views are nothing to worry about (relief is expressed as laughter), it puts the outsiders on the defensive. This means that they are not in a good frame of mind to assess carefully their own ideas or to learn from us—and, the natural impulse is to counterattack. This leads to a self-amplifying positive feedback system (Grinspoon 2003). That is, UFOlogists make louder and more insistent claims that elicit ever-greater outrage on the part of the skeptics, which further escalate the dispute with both sides overstating their position. Furthermore, escalating the conflict raises the stakes. The sharper the dispute, the greater the loss of face if one is proven wrong. This recognition, too, helps push emotion ahead of reason. None of this is to say that scientists should overlook claims that are foolish or dishonest. But, in the history of UFOlogy, aggressive debunking can backfire (Craig 1996). This happens, for example, when the public sees the skeptical alternative (such as fireflies and swamp gas) as less plausible than the initial claim.

Ignoring fanciful theories and outrageous claims is simple and—for certain purposes—effective. It leaves scientists free to do what they do best. In behaviorist psychology this tactic is known as the "withdrawal of reinforcement." Whether we ignore a child having a tantrum or someone collecting donations for a charity that does not interest us, the likely reaction is a brief intensification of the activity followed by its disappearance. There is truth in the cliché "Ignore them and they will go away."

While skirting the issue saves time and offers a measure of protection from counterattack, it does little to build public support. UFOlogists can claim that the professional scientists have not taken the time to examine the evidence, the implication being that if they had they would change their views. (David Morrison points out scientists will not take the time to look at this evidence because, on the basis of sampling a small amount of such evidence, they know that it is worthless [2001]. It is not necessary to consume an entire bowl of soup to discover that it is rancid.) Members of the public may wonder why scientists seem ignorant of widespread "common knowledge" or become susceptible to claims that astronomers are involved in "cover-up." Remaining aloof from the fray offers certain benefits—it reduces demands on the scientists' valuable time and diminishes the likelihood that he or she will be repeatedly attacked—but it leaves the public at the mercy of the opposition. Many pseudoscientists and alternative historians are cordial, welcoming, and good at marketing their ideas. They point out that they themselves are open-minded, and ask why they cannot get a fair hearing from their critics.

Education is an uphill battle because many segments of the public are not particularly well versed in science. We live in an era of relentless pressures to overlook mediocre performance, and we are about sixty years into rating inflation of employees, military personnel, and students. (In this last case, rating inflation is known as "grade creep.") Today, many K–12 educators are more concerned about sustaining a sense of personal worth than delivering honest feedback concerning academic performance. Books and magazines lower their sights to accommodate a broader audience (Raybeck 2000). Comparisons of contemporary issues of news magazines with issues published years ago are likely to reveal that today's articles are brief, use a more limited vocabulary, and contain more pictures. Many contemporary textbooks send difficult material to sidebars or appendices, if it is retained at all. Similarly, on the average, today's news broadcasts are pitched at a lower level than before. Soundbites have replaced careful analysis and complex issues. It is increasingly difficult to separate fact and fiction, as evidenced by countless documentaries on "life in space" that mix astrobiology, SETI, and UFOlogy, assigning sensationalism greater weight than accuracy. Not every research scientist needs to engage in public education. But many SETI scientists do—Carl Sagan was a leader in this regard—and they are joined by a vast network of professional educators and skeptics.

Noting that students deserve more than silence or a scoffing response to questions about UFOs, alien abductions, and other paranormal phenomena, Andrew Fraknoi points out that the same interests that are inspired by a shameless media can be used as a point of entrée for science education (2003). Many students look for a connection between science and pseudoscience. Over the years, he continues, astronomers, educators, and librarians have developed a wealth of educational material for use at public assemblies, on television, in planetaria, and in the classroom. He writes:

> I think that there is more that we can do in this area than simply point out the fact that astrology has now flunked dozens of scientific tests, that Jimmy Carter's UFO turned out to be the planet Venus, or that what crashed at Roswell, New Mexico was a then top secret balloon experiment trying to develop an early warning system about Russian nuclear tests. Clear explanations of how scientists or statisticians deal with claims about astrology and UFOs as alien spaceships can also give our students insights into how science really works—how to frame hypotheses, how to gather evidence and do experiments, how to make judgments about the statistical validity of those experiments, and how ultimately to decide what to believe about how the world works. (Fraknoi 2003: 4–5)

Conclusion

At the frontier, it can be very difficult to separate science from religion, myth, and wish. This is especially so in our age where scientists write books about quantum phenomena, multiple dimensions of reality, hidden universes, and other topics that impinge on myth and create a mirage of endless possibilities (Harrison 2007). Lines between science and non-science are blurred further by science books with titles alluding to God, spirituality, and immortality; by media exploitation of sensationalistic ideas; and by unedited websites that can claim anything. Scientists learn early on to define terms so that they do not have surplus or excess meaning, to avoid treating hypothetical constructs as real, and not go too far beyond the data. For non-scientists, these principles are not second nature, and in this era of multiculturalism science must compete with indigenous knowledge. Despite crucial metaphysical and epistemological differences, from the public's perspective SETI taps into many of the same emotions that sustain UFOlogy: a desire not to be alone in the universe, a hope for proof that civilizations can solve their problems and achieve great longevity, and a wish for guidance from superior, non-human forms of intelligence. Under these conditions, SETI's success at overcoming the image of "Little Green Men" has been truly remarkable.

But the battle will be unending. Lines separating science and non-science will change as new theories and methods take hold and as observations make the transition from fiction to fact (and in some cases from fact back to fiction). Border work will change accordingly. Whereas scientists are able to reach people who are already inclined to science or who need only a little more education to think scientifically, vast numbers of the populace are not naturally inclined to think like scientists and skeptics. Their thinking is intuitive and holistic. They are more influenced by stories and impressions than by rigorous quantitative analysis. They are enamored by possibilities rather than by findings. They know and interpret the world in ways that seem foreign to most scientists. They tend to be drawn to artistic and religious pursuits. Most likely these differences are hard-wired, and it is more appropriate to think of these as differences in style, rather than differences in intelligence. If, as scientists, we tend to be annoyed by intuitive or artistic people we should keep in mind that the controversies between science and non-science are healthy in that they force us to think very carefully about our own assumptions, theories, and methods.

Bibliography

Achenbach, Joel. 1999. *Captured by Aliens*. New York: Simon and Schuster.

Blum, Howard. 1990. *Out There*. New York: Pocket Books.

Clancy, Susan A. 2005. *Abducted: How People Come to Believe They Were Kidnapped by Aliens*. Cambridge, MA: Harvard University Press.

Cocconi, Giuseppe, and Philip Morrison. 1959. "Searching for Interstellar Communications." *Nature* 184: 844–846.

Craig, Roy. 1995. *UFOs: An Insider's View of the Official Quest for Evidence*. North Denton, TX: University of North Texas Press.

Denzler, Brenda. 2001. *The Lure of the Edge: Scientific Passions, Religious Beliefs, and the Pursuit of UFOs*. Berkeley, CA: University of California Press.

Dick, Steven J. 1996. *The Biological Universe: The Twentieth Century Extraterrestrial Life Debate and the Limits of Science*. Cambridge: Cambridge University Press.

Dick, Steven J., and Strick, James E. 2005. *The Living Universe: NASA and the Development of Astrobiology*. Piscataway, NJ: Rutgers University Press.

Fraknoi, Andrew. 2003. "Dealing with Astrology, UFOs, and Faces on Other Worlds: A Guide to Addressing Astronomical Pseudoscience in the Classroom." *Astronomy Education Review* 2, no 2: 150. http://dx.doi.org/10.3847/AER2003022. Accessed on 18 April 2011.

Friedlander, Michael W. 1995. *At the Fringes of Science*. Boulder, CO: Westview Press.

Gieryn, Thomas F. 1983. "Boundary Work and the Demarcation of Science from Non-Science: Strains and Interests in Professional Ideologies of Scientists." *American Sociological Review* 48: 781–795.

Goode, Erich. 2000. *Paranormal Beliefs*. Prospect Heights, IL: Waveland Press.

Hansen, George P. 2001. *The Trickster and the Paranormal*. Lincoln, NB: Ex Libris.

Harrison, Albert A. 2007. *Starstruck: Cosmic Visions in Science, Religion, and Popular Culture*. New York: Berghahn.

Howard, Graham. 2004. "Legitimating Astronomy." Doctoral dissertation, University of Wollongon.

Jacobs, David M. 2000. *UFOs and Abductions: Challenging the Borders of Knowledge*. Lawrence, KS: University Press of Kansas.

Kelleher, Colm, and George Knapp. 2005. *Hunt for Skinwalker: Science Confronts the Unexplained at a Remote Ranch in Utah*. New York: Paraview.

Martin, Brian. 2005. "Grassroots Science." In *Science, Technology and Society: An Encyclopedia*, ed. Sal Restivo, 175–181. Oxford: Oxford University Press.

Moldwin, Mark. 2004. "Why SETI is Science and UFOlogy is Not." *Skeptical Inquirer* 28, no. 6: 40–42.

Morrison, David. 2001. "Killer-Comets, Pseudocosmogony, and Little Green Men." In *Skeptical Odysseys: Personal Inquiries by the World's Leading Paranormal Inquirers*, ed. Paul Kurtz, 161–175. Buffalo, NY: Prometheus Books.

Palmer, Carole L. 1999. "Structures and Strategies of Interdisciplinary Science." Journal of the American Society for Information Science 50, no. 3: 242–253.

Peebles, Curtis. 1994. *Watch the Skies! A Chronicle of the Flying Saucer Myth*. Washington, DC: Smithsonian Institution Press.

Randle, Kevin D., Russ Estes, and William P. McCone. 1999. *The Abduction Enigma: The Truth Behind the Mass Alien Abductions of the Late Twentieth Century*. New York: Forge Books.

Raybeck, Douglas. 2000. *Looking Down the Road*. Prospect Heights, IL: Waveland Press.

Sagan, Carl. 1996. *This Demon Haunted World: Science as a Candle in the Dark*. New York: Ballantine Books.

Shermer, Michael. 2000. *The Borderlands of Science: Where Sense Meets Nonsense*. New York: Oxford University Press.

Strick, James E. 2004. "Creating a Cosmic Discipline: The Crystallization and Consolidation of Exobiology, 1957–1973." *Journal of the History of Biology* 37: 131–180.

Sturrock, Peter A. 1999. *The UFO Enigma: A New Review of the Physical Evidence*. New York: Warner Books.

Swift, David. 1990. *SETI Pioneers*. Tempe, AZ: University of Arizona Press.

Velikovsky, Immanuel. 1950. *Worlds in Collision*. New York: Macmillan.

Part III

COMMUNICATION WITH EXTRATERRESTRIAL INTELLIGENCE

Chapter 9

CULTURAL ASPECTS OF INTERSTELLAR COMMUNICATION

Carl L. DeVito

In our discussions of the search for extraterrestrial intelligence (SETI), particularly when we focus on the technical problems posed by interstellar communication, we can easily forget just what a momentous event the detection of an alien signal would be. Reactions would range from strong positive interest all the way to fear and paranoia (Harrison 1997).

Some will want to study the signal, seeking assurance that it is real. Some will caution against any response, feeling that it is better to listen silently and learn all we can before we even consider communication (Shklovskiĭ and Sagan 1966). There are many ways to look at this question. On the one hand we have here the opportunity to learn about, and learn from, a new, perhaps older civilization. On the other hand, they may be hostile or aggressive, perhaps even expansionist in their thinking (Clark 2000; Harrison 1997).

These reactions are, of course, understandable given the fact that we are considering here something totally new in human experience. Some of the more extreme reactions are, however, due to a misunderstanding of the physical facts underlying the SETI endeavor. Our purpose here is to recall, briefly, these physical facts and then explore how they affect this kind of communication.

The Physical Setting

The stars, as we all know, are very far away. It is not only a matter of few thousand miles or a few million, but many trillions of miles away. Such distances are measured in light-years. Light, and all other forms of electromagnetic radiation (radio waves, gamma rays, x-rays, etc.) travel at more than 186,000 miles per second. Thus, the distance such radiation travels in one Earth year, the light-year, is about six trillion miles (Kaufmann 1994). At the time of this writing, we have sent men 250,000 miles away to the moon, and sent unmanned spacecraft to the outer planets, less than five billion miles out, but no human probe has reached even the nearest star (Proxima Centuri, four light-years distant). It is clear from these considerations that reaching the stars by spacecraft is well beyond our current abilities and will remain so for the foreseeable future. Thus, if we are to contact extraterrestrial intelligence (ETI), we must do it by means of radio or perhaps some other type of electromagnetic radiation. Let us simply refer to this as radio communication. These facts limit the kind of civilization we can hope to find. There may be many races out there that excel in philosophy, art, music, or literature that do not send radio waves into space. Many of us would love to contact such a race, but the fact is, we simply are unable, at present, to do so.

The facts sketched above have other consequences as well. The distance that separates us from ETI also protects us from any form of interstellar aggression. The expense and energy required to mount an expedition across these vast gulfs will far exceed any possible gain. This fact should mollify those who fear extraterrestrial aggression. Also, our radio broadcasts have been leaking into space for almost a century. ETI may have already detected us, hence being silent, pretending we aren't here, seems pointless.

There are one or two other consequences that are relevant here. First, any society we detect will have the ability to broadcast radio waves into space. This implies at least a rudimentary technology, although given the distances involved I'd guess that their technology would be far beyond "rudimentary." Such a technology must, in my view, be based on some knowledge of science and it is this knowledge that will provide the basis for a mutually understandable language; more on this later.

The second consequence shows why the expertise of the social scientist is needed in the SETI enterprise. Interstellar communication will not be a dialogue in the usual sense. If we hear from a society that is, say, ten light-years away, we will not send a message, then wait twenty years or more for a reply, then send another message and so on. What we should do, in my opinion, and what I believe the aliens will also do, is immediately send a series of messages, perhaps a week or a few days apart, each containing more information than the last, but each containing some redundancy as a check on understanding. I don't see contact with an alien society as a path to mystical enlightenment, nor do I expect to hear from an all-wise guru who, knowing nothing about us, will somehow have the answer to all our problems. It is rather a way to pass on a "legacy" to other intelligences. It is a way to let them know we were/are here, that we lived and learned and did things, and experienced life. It is a way of extending the life span of humanity and a necessary one because the Earth will not last long by cosmic standards and once it is gone, so is all human accomplishment. Presumably, our alien contactees will do the same, giving us some knowledge of their totally alien society. We want to know about them just as we want to know about the Mayans, Egyptians, Greeks, and Romans. Not because this knowledge will "save" or even change us, but because they lived. Just knowing they exist will enrich our thinking and broaden our understanding of the nature of life.

My allusion to the ancient peoples listed above shows why we need social scientists on any "SETI team." This kind of communication will be, at least for quite a while, one way, much as is our communication with past societies on Earth. We will have to glean what we can from the messages they send us, extracting some understanding of their sense organs, their psychology, and their social structures along with what we learn of their physics, chemistry, and mathematics. There is so much we'd like to know about the aliens. What do they look like? Do they have sex? What are their social organizations like? Do they have a military? Do they have television? What is their music like? Their art? What are their theological ideas, their political ideas, their scientific theories, etc.? Unfortunately, there is no easy way to obtain such knowledge. We must patiently await their messages and deduce what we can from what they tell us. Turning this around we will want to tell them "all" about us. But this must be done systematically in small, easily understandable increments so that they can absorb the information we send them and gradually build up a "picture" of humanity that is more and more nearly complete.

There are some who resist this idea, insisting that the problem is easily solved by just sending an encyclopedia or some other vast tome to the aliens. This is an example of "royal road" thinking. The story goes that Alexander the Great studied geometry and at one point Memaechmus, his tutor, tried to teach him some proofs. He found them difficult and complained, "Master, in my kingdom there are royal roads built smoothly, as short cuts for the king. Can you not make this task easier for me?" To this Memaechmus replied, "Sire, there is no royal road to geometry." This is an important lesson, and very relevant to the present context.

Archaeologists study ancient societies in many ways. If, however, the society had a written language and if we can learn to read it, then our knowledge and understanding of that society is increased many fold. Deciphering an ancient language can be very difficult (Solé and Valbelle 2001), even though the society that created it was a human society. In SETI communication we must try to devise a language that we can teach our correspondents, a language they can then use to interpret our subsequent messages. This must begin at a low level and gradually build to increase the vocabulary and expressive power of the language so that more and more sophisticated messages can be sent. Now before I am accused of some horrible form of chauvinism, let me repeat that I expect the aliens to do the same thing, i.e., send us their version of a cosmic language so that we can better understand their subsequent messages. I think I speak for many when I say every effort would be made to learn that language. Until the aliens oblige, however, all we can do is form our own ideas on how to construct a language that can be taught to someone who is non-human and many light-years away. It is clear that no Earth language will do. Imagine that you speak only English and someone who speaks only Japanese is trying to teach you his language. This would be difficult enough even face to face, but now suppose you are in contact only by telephone! The problem we have set ourselves is even more difficult. The language we want to construct must be based, as far as this is possible, on the knowledge we and the aliens share. They won't know any human language. They won't know anything about our society, its customs, or its history. They won't know anything about human biology, human psychology, human music, or human art. So what is there that we and an alien race might have in common? Two things come to mind as possibilities: our mathematics and our physical sciences. These are, unfortunately sometimes very glibly, assumed to be universal (DeVito 2011). I think it important that we examine much more closely what it is we are saying here.

The Logic of Science

Physical reality has a logic of its own. One of Galileo's principal contributions to science was his insistence that the world can be understood (Hawking 1988). Subsequent developments have proved him right. Our engineers and scientists have designed probes to visit the other planets of our solar system. These probes have gone where they were designed to go, done what they were designed to do, and sent much information back to Earth. We have learned to understand physical reality at the level at which we experience it, and if our aliens have a science then they must have learned to understand reality as well. Of course, as psychologists tell us, human emotions have a logic all their own, and human politics has its own logic. But we are not concerned with these things here although at some later stage we may have to be concerned with them. Here we are talking only about understanding physical reality at the level of human experience (on the atomic level things get complicated, but we have learned to understand things at this level as well [Ebbing 1987]).

Our alien correspondents have also learned the logic of physical reality—they have a science so they must have—and so this logic, this way of thinking, is something we share because we share the same physical reality. This same logic underlies our mathematics: Now at the turn of the nineteenth century, mathematicians devised languages based on logic and used them to investigate certain problems in the foundations of mathematics (Freudenthal 1960). These so-called logistic languages morphed—due to the efforts of a great many very talented people—into the computer languages of today (Mamma and Waldinger 1985). There are some profound ideas here (Hamilton 1980), but we shall need only the most elementary aspects of the subject. By giving many examples using only simple arithmetic (the arithmetic of the counting numbers, what mathematicians call "natural" numbers, 1, 2, 3, ...) one can communicate the logical connectives (and, or, not, implies) and the quantifiers (for every, there is). Let me give an example: If $\mathbb{R}$ denotes the real numbers and $\mathbb{N}$ the natural numbers, then

$$(\forall r \varepsilon \mathbb{R})(\exists n \varepsilon \mathbb{N})(r < n)$$

The symbols give a false—and unfortunate—sense of sophistication. All this says is: "For every real number r there is a natural number n that is bigger than r." This rudimentary language can be expanded to enable one to say quite a bit about elementary science (DeVito and Oehrle 1990). So assuming our aliens are familiar with the natural numbers, supposing, that is, that they can count, we can teach them a very simple language. Unfortunately the expressive power of this language, what one can say with it, is not very great. It can, however, be easily improved as we shall see.

It has often been suggested that an alien society would share a great deal of mathematics with us. We need not concern ourselves with this. As we have said above, this kind of communication will be one way, so we should ask what aspects of human mathematics we can teach our correspondents. Assuming, as we have, that they can count, there is virtually no limit to what we can teach them, and a great deal of it can be expressed in the simple language sketched above (Freudenthal 1960).

It might be appropriate here to say a word about notation—an often confusing point even among humans. The natural numbers can be written in many ways, and various societies have used very different systems of notation. The underlying concepts, however, are the same. So while an ancient Roman might not understand the symbol "123," he or she did understand "one hundred and twenty three," and would have written it "CXXIII." The system of notation now in use worldwide is based on ten. So we all understand "123" to mean "1x(10x10) + 2x(10) +3." This convention is so ingrained in us today that we are rarely aware of it. But systems based on five or twenty (or any whole number from 2 on) are possible, and several have been used in the past. In a quinary (base five) system "123" would be understood to mean "1x(5x5) +2x(5) +3," which, of course, is "38" in base ten; and in a vigesimal (base twenty) system "123" would be understood to mean "1x(20x20) +2x(20) +3," which is "443" in base ten. These systems may have arisen because some people counted on one hand while, in other places, people used both their fingers and toes (see Dantzig 2005). Other systems have been used and vestiges of them remain with us even today. Our use of sixty to measure time and angles comes from the sexagesimal (base sixty) system devised by the ancient Sumerians (see Krupp 2007). In the kind of communication that I am discussing here, we would teach the aliens our notation for the natural numbers and they would teach us their notation. Since the underlying concepts are the same, learning each other's notation should not be an insurmountable problem.

So here we see how, since the aliens understand physical reality, we can begin constructing a language and communicate with it whatever amount of mathematics we feel is necessary. The problem, and it is a difficult one, is how to go from a discussion of mathematics to a discussion of other aspects of human civilization. We shall sketch one approach below.

The Material World

Matter presents itself in myriad forms and three states: solid, liquid, and gas. But chemists have learned that all matter is made up of just ninety-two elements. Spectroscopic studies have shown that these same ninety-two elements, and only these, occur throughout the visible universe (Kaufmann 1994). The laws of chemistry, then, are truly universal. It was noted by many that the properties of the elements vary in a fairly regular way, and in the nineteenth century, the Russian chemist Dimitri Ivanovich Mendeleev constructed a table based on these properties and the way they changed. My colleagues in chemistry tell me that it is difficult to overestimate the importance of this table for the development of their science (Ebbing 1987). Furthermore, this table enabled Mendeleev to predict the existence of at least three as yet undiscovered elements and to sketch their properties. In all three cases he was later proved to be correct. It may be that any race that has a science will discover this table. But even if they are familiar only with the properties of the elements they may be able to see the "logic" of the table and understand something of its significance. By communicating this table we may call attention to information about the material world that is shared by our societies. Moreover, once we can talk about the elements we can begin discussing chemical reactions, enhancing the expressive power of our language even more.

Chemistry is important in connection with SETI for another reason. Whether one has hands, tentacles, or claws, one cannot manipulate individual molecules. In order to make meaningful chemical calculations (how many grams of iron and how many grams of sulfur must be combined to produce five hundred grams of iron sulfide?) one must learn something about the laws of chemical combination (such laws are universal remember), one must learn something about the relative weights of atoms and one must understand the significance of the Avogadro Number. One can communicate, to anyone having this understanding, the basic human convention for measuring mass, the gram (DeVito and Oehrle 1990). This is a major step in communication because it changes the focus from the qualitative to the quantitative.

One can carry these ideas further. It is well known that adding one calorie of heat to one gram of ice raises its temperature by one degree Celsius. This is so until we reach 0°C. Then all additional heat goes into changing the state of the ice. It takes about eighty calories of heat to change one gram of ice at 0°C to one gram of liquid water at this same temperature. Then each calorie added raises the temperature one degree until 100°C is reached. It takes about five hundred forty calories of heat to change one gram of liquid water at 100°C to one gram of steam at 100°C, which explains why a steam burn is generally so much worse than a hot water burn. Many substances change states in a manner analogous to water, although the quantities of heat and the melting and boiling points differ. By calling attention to these facts one can communicate many important human conventions; e.g., the calorie, the degree, and even our units of pressure.

The ability to communicate our units, which are, after all, merely human conventions, enables us to present precise scientific information to our contactees. This would be of considerable interest to a scientific society. Imagine the joy of our scientists if they could receive precise detailed information about a distant star, a distant planet, or a distant solar system. Our astronomers, planetary scientists, and even our meteorologists would be ecstatic.

The SETI Team

The construction of a language based on the facts sketched above will take extreme care and will probably become the task of a group of specialists. This group will have two problems: How to communicate what they learn from the aliens to humanity, and how to communicate something about the nature of humanity to the aliens. Both of these problems require the expertise of cross-cultural researchers and other social scientists.

Let us look at these problems one at a time. Assume that we receive a communication similar to that discussed above. Our task will be one that is familiar to the historian and archaeologist. We must learn a "foreign" language and then use it to understand subsequent messages. Simultaneously, we will try to glean what we can about the alien society sending the message. If the messages follow the pattern given above, they will begin with elementary facts about physics and chemistry. This is a very good thing for several reasons. Many of my Mexican neighbors here in Southern Arizona are very sensitive to what they see as the cultural dominance of the "Anglo" community. They feel that Anglos believe, although they are often unaware of it, that their ways are the only ways and that other cultures are inferior and inconsequential. Some of my colleagues at the University of Arizona—we have a number of native French speakers on our faculty—express similar concerns. It would be a mistake, given this sensitivity, to present to the world messages from the aliens in English or any other Earth language. Fortunately, the early messages will be expressed in some formal language like the one sampled above. Thus the messages can be presented, or released to the press, in this abstract form allowing each country to translate them for their citizens. In this way we avoid even an appearance, however unintentional, of "cultural bullying." The early stages of this kind of communication must, it would seem, move from a logic-based formal language to a discussion of science. This is also a distinct advantage for another reason. If the early messages contained anything that could remotely be interpreted as "moral" the consequences could be catastrophic. Those who agree with the message will claim that God herself is showing her support for their views, and those who disagree will allege that the message comes from the evil one and is an attempt to lead the faithful astray. Expensive radio telescopes may be destroyed by people with this mind-set. It is better that the early messages be something like this:

$$(t>405)\rightarrow(\forall p)(NH_3 @t\ deg@p\ atm) = \gamma NH_3$$
$$(t\leq405)\rightarrow(\exists p)(NH_3 @t\ deg@p\ atm) = \lambda NH_3$$

No one will attach religious or moral significance to such statements and in this way the human race will have the time, and the emotional distance, to come to terms with the fact that we are dealing with material creatures and not angels or devils. We should note, however, that even a series of scientific messages may give us clues to the psychology of the aliens, the nature of their sense organs, perhaps even their evolutionary history; a strongly mechanistic science may indicate a race that has internalized the properties of motion and so at some point in their history played the role of predator, and at some point that of prey. Again we see why it is so important to have social scientists on the "team."

The second problem is equally challenging. To get an understanding of it we might imagine how we would react to pictures from the aliens. There seems to be an inherent discontinuity in trying to build a language from simple science to the point where biological information can be discussed. At some point we must show pictures of our world, our biosphere, and ourselves. The plaques sent into space aboard the Pioneer spacecraft have pictures of humans on them (Basalla 2006) and the message sent from Arecibo, based on primes, is also a picture. How one can try to make sure any picture sent is correctly interpreted has been discussed previously (Benford 2000; DeVito 1990). I have been saying that we expect our correspondents to learn our conventions as we are learning theirs. This is also true for any pictures we exchange. We, and they, must learn how to correctly interpret any pictures that are sent. The problem of how to teach our correspondents to do this has been treated in the SETI literature (see Vakoch 2000, 2011). So let us, for the rest of this discussion, suppose that pictures are being received and sent. Here, the cross-cultural researcher will play a major role. Suppose that the first pictures of the aliens show a humanoid with some feature we find disturbing, frightening, or even disgusting. Suppose, for example, that they have horns. These may be simply sense organs, perhaps their ears happen to be located on the top of their heads. Imagine the consternation this will cause in some places. Other, more subtle problems may also arise. Perhaps they have a different skin color. How will people feel about that (Harrison 1997)? Maybe, in a series of pictures, we see that the aliens are left-handed, or perhaps they are bisexual and the female is very obviously the dominant gender? Such pictures will be very disturbing in some cultures, and I'm sure I haven't thought of a great many other, similar, problems. The pictures received can be examined by cross-cultural researchers before they are released, so that images that might be troubling can be identified and the public prepared for what they will see. Turning this around we may wonder how pictures of ourselves, or our social interactions, pictures we find commonplace or even banal, might affect our alien correspondents. I would suggest that we begin with pictures of the Earth showing large-scale, gross, features of the planet—its seas, deserts, polar regions, rain forests, and jungles. The seasonal cycles of these regions can be shown in a series of pictures telling our correspondents that they are seeing, in broad outline, an eco-system. These pictures can be repeated but shown in somewhat finer detail, showing birds and insects perhaps. Aquatic life, small reptiles, and mammals could then be shown, gradually informing our correspondents of the variety of our biosphere. We could follow this up with pictures of larger animals like herds of deer, bison, horses, and elephants. We might also consider sending pictures that show how the different life forms inter-relate. But before we show humans we may want to show evidence of our existence. We could show early, primitive, human dwellings; e.g., huts in the forest, cliff dwellings in the desert, igloos in the Arctic. We may then show farms and ranches with humans working in these places, but shown from a distance. In this way we emphasize the fact that humans are part of the biosphere, dependent on other members of that sphere, but able to adapt their surroundings to their needs. Thus we want to show man in a biological context. The human race may not seem so threatening when seen in such a context, and it is clear that there is nothing supernatural about us. Eventually we will want to show pictures of our cities, our vehicles (ships, planes, trains, etc.) and of ourselves. It may be possible to use pictures to place our social interactions in a context that shows them to be influenced by our climate, our basic biology, and our early history so that they do not seem unduly strange or capricious. If the aliens send pictures of themselves, their world and its biosphere, perhaps they will not seem quite so alien.

The suggestions above are just that, suggestions. My feeling is that cross-cultural researchers can perfect and expand on these ideas. I feel that the exchange of information becomes more meaningful, and less weird, if it is placed in the proper context. There is much to be learned here and we must do all we can to insure that a mutually beneficial exchange continues over many decades. This can be achieved by presenting the Earth, its place in space, its physical characteristics, and its biosphere as an integrated whole, a fascinating, richly varied system whose dominant life form recognizes this variety, recognizes our place in it and its importance for our well-being. We wish to present ourselves as a highly intelligent race. A race that has accomplished much, learned much, but is wise enough to realize that it has much more to learn. Communication with another, totally different, race is a wonderful opportunity to increase our knowledge of astronomy, of biology, and other sciences, but it will also enhance our understanding of our society, our place in the universe and, perhaps, our humanity.

Bibliography

Basalla, George. 2006. *Civilized Life in the Universe*. Oxford: Oxford University Press.

Benford, Gregory. 2000. *Deep Time*. New York: Harper Collins.

Clark, Stuart. 2000. *Life on Other Worlds and How to Find It*. London: Springer.

Dantzig, Tobias. 2005. *Number: The Language of Science*. New York: Penguin Group.

DeVito, Carl L. 1990. "Languages Based on Science." *Proceedings of the International Astronautical Federation Symposium*. Dresden, Germany.

———. 2011. "On the Universality of Human Mathematics." In *Communication with Extraterrestrial Intelligence*, ed. Douglas A. Vakoch, 439–448. Albany, NY: State University of New York Press.

DeVito, Carl L., and Richard T. Oehrle 1990. "A Language Based on the Fundamental Facts of Science." *Journal of the British Interplanetary Society* 43: 561–568.

Ebbing, Darrell D. 1987. *General Chemistry*. Boston, MA: Houghton Mifflin.

Freudenthal, Hans. 1960. *Lincos*. Amsterdam: North Holland.

Hamilton, A. G. 1980. *Logic for Mathematicians*. Cambridge: Cambridge University Press.

Harrison, Albert A. 1997. *After Contact*. New York: Plenum.

Kaufmann, William J. 1994. *Universe*. New York: Freeman.

Krupp, E. C. 2007. "Rambling through the Skies: Going Like Sixty." *Sky and Telescope* 114, no. 5: 47–48.

Mamma, Zohar, and Richard Waldinger. 1985. *The Logical Basis for Computer Programming*. Reading, MA: Addison-Wesley.

Shklovskiĭ, Iosif S., and Carl Sagan. 1996. *Intelligent Life in the Universe*. San Francisco, CA: Holden-Day.

Solé, Robert, and Dominique Valbelle. 2001. *The Rosetta Stone*, trans. Steven Randall. London: Profile Books.

Vakoch, Douglas A. 2000. "The Conventionality of Pictorial Representation in Interstellar Messages." *Acta Astronautica* 46, no. 10–12: 733–736.

———. 2011. "A Narratological Approach to Interpreting and Designing Interstellar Messages." *Acta Astronautica* 68, no. 3–4: 520–534.

Chapter 10

Cosmic Storytelling
Primitive Observables as Rosetta Analogies

Harry Letaw, Jr.

The mystique of imagined extraterrestrial civilizations living, dying, and conducting their affairs in far-distant kingdoms among the stars has likely stirred the minds of children for time immemorial. Their mothers have responded to the question "Do people live there?" by gently declaring that we do not know. And that answer stands today in the galactic realm, although it is now resolved negatively for our Moon and, arguably, for several of our planetary neighbors.

The literature of comic strips, motion pictures, and novels of the particularly wide-ranging genre of science fiction continues to feed the imaginations of both children and consenting adults. Beyond fiction, the question has drawn into its discussion serious physical and social scientists, philosophers, and politicians. In *Is Anyone Out There?*, Frank Drake and Dava Sobel (1992: 1) quote Metrodorus, a Greek philosopher of the fourth century BCE: "To consider the Earth as the only populated world in infinite space is as absurd as to assert that in an entire field of millet, only one grain will grow."

In the development of communications with an unknown, non-human race of intelligent beings, it is essential that we first know ourselves. This theme, should it be neglected, will surely defeat our best efforts to make ourselves understood. In his essay "Fragments of Paradise," Alberto Manguel (2007: 91) succinctly describes the lust of humanity for communication:

We come into this world as reading animals. Our first impulse is to decipher what we sense around us, as if everything in the universe carries meaning. We try to decode not only systems of signs created for that purpose—alphabets, hieroglyphs, pictographs, social gestures—but also the objects that surround us: the faces of others and our own reflection, the landscape through which we move, the shapes of clouds and trees, the changes in the weather, the flights of birds, the spoors of insects. Legend has it that cuneiform script, one of the earliest systems of writing, was invented by copying sparrows' footprints found in the mud of the Euphrates 5,000 years ago, prints that must have seemed to our remote ancestors not just casual markings but words in a mysterious and divine language. We lend moods to the seasons, significance to geographic settings, symbolic values to animals. Whether as trackers, poets, or shamans, we have intuited in the unfolding of Nature an endless book in which we, like every other thing, are written, but which we are also compelled to read.

Our purpose is to broaden modestly the continuing dialogue on strategies and concepts for creating messages presumably to be launched by humankind in response to receipt of an apparent message from extraterrestrial intelligence (ETI). There have been many ingenious and productive efforts in that direction by a highly talented corps of wise contributors. When one strives to add to that store of literature, it is very difficult to do much more than stir up well-plowed ground. Albert Harrison and Steven Dick (2000) provide an authoritative summary of the issues and impact of search for extraterrestrial intelligence (SETI). Other contributors to that volume are equally illuminating on the subject.

We are adapting an ancient practice to communicate with ETI, seizing upon storytelling, a modality that has met human needs from ages past. Many schemes and ideas are aimed at bridging the almost unimaginably wide gulf that may distinguish the human species from extraterrestrials sharing the universe. The means of composing suitable messages is far from being a cookbook recipe or even settled art and science. In the following sections, we will share with you our thinking on this matter in terms of both message content and structure. In particular, we will explore how simple (to us) primitive observables may serve as Rosetta analogies capable of cracking open the door to mutual understanding across the cosmos.

Messaging: Complex, Uncertain

Beyond proof of their existence, a principal rationale for investing in interstellar communications with races that we are unlikely ever to meet physically is to collect and use knowledge that such correspondents offer. Considering constraints of time and distance, the degree of information reciprocity tendered by human beings may be optional. Of course, a clutch-purse approach restricting the human contribution may terminate the encounter. Obviously, we cannot grasp authoritatively either the motives underlying or the likely content of any such communication that may be received by human beings. Speculation on this issue, as on others related to this matter, is useful in that it better prepares our minds should we be called upon to respond or even decide to initiate traffic.

Contributors to the field of message composition are working diligently to devise "intelligible" communications. Criteria proposed for content to be launched in such exchanges are broad and inclusive of elements of our perceived human condition and nature, our environment, and our experience, theories, and aspirations, all couched in diverse systems of symbols and images. It is useful in this "quiet time" to apply our critical faculties to the task of assembling a notional best-practices guide to aid future colleagues who may be challenged to compose messages under great political pressure.

In view of the state of our knowledge, however, it would be both illogical and unbecoming to eliminate any paradigm a priori. Any signal received from ETI will contain presently unforecastable cues, perhaps even direction, with respect to language and format choices and, indeed, initial content. While human beings will surely take all such offers of guidance under advisement, we here are not sanguine that our species will accept advice from the cosmos with any greater grace than is our terrestrial norm.

The path toward agreement on humanity's response to the "Signal from Elsewhere" may be a rocky one. It will begin in an environment of bewilderment and excitement consequent to the announcement that ETI has called. Difficult and numerous technical problems will emerge with it. The event will surface a host of security issues and call forth multinational, multilingual, international, and transconfessional reprimands and complexities instantly. If the decision is taken to respond, debates on message structure, transmission strategies, and media selection await. Should the absence of capacity for political and social compromise, prevalent in our world today, persist to that time, unanimity in any aspect of the matter will be achieved with difficulty, if at all.

A principal concern that arises as we consider the process of responding to the signal from ETI is: Will the content and format of, arguably, the most anticipated communication ever initiated by humankind be a "lowest-common-denominator" response crafted by a committee of bureaucrats, or will it be the best we can do? Harrison explored the issue, one of great and continuing concern, of societal-governmental response to the "confirmed" receipt of such a signal (2003). He examined the key question of who will be "in charge"—thus, who will exert final authority in selecting the message structures and content to be transmitted. At the root of the matter is whether or not any response at all will be sent. Harrison wrote:

> Perhaps the most crucial responses to the confirmation of extraterrestrial intelligence will come from organizations, rather than from individual people. Among the key organizations that will help shape humanity's response are political institutions such as the U.S. Congress, administrative bodies such as the U.S. Department of State, security agencies, the military, professional societies, and the media. Although popular culture and individual beliefs will affect organizational performance, organizational reactions will depend also on organizational cultures and traditions, administrative structures, communication patterns, decision-making processes, and the actions of other organizations. Prompt and effective responses may be blocked by sociopolitical constraints, jurisdictional disputes, cumbersome structures and procedures, stresses that frequently slow and distort information processing, and potentially counterproductive efforts to maintain positive organizational images. (2003: 229)

Douglas Vakoch has analyzed the dimensionalities of cross-cultural influences on message content, invoking both international and intercultural variables. In "The Art and Science of Interstellar Message Composition: A Report on International Workshops to Encourage Multidisciplinary Discussion," Vakoch (2011) reviewed "the SETI Institute's efforts to increase broad-based, international discussion of the societal implications of detecting extraterrestrial intelligence." The approach envisioned increases the involvement of social scientists in the process of message generation. While such a program clearly benefits output quality, it also highlights the vast realms of stakeholders who will wish to participate in the process of message generation and selection.

The effort to articulate humanness has also been pioneered by Vakoch in the particular context of such selfless, highly nuanced behaviors as altruism (2008; Vakoch and Matessa 2011). The benefits of considering and dealing with such issues, perhaps defensively, are self-evident in the context of transmitting, whether immediately or later, full knowledge of ourselves as well as of externals. In all likelihood, content dealing with human speciography is at the heart of the corpus of information most prized by our distant correspondents. They may know in advance that we are a far-younger civilization than they, unlikely to possess general scientific knowledge of great value. The essential utility of the objective set forth by Vakoch is obvious; however, it is evident that in its implementation, multiculturalism will add greatly to the complexity of the processes of message creation and approval.

Awareness on the part of the SETI community of the multivariate nature of the parameters of message composition and approval processes is highly beneficial. It argues for and stimulates preparedness. The large menu of message structure and content choices presently available will grow steadily in ratio to the numbers of members of both the physical and social sciences communities and national and international political bodies interested in exploring the prospect of receipt of such a signal and increasingly persuaded that its probability is greater than zero.

Undetermined and remaining in the balance is the question of how many independent transmission authorities might become active with little to no coordination of effort. In the anticipated environment, cost of such apparatus will be seen as a trivial constraint in comparison to "getting out the *right* message." One might speculate that dozens of transmitters would become active in due course, some likely secular, but others perhaps confessional in origin. The consequences of such diversity are unclear. In any case, uncoordinated multitasking would certainly reveal a valid aspect of our nature. Whatever obstacles it may encounter, it is incumbent upon the SETI community to pursue the mission inclusively and vigorously, trusting that the Signal from Elsewhere may sharpen our thought processes and, perhaps, encourage our better natures.

Teaching ET to Read Our Way

The objective of each candidate message concept created in anticipation of receipt of a signal is to make a best effort to ensure its intelligibility to ETI. We cannot know in advance what will "work," although as noted above, a significant narrowing of options may arise after a received message is decoded, formatted, read, and understood. The uncertainty inherent in our overall objective of being understood has prompted the generation of a productive literature featuring highly creative initiatives aimed at teaching ET to read our way.

Somewhat at odds with this effort is the widely held belief that the civilization(s) to whose signal we are considering our response may be far older and wiser than we. When dealing with beings who are our informational and intellectual superiors, one wonders whether our seemingly erudite efforts to make ourselves understood will be interpreted by the savants of ETI as demeaning claptrap. We have no idea what they know or will learn of us before communicating. Would it be entirely surprising should their second message, if not their first, be couched in superb diplomatic French?

An alternative possibility is the superannuation of the initial signaling civilization in the period elapsing during two-way transmission, not to mention Harrison's time delays incurred in burrowing through the bureaucratic thicket as SETI seeks message approval. In such a case, a perhaps marginally evolved successor civilization may need all of the help we can provide to decode our response, perhaps presented to them by an ancient system operating on autopilot. Erring on the side of caution, we find no fault with the idea that the principal information content of early messages should be designed with guideposts on the path to understanding. We trust that such attention to detail will be received with the respect with which we submit it for review.

While considering the classes of reading primers that might be composed, it is useful to consider Kathryn Denning's (forthcoming) caution that we attend carefully to the lessons of archaeology, the essence of which we paraphrase: it is seemly to maintain great humility in estimating both the elegance and utility of one's message constructs. Its symbology may be clearly "readable," yet defeat all efforts to translate it into meaningful text, even granting super-human brilliance to its recipients. The following passage highlights the danger of assuming too much about the efficacy of symbols, alphabets, and pictures we create in composing messages intelligible to the non-acculturated ETI:

> There are cases where decipherment has not yet been possible or is only beginning, such as the Indus script, the Rongorongo script, Linear A, Linear Elamite, Jurchen, Khitan, and some Mesoamerican scripts. Sometimes we are missing a key piece of information, such as the language being represented. Sometimes there just isn't enough of a script to do much with it. The best methods in the world cannot bridge certain gaps. This is humbling. ... For example, in the case of the Indus script, we have 4000 texts with plenty of redundancy, but the sheer quantity of information has not helped. Recent analyses suggest that the entire framing of the Indus script has been incorrect, which might explain why none of the many attempts at decipherment (over 100 published since the 1800s), has met with much acceptance. (Denning forthcoming)

The immense literature dealing with composing effective communications features a host of approaches created to ensure intellectual lock with our correspondents (Vakoch 2011). The complexity of surmounting this presumed highest hurdle has elicited new languages based upon a variety of assumptions. Mathematics is considered by some to be a vessel of universal language. An ETI capable of transmitting messages that can be extracted from background noise and recognized as such by terrestrial researchers, it is hypothesized, would have identified, derived, and codified mathematical propositions in forms that are, at least somewhat, analogous to terrestrial mathematics. This assumption has been questioned (Vakoch 1998; DeVito 2011), but it is a reasonable starting point.

Hans Freudenthal's seminal effort in the field was the creation of a language based upon mathematics and logic. It was a highly rigorous effort designed for the purpose of communicating with races having neither contact with nor knowledge of human beings and their works. He named the language *Lingua Cosmica,* contracted into the term "LINCOS" (1960). This work has been cited by numerous authors, many of whom went on to create their own useful and productive approaches to the problem.

Carl DeVito (forthcoming) and Richard Oehrle (DeVito and Oehrle 1990) developed and systematically extended a language based upon logic, mathematics, and the physical sciences. Its multiple purposes include communication with a hypothetical intelligent extraterrestrial race as well as future terrestrial computers able to do science at human or near-human levels. DeVito and Oehrle encapsulated their approach in the following abstract:

> The problem of how to communicate with the members of an alien society has been discussed by many authors but only one, Hans Freudenthal, has constructed a language for this purpose. Freudenthal assumes nothing other than the ability to reason as humans do and, because he assumes so little, it is necessary to communicate a great deal about the language itself before being able to communicate any interesting information. The problem is here approached differently. Since it is likely that contact between our civilization and an alien one would be *via* radio, potential correspondents would have a basic knowledge of science. It is assumed, more specifically, that our correspondents can count, understand chemical elements, are familiar with the melting and boiling behavior of a pure substance and understand the properties of the gaseous state. All this should be known to any society capable of developing the radio telescope. By systematically using this common knowledge one can communicate the notation for numbers and chemical elements and then communicate our basic physical units; i.e., the gram, the calorie, the degree (Kelvin), etc. Once this is done more interesting information can be exchanged (DeVito and Oehrle 1990).

The composition of messages includes media and concepts that move beyond the structure of mathematics. Vakoch has created numerous message concepts and structures and, additionally, has extensively explored the literature of such efforts as well as multidisciplinary venues structured to encourage and facilitate the creation of new message composition modalities and content (2011). Vakoch and his collaborators have focused strongly on modalities capable of communicating such human behaviors as altruism and the elements of the social sciences. Proposed message structures include symbology, artistic imagery, music, and a host of other strategies designed to unfold and render understandable more complex human behavioral elements.

Our Chosen Symbology

There is existential tension between symbolic language and imagery. In the present case, this does not appear to arise from the question of comparative technical difficulties that may be perceived between transmitting or receiving and decoding radio and video technologies. The SETI Institute's Seth Shostak asserts that a qualified extraterrestrial engineer can readily deal with either (1995, 2011). Arguments favoring one or the other approach may be drawn in rigid terms despite the fact that the state of our knowledge of ETI provides no a priori rationale for limiting oneself to one or the other. Nevertheless, the question demands consideration before message composition is undertaken.

The following brief excerpt from Michael Arbib (1979: 21–22) is a rationale stated in support of one choice of "sign" presumed to be the most appropriate for communicating with ETI:

> One needs a language made of symbols which can be rearranged in arbitrary fashion, thus transcending imitation or the transmission of pictures of actual events. The trouble with pictures is that they are too literal to communicate general truths: imagine a picture which adequately conveys a theorem about polynomials, or which conveys the negation of a statement. We [suggest] that pictorial information will not be sufficient for interstellar communication, and that a rich symbol system based language will also be required.

Clearly, Arbib's terminal *also* avoids foreclosing the use of imagery in communicating the extraordinarily diverse field of concepts, ranging from one-on-one correspondence to altruism and beyond. It may be difficult, as Arbib states, to convey a theorem about polynomials solely in pictures. Such propositions, however, are not readily proved. It is reasonable to suggest that the concept of "mountain range" may be somewhat more effectively communicated in pictures than in words. That, too, remains to be proven and is, in the end, dependent upon audience acculturation.

Visuals are critical to our paradigm, a choice that we have not taken lightly. We have concluded that our storytelling modality can best be used with rich illustration. As we shall see, the methodology also lends itself to the use of signs in mathematics and symbolic language and, perhaps, in sound. We have consulted studies in the cinematic arts for guidance and insights, from a terrestrial point of view, of course, on the nature of communicating by use of imagery, "moving" or not.

In their article "Symbolic Strategies," Sol Worth and Larry Gross analyzed the semiotic underpinnings of cinematic imagery, producing the following definition: "Communication is a social process, within a context, in which signs are produced and transmitted, perceived, and treated as messages from which meaning can be inferred" (1974: 14). This clarifies our task. We have no assurance that communicating with ETI is a social process. We hope that is the case as it would bode well for the utility of storytelling, a participative art. However, even if ETI receives information with that absence of emotion encountered by a byte in its handshake with the next chip on the board, we do not despair as long as other key criteria of the definition are met. After all, even a lowly byte, with its congeners, can quite asocially, but effectively, call forth a search engine.

Clearly, any signal from here to there is fraught with context. Once verified, there will be no doubt that an intelligence, organic or not, has produced a signal and the signal has been transmitted, else ETI should not have detected it. ETI has perceived, and noted, the signal and, again, after ascertaining that it is, indeed, a valid communication, will very likely proceed to attempt to infer its intended meaning within context. To the degree that the attempt is successful, communication will have taken place, which is precisely our objective.

Considering cinema, the notation proposed (Worth and Gross 1974) facilitates analysis of the semiotics of "events" into sign events and non-sign events. The latter are everyday activities whose meanings are clear without conscious analysis. Sign events may be either natural or symbolic, but are always used to interpret meaning. If an event is deemed natural, the observer adapts to it appropriately, but if deemed symbolic, the observer "consciously or tacitly assumes implicative intent and call[s] into play those interpretive strategies by which we *infer meaning* from communicative events."

We must presume that quite ordinary non-sign events automatically become sign events when they are received elements of an interstellar message between human beings and ETI. An example of a natural, non-sign event is a worker, paying no attention to the observer, chopping wood in an appropriate setting. A representation of this event in an interstellar transmission, however, is converted instantly upon reception into an important sign event to be interpreted. The content in such signals, therefore, will "call into play ... [those] interpretive strategies ... that we wish to facilitate by message design" (Worth and Gross 1974).

Worth's valuable exploration of the multicultural aspects of communication by film are summarized in Gross's introduction to *Studying Visual Communication* (Worth 1981). Worth's research on bioethnography of the Navajo Nation provides insights into the difficult task that we are addressing. He stated that film images are not "exclusively and naively" *about* culture, but a record *of* culture, observing that they represent the picture maker's "dialogue with the world" (1981: 16). Worth denied "the possibility of an objective, value-free film record [with] the assertion that every filmmaker has an inherent cultural bias" (1981: 7).

This distinction was crystallized in post-viewing comments collected from Navajo audience members shown films shot and edited by non-Navajo picture makers. Tellingly, one Navajo observer reported that he could not grasp the meanings in those films, in contrast to those by Navajo picture makers, because the former were in English. There were no sound tracks at all. This underscores the necessity that our compositions must teach our metaphors, to the extent that we include them in our messages, as well as reading skills, else they may not be understood by ETI.

A question not operative in terrestrial multicultural research is that of the intrinsic utility of any image or writing falling onto the ETI message desk. Is "seeing" an element of their physiology and psychology? Do ETI study, produce, or otherwise deal with imagery? In raising the question, we note that our Milky Way is awash in energy of the entire electromagnetic spectrum. It would be an evolutionary oversight of some magnitude should a race that caps its food chain be totally unmindful of such energy.

It is possible, perhaps, that a civilization might have lost the need for and abandoned its capacity to produce or use visual signs. That would in no way cripple their ability to build radio telescopes. Instruction sets devoid of visual content may be entered by numerous means into automated manufacturing systems that fabricate and assemble equipment. Human beings presently apply such techniques in a variety of physical and biological fields including the construction of scientific apparatus.

Whatever the organic capacities of ETI, one would expect electromagnetic data collection to be an integral part of their astronomy or intelligence operations, assuring situational awareness. This does not presuppose warfare in the cosmos, but suggests use of observational techniques to track such threats as asteroids. State-of-the-art terrestrial sensors, for example, collect and analyze information from ever-wider energy bands without human intervention. Those technologies are being extrapolated to provide rudimentary sight to visually challenged human beings. It seems highly unlikely to us that exploitation of a human message would fail because it is "invisible" to ETI.

As we accept the burden of SETI to go forth and explore message composition, we cannot afford to believe that we are uniquely objective. Each day, we bring to our desks our innate selves, understanding that many of our traits remain hidden, qualitatively and quantitatively unknown even to us. While wishing to avoid the pitfalls of loading messages with hidden meaning, we assert our overarching goal to communicate faithfully our humanness, those characteristics with which evolution freshens and enriches the sentient content of our niche in the universe. We must make a conscious effort to render our reading lessons understandable. In the process, we also struggle to avoid burying meaning in metaphors clearly indecipherable to those unversed in our alien culture.

Primitive Observables

The term *primitive observables* is not contrived to induce the reader to agree that those values are so fundamental that observing them, or their fair representation, leaves no doubt as to their nature and meaning in an extraterrestrial context. We wish to use them to create Rosetta elements containing as few cultural metaphors as possible with the hope that they can communicate by analogy. In some cases, however, key metaphors may transfer directly into the context of other cultures. An example might be images of an individual erecting a four-post shelter, placing a blanket beneath it, and lying upon it. The sequence may be clear to one or more cultures and mysterious to others.

The highest hurdle in formulating a strategy of interstellar storytelling is to define effective Rosetta elements. These are the production values deemed to render human stories intelligible to extraterrestrials. We present an open set of primitive observables that are fundamental to sentient activity on Earth. We propose composing messages containing a rich mix of representations of such key signs, hypothesizing that some or many are analogous to sentient activities in some or many accessible ETI civilizations.

Primitive observables are drawn from such sets as:

1. physical observables, such as terrain features, weather events, light and shadow, changes of state, fluid flow, buoyancy, and wave motion;

2. simple machines and tools, such as levers, wheels, ropes, pulleys, sails, screws, hammers, saws, and containers;

3. basic physical activities, such as grasping, walking, running, lifting, climbing, throwing, playing, eating, and sleeping;

4. domestic pursuits, such as erecting shelters, collecting, hunting, preparing and ingesting food and water, agriculture, animal husbandry, weaving, mining, shaping, and transporting by wheelbarrow, quadruped-drawn cart or boat.

As story development evolves and branches, higher, more complex activities and technologies may be tapped.

We postulate an accessible ETI who does not live within an exotic environment such as the maw of a black hole, but on a hypothetical planet that we may call γ-Tenalp, engaged by a star in our galaxy that may be light-centuries distant. From the point of view of ETI, and perhaps from ours, too, γ-Tenalp has a reasonable, not to say Earth-like, environment in terms of its gravity, insolation, range of temperature, atmosphere, resources, agriculture, and, perhaps, chemistry. While few of our assumptions may apply to all ETI abodes, we posit a reasonable probability that extra-solar system planets supporting accessible, intelligent life with which we can engage may fit such a mold.

Although the intelligent organism to which we respond may be neither carbon nor water based, it is likely to include a cellular liquid transport medium. A useful planet such as γ-Tenalp, then, probably features a liquid circulation cycle among atmospheric, oceanic, and land reservoirs. With a sun, gravity, atmosphere, and ocean, its weather will include rainfall. Rain on γ-Tenalp may not look or smell or feel or run off exactly like Earth rain, but when it falls, it will do so in drops that splash on solid terrain or in pools of liquid. Such drops, despite differences in gravity, chemistry, density, viscosity, and surface tension, are unlikely to differ markedly in appearance from water or liquid drops with similar properties on Earth.

We select the first Primitive Observable to present here on the basis of our estimate that a liquid cycle is prevalent on γ-Tenalp. Figure 10.1 is a representation of a high-speed photograph of a falling drop of liquid and figure 10.2, its recoil after striking a pool of liquid. These icons, well known to Earth scholars, scientists, and lay observers, may require future adjustment to be fully generalized. While maintaining deep humility with respect to our objectivity, we suggest that liquid drops are primitive observables that, exclusive of their means of representation, may be only lightly encumbered by Earth-culture metaphors. No analogy is a perfect identity, but it would not surprise us to find that high-speed images of liquid drops would be recognizable to denizens of γ-Tenalp. If so, they would serve as effective Rosetta analogies, providing a small link of understanding, the beginning of a connection of the cultures of our planets.

Figure 10.1. Representation of a high-speed photograph of a falling liquid drop. Credit: Michael H. Mower.

Further exploring the drop images as primitive observables, we note additional benefits. The figures do not describe the physics and chemistry of drop formation, but represent the drop process itself. The figures are not mathematical abstractions, but frames of a potentially cinematic process that may be used to show motion, and are a visual impression of the calculus of a raindrop falling into a pool. Such images, or duplicate following sequences, may include symbolic language overlays, e.g., "drop" or "liquid," presuming the use of English, or appropriate mathematics. Further enrichment might include audio tracks enunciating words in synchrony with their appearance, as well as inclusion of short written and spoken sentences, such as, "Drop falling into liquid."

Figure 10.3 represents a human-like creature using a lever to dislodge or move an object. This figure introduces both the human form and a simple machine. We call the creature a *Phoid*, our abbreviation of the term *Anthropomorphoid*, the name chosen by Vakoch for the form of his design. Gratefully and with permission of its author (2005), we have adapted the Phoid figure to our purposes. The lever is as simple a machine as one might offer, but the biological Phoid is a major complication.

Standing alone in this single image, the Phoid is an indecipherable icon, of course depending upon the anatomic structure of denizens of γ-Tenalp

Figure 10.2. Representation of a high-speed photograph of the recoil of a liquid drop falling into a liquid pool. Credit: Michael H. Mower.

Figure 10.3. A Phoid using a lever on a stone fulcrum to move a stone. Credit: Michael H. Mower.

or their beasts. We do not deal with single frames, however, but create strings not unlike a "flip book" or a comic strip of indeterminate length. The Phoid will be shown to be the actor, shaker, and mover in such sequences. It is unlikely that the inanimate tools, carts, shelters, and other items that will appear from time to time will be thought to be intelligent, except perhaps early on initial exposure. Viewers will nominate the Phoid as the agent of change.

The list of candidate primitive observables is both long and rich. As the initial entries are established, additions and extrapolations of such icons will be introduced. For example, in the figures presented, we have introduced liquid, drops, levers, and Phoids. In a further step forward, as presented in the following section, we will place the Phoid in a boat floating on liquid. The motive power for the boat will be a pole not unlike the lever. In combination, they will move along the liquid surface and ultimately into startling adventures. As stories are developed, the Phoid will be seen to be endowed with faculties of reasoning and choice that, we trust, will serve as a rudimentary Turing test establishing its bonafides as an intelligent operator.

Creating Stories

A principal development criterion for message content composed to respond to a signal from an extraterrestrial intelligence is that it encompass the human condition and provide a kaleidoscopic view of wit, intelligence, creativity, technology, history, behavior, biology, customs, and environment along with a host of other traits, qualities, and factors. We have long woven perceptions of our humanity into stories mediated by narrative, poetry, song, drama and dance, cave paintings, steles, print, tapestries, and video as each new medium emerges. The present modality is based on mediation by cinematic, initially image-only, cartoon narratives transmitted in frame-by-frame progression.

Storytelling powerfully communicates hard facts, states of mind, and the bounds of acceptable behaviors—humanness in its entirety. Stories creatively interrelate human beings, other animals, and inanimate objects and their thoughts, responses, and outcomes in bounded environments. Illustrated stories can present primitive observables in a real-world context: simple machines in use and basic physical activities in simple cartoon form. Cinematic chains and trees of such sequences have unlimited capacity to expand, embracing the human condition and, ultimately, all of our knowledge by example as the symbology grows in complexity and richness. Should an interstellar partner share stories with us, it would facilitate our capturing their essence as well as their knowledge.

Cinematic "narration" is a modality that, picture-only, frame-by-frame advances the action of a story at a desired rate, absent language and nuanced discourse. The vibrant Bayeaux Tapestry is a stunning example of such a storytelling modality, although it is captioned and its imagery in many places is somewhat more detailed than that which we envision here. Simplicity and intelligibility can be served by the reuse of standardized images. Repetitive image elements may be thinned in detail, retaining only line and form essential to decoding. Such strategies contain cost and complexity.

There is initially no verbal component in these cinematic stories. Comic-strip and flip-book artists communicate complex ideas to human beings using image frames without speech balloons. In this context, it is informative to "mute" a television advertisement and compare that experience to listening to its audio track in the absence of video. The two messages are often quite different. Imagery, for example, may use dancers to attract attention or actors to demonstrate ease of product use, while the accompanying audio proclaims product economy.

Imagery, created frame by frame, is rendered with relative artistic economy and varying degrees of "magnification" as detail is revealed by close-up views, shown as extensions of preceding frames at lower magnification. Sequences may feature such physical observables as terrain and weather effects. Sunlit terrain with a mountainous background may be changed stepwise: developing as the sun transits, clouds gathering, lightning striking, raindrops falling, splashes, liquid runoff, water courses, and lakes.

We populate stories with Phoids who can become involved in basic physical activities, quite normal to us, such as collecting and drinking liquid, wading into liquid and launching and poling boats. Such activities are enriched with associated physical observables: wading feet occulted by liquids, wakes emanating from moving legs, air bubbling from dipped containers filling with water, and fluid whorls and wakes about moving poles and boats. The physical observables are deemed critically important cues in that they would be expected to resemble many accessible alien environments.

Basic human activities may have analogs in many, if not all, ETI societies. These are shown as Phoids pitch and strike camp, load carts, and travel. They perform human tasks associated with daily living and travel. Their stories can be enriched by encounters with other Phoid bands, perhaps discriminated by attire clarified as such by its removal in certain sequences. They meet physical challenges, surmounting mountainous terrain and undertaking complex, perhaps behaviorally unique, activities such as rescuing a Phoid who has fallen off of a trail (Vakoch 2005). Stories with such sequences present examples of rudimentary human activities as well as such complex human qualities as species altruism, thus presenting the desired kaleidoscopic view of the human condition.

Story Structures

After transmitting early message strings, we can weave examples of human behavior into a cinematic story. We can present domestic pursuits, frame by frame, in primitive context, later adding trappings of technology. Slowly changing sequences are designed to help our correspondents grasp a global perception of the basics of humanity, human knowledge, and human behavior.

Such communication can begin on a very basic level, not unlike that of encountering for the first time and enjoying the mandatory hospitality of an encampment of nomadic human beings. Learning would begin immediately and slowly—very slowly—expand into multidimensions. As we have noted, relatively primitive human activities provide a rich structure from which to devise and present virtually inexhaustible menus of behaviors, customs, techniques, environments, and topographic settings.

In reliance upon early transmissions having advanced the conversation and image conventions, a simple story can be told with frames initially showing flat, featureless foreground with elevated terrain in the distance. A Sun image is above. Small clouds appear in the sky. Cloud cover builds, occulting the sun. Following frames show intermittent lightning illustrated by conventional strokes. Rain begins to fall. Liquid collects in a depression into which rain drops splash as shown in figures 10.1 and 10.2.

We introduce a Phoid catching rain in hands or cup and drinking. A juvenile Phoid enters. The mature Phoid allows the juvenile to drink from hands or a cup. Water runs down a narrow course into a lake. A Phoid wades into the shallow lake, illustrated by occulted feet and ankle wakes. As represented in figure 10.4, the Phoid, after launching a small boat and boarding it, creates wakes and water whorls as he poles ahead. Such a compact story, illustrated largely by liquid-cycle elements, can move the ball a fair distance within a reasonable number of frames, perhaps accompanied with well-chosen phrases from Smetana, Debussy, or Vivaldi that we find to be pleasant.

Storytelling portrays space, time, and action with flexibility, providing a wide-ranging view of the human condition and activities that may represent experiences shared in common with our distant neighbors. Many

Figure 10.4. A Phoid poling a boat on a body of liquid. Credit: Michael H. Mower.

behaviors can be illustrated in the context of a single storyline. Root analogies may allow the Phoid environment and practices to be compared to those of extraterrestrials in settings of high heuristic value. Root analogies can be conceptualized into succeeding story sequences in a system of chains and trees. Careful branching can carry the story forward in any desired direction.

An Altruism Story

Our purpose is to create an exemplary story plot to illustrate the evolutionary potential of the cosmic storytelling modality described. The storyline involves a dangerous trip away from an established water-rich environment into a rugged, waterless desert. Customs, geography, and normal and abnormal behaviors can be illustrated in such stories. How Phoids deal with strangers from other bands, share with them, and succor them in distress is designed to suggest altruistic behavior. Projected in highly redundant fashion, it is our aim to render a long story reasonably easy to decode, step by step, although such behaviors may be exceedingly difficult to understand at the outset depending upon the norms of the ETI society contacted.

Proceeding into the plot, once upon a time, a band of Phoids were equipped by their haberdasher with turbans, earlier established to be clothing items. Turbans will discriminate them from members of other Phoid bands whom they will soon encounter. They prepare to set out on a journey taking them into a desert area from their present encampment on the shore of a lake featuring leafy trees and other vegetation. They fill many containers with liquid from the lake. As the containers are immersed, air displaced by liquid visibly bubbles out of them. The filled containers are loaded onto quadruped-drawn carts. Food and equipment items, their form and function having been established previously, are also loaded.

The Phoid band jumps into their carts and depart. As the caravan moves away from the lake, traveling on a cart track, terrain relief soon changes, dust clouds rise, and prevalent vegetation becomes succulent-like, all perhaps helpful in communicating the idea that the band is entering a dry country. Bold shadows beneath carts and draft animals indicate strong sunlight. Gradually shifting shadows can communicate changes in direction or passing time. As the Sun drops low in the sky, the Phoids raise shelters such as yurts or tepees. They build fires, cook, eat, and retire for the night.

The next morning, as the sun rises, they strike camp and set out again. The caravan comes upon a differently dressed, lone Phoid, wearing a unique headdress, lying on the ground. Phoids dismount and investigate the stranger. Two Phoids lift the stranger and place him in the shade under a cart. They remove the headdress, ensuring that the stranger is seen to be a Phoid and not mistaken for another species. They sprinkle liquid upon the stranger, elevate his head and help him drink. They assist the stranger to stand. The stranger replaces his or her unique headdress. The host Phoids assist the stranger into a cart. The caravan resumes travel.

Story imagery is highly redundant in the interest of facilitating frame-to-frame continuity. Creation of such stories can be accomplished in an open-source environment. It is unnecessary to centralize or control story origins—the more, the better. Evidently, it would be useful for formats to be adhered to, image conventions conserved, and transmission orderly to avoid chaos and a major sorting task at the receiving end. We suggest that our classically slow, deliberate story progression may speed understanding and grasp of quite subtle nuances of human thought and behavior as well as of our rational, computational, and observational skills. We note in closing that no matter how clever our capacity to communicate, we cannot communicate that which we do not know nor can we assure understanding on the part of the ETI.

Afterword

We have explored the application of one of our oldest communications strategies, storytelling, to exchange perceptions and knowledge with a presently unknown, as yet unrevealed, and possibly non-existent cosmic neighbor. This exploration, itself the telling of a story, is a product of the hope that humankind is not a lone seeker in the universe, but one of many who share its breathtaking beauty, unbounded promise, and mythic grandeur.

The brief span of human life and the fragility of our works and civilizations call into question whether or not we will ever greet a fellow species, and in meeting, wonder at our unplumbable differences while glorying in our shared intelligence. The prospects of such contact and the spirit of optimism thereby engendered greatly enrich the lives of those of us who relish the thought of the childlike pleasure that would come from sharing our story with such distant friends.

Acknowledgments

We acknowledge with gratitude the patient encouragement generously extended to us by our friend and mentor, Dr. Douglas A. Vakoch of the SETI Institute, as we have sought a modest niche in the great argosy of this uplifting search. We gratefully acknowledge our indebtedness to Mr. Michael H. Mower of Crofton, Maryland, our friend and highly talented computer-graphic illustrator whose extraordinary skills bring life to elements of messages that we hope may one day be launched beyond our farthest reach.

Bibliography

Arbib, Michael. 1979. "Minds and Millennia: The Psychology of Interstellar Communication." *Cosmic Search* 1, no. 3: 21–24, 47–48.

Denning, Kathryn. Forthcoming. "Learning to Read: Interstellar Message Decipherment from an Anthropological Perspective." In *Archaeology, Anthropology, and Interstellar Communication*, ed. Douglas A. Vakoch. Washington, DC: National Aeronautics and Space Administration.

DeVito, Carl L. 2011. "On the Universality of Human Mathematics." In *Communication with Extraterrestrial Intelligence*, ed. Douglas A. Vakoch, 439–448. Albany, NY: State University of New York Press.

—————. Forthcoming. "Overcoming the Language Problem: Modeling Time and Space in Interstellar Messages." In *Between Worlds: The Art and Science of Interstellar Message Composition*, ed. D. A. Vakoch. Cambridge, MA: MIT Press.

DeVito, Carl L., and Richard Oehrle. 1990. "A Language Based on the Fundamental Facts of Science." *Journal of the British Interplanetary Society* 43: 561–568.

Drake, Frank, and Dava Sobel. 1992. *Is Anyone Out There?* New York: Delacorte Press.

Freudenthal, Hans. 1960. *LINCOS: Design of a Language for Cosmic Intercourse*. Amsterdam: North-Holland.

Harrison, Albert A. 2003. "Confirmation of ETI: Initial Organizational Response." *Acta Astronautica* 53: 229–236.

Harrison, Albert A., and Steven J. Dick. 2000. "Contact: Long Term Implications for Humanity." In *When SETI Succeeds: The Impact of High-Information Contact*, ed. A. Tough, 7–31. Bellevue, WA: Foundation For the Future.

Manguel, Alberto. 2007. "Fragments of Paradise." *The American Scholar* 76, no. 3: 91–97.

Shostak, Seth. 1995. "SETI at Wider Bandwidths?" *Progress in the Search for Extraterrestrial Life*. ASP Conference Series 74, ed. G. S. Shostak, 447–454. San Francisco, CA: Astronomical Society of the Pacific.

—————. 2011. "Limits on Interstellar Messages." In *Communication with Extraterrestrial Intelligence*, ed. Douglas A. Vakoch, 357–369. Albany, NY: State University of New York Press.

Vakoch, Douglas A. 1998. "Constructing Messages to Extraterrestrials: An Exosemiotic Perspective." *Acta Astronautica* 42: 697–704.

—————. 2005. Private Communication.

—————. 2008. "Representing Culture in Interstellar Messages." *Acta Astronautica* 63: 657–664.

—————. 2011. "The Art and Science of Interstellar Message Composition: A Report on International Workshops to Encourage Multidisciplinary Discussion." *Acta Astronautica* 68: 451–458.

Vakoch, Douglas A., and Michael Matessa. 2011. "An Algorithmic Approach to Communicating Reciprocal Altruism in Interstellar Messages: Drawing Analogies between Social and Astrophysical Phenomena." *Acta Astronautica* 68: 459–475.

Worth, Sol. 1981. *Studying Visual Communications*, ed. Larry Gross. Philadelphia, PA: University of Pennsylvania Press. http://astro.temple.edu/~ruby/wava/worth/svscom.html#tblc. Accessed on 18 April 2011.

Worth, Sol, and Larry Gross. 1974. "Symbolic Strategies," *Journal of Communications* 24, no. 4: 27–39.

Chapter 11

Direct Contact with Extraterrestrials via Computer Emulation

William Sims Bainbridge

Radio transmission of human personalities to other stars is a logical corol-lary of personality capture, the process of gathering sufficient information about a human being's memories, thoughts, and feelings to allow emula-tion of the person in a computer, information system, or robot. Steady progress in artificial intelligence, cognitive science, and personality cap-ture raises the very real possibility of transmitting functional avatars of human beings to corresponding extraterrestrial civilizations, and vice versa. These avatars would be high-fidelity autonomous agents capable of perceiving, thinking, and acting in manners very similar to the humans and ETs on which they are based.

Historical Background

When I first seriously proposed personality capture in 1993, I did so in the form of a parable about a fictitious engineer who had been working on a NASA Search for Extraterrestrial Intelligence (SETI) project to de-tect radio signals from extraterrestrial civilizations. In the story, he under-goes an experience of almost religious revelation, standing on the actual surface of the great Arecibo radio telescope, realizing that he personally could travel to the stars if he scanned his personality into a computer and had it sent, perhaps centuries later, on an interstellar probe. After eight years of research, I presented a more-grounded version of the idea at a NASA conference:

> We have the technology, already today, to begin archiving human personalities at low fidelity within what I call *Starbase*, a database destined eventually to be transported to the stars. To gain entry to Starbase, a person must contribute significantly in some way to the creation of interstellar civilization. One way is to help develop technologies for archiving and reanimating human personalities at ever higher fidelity. Another is to work toward the establishment of small human colonies, first on the Moon and Mars, where Starbase can be headquartered and where serious work on reanimation can begin.
>
> When the time comes for the first interstellar expeditions, they will be carried out not by biologically based humans in their first brief lifetimes, but by eternal Starbase modules incorporating the archived but active personalities of the crew and colonists. At the destination, the crew will not waste its time terraforming planets, but will adapt the colonist into whatever form (biological, robot, cyborg) can thrive in the alien environment. Subsequent waves of colonists can be sent as radioed datafiles, in a technically feasible version of the old science fiction dream of teleportation. (Bainbridge 2002b: 61–62)

I am sure that many visionaries and science fiction writers have had similar ideas. Back in 1966, Roger MacGowan and Frederick Ordway argued that interstellar explorers will be robots rather than biological organisms, for example. Recently, Steven J. Dick (2003) has argued that the dominant forms of intelligence in the universe may be "postbiological," raising the question of whether our own species is ready to transition away from its traditional biological form.

The crucial point is that the convergence of cognitive science, uniting cognitive psychology with artificial intelligence and cognitive neuroscience, has prepared a basis for rapid and very practical progress in personality capture and emulation. In partnership with Mihail Roco, the charismatic leader of the National Nanotechnology Initiative, I have been able to organize a series of scientific conferences exploring the convergence of nanotechnology, biotechnology, information technology, and new technologies based in cognitive science. At the first of these Converging Technologies conferences, sponsored by the National Science Foundation, computer graphics pioneer Warren Robinett projected the consequences of understanding how the human brain actually works. He noted: "If a mind is data that runs on a processor (and its sensors and actuators), then that data—that mind—can travel at the speed of light as bits in a communication path. Thus, Mars is less than an hour away at light speed. (We need a rocket to get the first receiver there.) You could go there, have experiences (in a body you reserved), and then bring the experience-data back with you on return" (2003: 169). Robinett and I both assumed it would be necessary to transport a receiver and many support systems to the destination, but that would not be the case if an extraterrestrial civilization were willing to serve as a host for interstellar informatic travelers, or "infonauts." With that possibility in mind, we can consider what actually would be involved in capture, transmission, and emulation of human personalities.

Personality Capture Methodologies

To introduce personality capture efficiently, I will explain my own personal approach to it. My family has always placed great emphasis on preserving personal historical records, and my entire life has been spent surrounded by ancestor's publications dating back to 1856, photos from the same decade, diaries and scrapbooks to 1870, and home movies to 1928. Among the dozen members of my immediate family who have published, several count as historians, but several also as scientists, and I have worked extensively in both genres. In the 1980s I became interested in computational social science, and I programmed questionnaire-writing software for two of my books, published in 1986 and 1989. This software offered the user several question formats, multiple response formats, and opportunities to write in text. For example, the user might want a series of agree/disagree items, with a particular number of responses (e.g., Strongly agree, Agree, Neutral, Disagree, Strongly disagree—or leaving out Neutral to force a positive or negative choice), and would write in a statement for each question to which the respondent would react. The software would save the questionnaire in a special format, display it so a person could answer the questions on the computer, then save the data for later analysis by another part of the software.

Simultaneously, I was working in the area of artificial intelligence called neural networks, publishing some neural net multi-agent system software as early as 1987. This got me thinking again about the field in which I had done my Harvard doctoral oral exam, ethnopsychiatry, the sociology and anthropology of mental disorder with an emphasis on the interplay of culture and personality. After I came to the National Science Foundation in 1992, the first workshop I funded was about artificial social intelligence, the application of machine intelligence techniques to social phenomena, including both theory building and data analysis. Shortly afterward I be-came involved in the Digital Library Initiative, just at the time the World Wide Web was being born, and I quickly saw the opportunity to use on-line questionnaires to develop culturally rooted questions for archiving individual beliefs, attitudes, and values. In 1997, I launched a website called *The Question Factory* for this purpose, and a year later joined the team sponsored by the National Geographic Society that was planning the first of a pair of massive online questionnaires.

Individual human personalities are formed in a sociocultural context, and societies vary, so many measures of personality must be culturogenic. That is, the questions must be drawn from the same sociocultural con-text as the respondent, and cannot simply be invented by the researcher. For example, in *Survey2000*, the first major NGS online questionnaire, I included an open-ended item, asking people to predict what the world would be like in a century. I then went through the responses of something approaching twenty thousand people, gleaning and collating statements about the future, resulting in two thousand distinct statements. I then wrote software called *The Year 2100* to administer these as questionnaire items. The respondent was asked to judge how good each idea was, on an eight-point scale, thereby measuring the person's values in terms of the issues the surrounding culture thought would be important for the long-term future. On another eight-point scale, respondents also rated how likely each prediction was to come true. The correlation between these two scales represents the person's optimism, that is, believing good things will happen, normed in terms of the respondent's own beliefs and values. The software permits analysis of optimism in each of twenty areas of life, and research I have done with it confirms that people may have complex patterns of optimism and pessimism across domains of experience.

Subsequently, I assembled materials from other cultural sources for nine more software modules, a total of twenty thousand stimuli, each with two responses, for forty thousand measurements. Although standard psycho-logical tests lack fine detail and are somewhat abstract, they are also useful for personality capture, so an eleventh module incorporates two thousand public domain personality measures from the International Personality Item Pool (http://ipip.ori.org/) created by Lewis R. Goldberg (1999). An-other module explores the individual's short-term memory, inspired by the classic work by Saul Sternberg (1966), asking the individual to memorize 5,760 strings of digits or letters, measuring both accuracy and swiftness of recall. A new area of research is the emotional connotations of autobio-graphic memories (Bainbridge 2006). Complete personality capture will also need to incorporate natural language-processing voice-recognition work on the person's speech; motion capture of gestures, facial expressions, and task-oriented movements; and metabolic, anthropometric, and genetic measurements of the individual's physical body. This sounds like a lot of effort, but with automation it could be finished within two or three months of the person's effort, and might be scheduled as a free-time activity over several years.

Increasingly, we will archive ourselves as an incidental byproduct of interacting with our machines. For example, the Teachable Agents Group at Vanderbilt University has been exploring how to help students learn by having them teach science and math to a computer-animated artificial agent named Betty (Biswas et al. 2005). By recording the detailed interactions between Betty and the student, the system learns much about the student's deep thought processes, precisely in a context where an artificial intelligence is learning to think like a person. A team at the University of Southern California has been recording the behavior of students in educational immersive game environments, in order to design better instructional games but incidentally recording much about the students (Yang et al. 2005). John Smart has argued that human-computer interaction technologies will continue to advance in the coming decades, and soon we will be using a linguistic user interface to converse with our machines: "As our own most-preferred digital personal interface (our 'Digital Me') gains exponentially more storage and processing capacity, it will incrementally engage in a process that William Sims Bainbridge calls 'personality capture.' Our DM's will carry an ever more valuable record of all the past communication we have had with them, and increasingly become our best professional representatives, coaches, managers, and extended memory for important events" (2004).

Rough calculations suggest that a medium- to high-fidelity copy of a single personality could constitute less than a gigabyte of data, perhaps ten gigabytes if this estimate is too low and the person's genetic code and other physical data were included. The code to create the artificial intelligence personality-emulation system, and the messages to tell extraterrestrials how to assemble the system, would add several more gigabytes. There would be economies of scale in sending information about many human beings, especially because many of the individual measurements are comparative with other humans. For example, it could be more efficient to send the genetic code as a list of the person's fifty thousand or so genes, rather than the three billion base pairs, but this assumes that a key to the genes has been sent separately. Fidelity of each avatar could increase as the number of people to be emulated increased, and as our artificial intelligence technology improved. These facts are quite compatible with interstellar transmission, because the recipient civilization would want time to study the information as it came in, and would probably learn much from low fidelity emulations of humans, increasing the fidelity as time passed.

Cosmopolis: The Emulation System

Many writers have speculated that a number of civilizations are already in radio communication with each other, and that we could join their cosmic club. I will now suggest that a club needs a clubhouse, and that each such civilization will establish a vast virtual reality world, perhaps on an unused asteroid or specially built space station, call it *Cosmopolis*. Here, computer-emulated representatives of each of the communicating civilizations would live and work together, serving to link the intelligent species of that solar system with the rest of the galaxy. Whether by local (i.e., interplanetary) radio or in person, members of the host civilization would interact with the avatars of other civilizations. But the hosts would also contribute their share of avatars to Cosmopolis. For many purposes, their AIs would need to be on an equal footing with the others.

Although contemporary radio technology could probably deliver information at a reasonable bitrate across one hundred parsecs, at this distance a single question-and-answer exchange would take six hundred and fifty years. Because the Cosmopolis avatars would reside locally, within information systems equipped with sensors and robots, communication would be instantaneous, rather than delayed by the speed-of-light limitation on interstellar radio, and they would be able to act within the host civilization. They would function in real time as ambassadors and as trading colonists providing translated versions of works of art, literature, and scientific discoveries.

When interacting with a biological being, a Cosmopolitan avatar would need the equivalent of a visual display and voice synthesis equipment. The technology for creating realistic avatars in collaborative virtual environments is already far advanced, and considerable research has examined the social implications of this technology (Bailenson et al. 2004, 2005). The areas where research is not far enough advanced are natural language processing by computerized dialogue systems, and the fundamental artificial intelligence technologies needed to emulate those parts of the human mind that cannot readily be captured in attitudes and preferences.

When the avatars are interacting with each other, and a biological being is not in the communication loop, there is no reason why the speed of thought and interaction could not be greatly accelerated. In discussing physical travel near the speed of light, we have become used to talking about time dilation. Inside Cosmopolis, we may encounter phenomena of time constriction. One possible paradox would be that the interacting cultures within the collaborative virtual environment would create fusion subcultures far more rapidly than the host civilization could assimilate their innovations. Thus, all of the participating civilizations could experience extreme cultural lag (Ogburn 1922) once the avatars were communicating with each other effectively. Of course, this assumes they will be able to communicate effectively enough in the beginning to develop a culturally catalytic relationship.

In his early novel *Iceworld*, Hal Clement suggested that the best way members of two very different intelligent species could begin to communicate would be by exchanging things of value. He understood that it might be difficult to predict what an extraterrestrial being would want. Technological inventions would be one possibility, but new technology depends so heavily upon existing industrial capacity, that only a few of our engineering triumphs might be valuable to extraterrestrials without requiring them to make a considerable investment in support infrastructure. Music is another possibility, and today's synthesizer technology could readily transpose Bach to different octaves in sounds that would be sweet to alien ears. Perhaps we could sell large prime numbers, on the assumption that the other civilization could not possibly devise mathematical means to mass produce them. My point is that our avatar ambassadors must be prepared to offer many kinds of information that might be of value, at the same time they evaluate the worth to humans of what the ETs are offering.

This raises the question of who shall represent each world. The term *ambassador* implies a representative of a government. Given the direction Earth history is taking, where global capitalism vies for supremacy with religious fundamentalism, one just as well might argue the ambassadors would be salespeople or evangelists. If a civilization has no central government, will it have several competing ambassadors, representing whatever factions it possesses? The answer may be that Cosmopolis will be a trading colony, representing whatever individuals and groups were sufficiently motivated to send their avatars to the stars. We might well recall the opening comment from the *Babylon 5* television series, about a place where humans and aliens could meet: "It's a port of call, home away from home for diplomats, hustlers, entrepreneurs and wanderers."

There are many good reasons to hope that well-established advanced civilizations will be able to develop cooperative relations with each other (Harrison 1997), but the chances for conflict would seem greater the more fragmented each civilization is. Perhaps interstellar war is possible, after all, but it will take the form of some forces trying to prevent others from getting or giving information through Cosmopolis. The weaponry could consist of computer viruses infiltrating the alien equivalent of the

World Wide Web. By placing the emulation system on an isolated asteroid, guarded by informatic firewalls, the host civilization would protect
itself against these possible dangers.

Plan for Action

It might seem that any work on developing interstellar embassies would
need to wait until after extraterrestrial civilizations had been contacted or
plans were well advanced for interstellar expeditions by means of highly
advanced spacecraft. I think the opposite is true: The goal of direct contact with extraterrestrials via computer emulation could motivate the
search for extraterrestrial intelligence.

Some individuals will want to invest energy and money in developing
the needed personality capture and emulation technology because they
personally hope to become interstellar ambassadors. If Cosmopolis would
be more like a trading colony than a mere diplomatic office, then its virtual population could be quite substantial. I like to imagine it like the city
of Hong Kong, trading between China and the world, which has a population of fully seven million. While most people might not be interested,
it would seem reasonable to expect that more than seven million people
alive today would be willing to invest significant sums if the direction
the research would take were well mapped out. If each of seven million
people invested ten thousand dollars, the total would be seventy billion
dollars. On an annual basis, even one thousandth of that could support
the early stages of a vigorous research program.

Of course, many people would not believe that any conceivable technology could actually grant immortality through personality capture.
Perhaps their religious views define immortality very differently, or they
see compelling philosophical arguments why their avatars could not be
themselves. When I published my factual article "A Question of Immortality" in *Analog* magazine, the title was chosen to reflect this controversy. The editor, Stanley Schmidt, insisted that I avoid claiming that
personality capture was the same thing as real immortality, and therefore
I ended the article with this paragraph: "We already possess technology
that can allow aspects of your personality to influence the world in a dynamic manner, even after you are no longer living in it. This falls short
of true immortality, because you (as conventionally defined) will not be
conscious of it. Your evaluation of the possibilities for future cybernetic
immortality will depend, therefore, not merely upon your estimate of the
technical possibilities but also upon your personal conception of yourself"
(Bainbridge, 2002a: 40).

Whether coincidentally or by design, the May 2002 issue of *Analog* that held my article also contained several stories about technological immortality, thereby illustrating the breadth of imagination that can be brought to bear on the topic. Sherry Turkle (1984) has argued that people who grow up from early childhood using a computer may come to feel it is a "second self." Some people may feel that their avatars are more like descendents than a second self, what Hans Moravec (1988) called "mind children." In the two decades since Turkle and Moravec wrote, a considerable literature has arisen in computer science about the nature of self-reference and the social-psychological relationship between people and their autonomous software agents or avatars (Dobbyn and Stuart 2003; Friedman and Nissenbaum 1997; Smith 1986).

The crucial point is that many people, guided by a range of beliefs about themselves, will identify to a significant extent with their avatars. Of these, a small percentage but large absolute number (given the population of our planet) could be enlisted in a social movement to send virtual ambassadors to the stars. Logically, they should invest their efforts along two parallel tracks: developing the cognitive and information technology needed for high-fidelity emulation of personality, and locating extraterrestrial civilizations while building the infrastructure to communicate with them. Both of these tracks offer ample opportunity for individuals and small groups to contribute.

As proponents of the search for extraterrestrial intelligence have found from bitter experience, governments are not reliable sources of funding for anything that requires imagination and an orientation toward the future. Governments do support some research on artificial intelligence, human-computer interaction, and information archiving technologies. However, government support for fundamental cognitive science is weak, and none of the research grants in that area are likely to go for personality capture or emulation. Thus, individuals and groups should identify research gaps that realistically could become the target of their own intellectual efforts. At the same time, leaders of the SETI movement and well-meaning entrepreneurs should be alert to opportunities to channel money and volunteer labor into projects that could have near-term success goals as well as aiming toward direct contact with extraterrestrials in the more distant future.

The broad plan described here could add motivation to invest in completing the instruments currently under construction or design to detect extraterrestrial radio signals. A logical next step is to beam radio messages outward, containing personality-capture information from individual investors, even though we do not yet know the most likely targets. Sending information for an avatar of oneself to the stars could have a symbolic benefit, very compelling for some wealthy visionaries, even if the realistic chances of the message being received are low. Some of their investment could go to search efforts, with the understanding that as soon as an extraterrestrial civilization were found, the messages would be re-sent in its precise direction.

If the next generation or two of attempts to detect extraterrestrial signals were unsuccessful, the campaign would merely move to a higher level. The efforts of amateurs, guided by a few scientists in the appropriate fields, could develop effective techniques for personality capture and emulation. People who wanted their personalities sent to the stars could assign investments over to special non-profit organizations that served as terrestrial personality archives and extraterrestrial development promoters. Once sufficient resources were concentrated, and space technology had advanced somewhat further, we could build our own Cosmopolis on the Moon.

Inside a functional lunar Cosmopolis, cognitive scientists and computer scientists could complete development of the needed Starbase technology. Either ordinary humans living in a lunar outpost, or the artificial intelligence agents dwelling in Cosmopolis themselves, could use teleoperation robots to build an exceedingly large SETI antenna array on the shielded far side of the Moon. Lunar and orbiting telescopes should, by that time, be able to identify nearby extrasolar planets capable of supporting life. If the lunar radio-detection effort failed, there would be no sense of defeat, but a redirection of efforts toward construction of a fleet of interstellar vehicles to send multiple Starbases on colonizing missions and in tireless search for other civilizations.

Author's Note

The views expressed in this chapter do not necessarily represent the views of the National Science Foundation or the United States.

Bibliography

Bailenson, Jeremy N., et al. 2004. "Transformed Social Interaction: Decoupling Representation from Behavior and Form in Collaborative Virtual Environments." *PRESENCE: Teleoperators and Virtual Environments* 13, no. 4: 428–441.

———. 2005. "Transformed Social Interaction, Augmented Gaze, and Social Influence in Immersive Virtual Environments." *Human Communication Research* 31: 511–537.

Bainbridge, William Sims. 1986. *Experiments in Psychology*. Belmont, CA: Wadsworth.

———. 1987. *Sociology Laboratory*. Belmont, CA: Wadsworth.

———. 1989. *Survey Research: A Computer-Assisted Introduction*. Belmont, CA: Wadsworth.

———. 1993. "New Religions, Science and Secularization," In *The Handbook of Cults and Sects in America*, ed. David G. Bromley and Jeffrey K. Hadden, 277–292. Greenwich, CT: JAI.

———. 1994. "Extraterrestrial Intelligence: Communication." In *The Encyclopedia of Language and Linguistics*, ed. R. E. Asher, 1200–1203. Oxford: Pergamon.

———. 2002a. "A Question of Immortality." *Analog* 122, no. 5: 40–49.

———. 2002b. "The Spaceflight Revolution Revisited." In *Looking Backward, Looking Forward*, ed. Stephen J. Garber, 39–64. Washington, DC: National Aeronautics and Space Administration.

———. 2003. "Massive Questionnaires for Personality Capture." *Social Science Computer Review* 21, no. 3: 267–280.

———. 2004. "The Future of the Internet: Cultural and Individual Conceptions." In *Society Online: The Internet in Context*, ed. Philip N. Howard and Steve Jones, 307–324. Thousand Oaks, CA: Sage.

———. 2006. "Cognitive Technologies." In *Managing Nano-Bio-Info-Cogno Innovations: Converging Technologies in Society*, ed. William Sims Bainbridge and Mihail Roco, 207–230. Berlin: Springer.

Bainbridge, William Sims, et al. 1994. "Artificial Social Intelligence." *Annual Review of Sociology* 20: 407–436.

Biswas, Gautam, et al. 2005. "Learning By Teaching: A New Agent Paradigm for Educational Software." *Applied Artificial Intelligence* 19: 363–392.

Clement, Hal. 1953. *Iceworld*. New York: Gnome Press.

Dick, Steven J. 2003. "Cultural Evolution, the Postbiological Universe and SETI." *International Journal of Astrobiology* 2, no. 1: 65–74.

Dobbyn, Chris, and Susan Stuart. 2003. "The Self as an Embedded Agent." *Minds and Machines* 13, no. 2: 187–201.

Friedman, Batya, and Helen Nissenbaum. 1997. "Software Agents and User Autonomy." In *Proceedings of the First International Conference on Autonomous Agents*, 466–469. New York: Association for Computing Machinery.

Goldberg, Lewis R. 1999. "A Broad-bandwidth, Public Domain, Personality Inventory Measuring the Lower-level Facets of Several Five-factor Models." In *Personality Psychology in Europe*, vol. 7. ed. I. Mervielde, et al., 7–28. Tilburg, The Netherlands: Tilburg University Press.

Harrison, Albert A. 1997. *After Contact: The Human Response to Extraterrestrial Life*. New York: Plenum.

Moravec, Hans. 1988. *Mind Children: The Future of Robot and Human Intelligence*. Cambridge, MA: Harvard University Press.

Ogburn, William Fielding. 1922. *Social Change with Respect to Culture and Original Nature*. New York: B. W. Huebsch.

Robinett, Warren. 2003. "The Consequences of Fully Understanding the Brain." In *Converging Technologies for Improving Human Performance*, ed. Mihail Roco and William Sims Bainbridge, 166–170. Dordrecht, Netherlands: Kluwer.

Smart, John. 2004. "Simulation, Agents, and Accelerating Change: Personality Capture and the Linguistic User Interface." Accelerating Change 2004 Conference, ITConversations. http://www.itconversations.com/shows/detail374.html. Accessed on 18 April 2011.

Smith, Brian Cantwell. 1986. "Varieties of Self-Reference." In *Proceedings of the 1986 Conference on Theoretical Aspects of Reasoning about Knowledge*, 19–43. New York: Association for Computing Machinery.

Sternberg, Saul. 1966. "High-Speed Scanning in Human Memory." *Science* 153: 652–654.

Turkle, Sherry. 1984. *The Second Self: Computers and the Human Spirit*. New York: Simon and Schuster.

Yang, Kiyoung, et al. 2005. "Continuous Archival and Analysis of User Data in Virtual and Immersive Game Environments." *Proceedings of CARPE '05*, 13–22.

Chapter 12

THE INSCRUTABLE NAMES OF GOD
The Jesuit Missions of New France as a Model for SETI-Related Spiritual Questions

Jason T. Kuznicki

To date, much of the literature about the search for extraterrestrial intelligence (SETI) produced in scientific circles has, predictably, revolved around the scientific and technical aspects of the endeavor. In a sense, this is perfectly natural, as we have only recently mastered some of the technologies that might allow communication in the first place. Yet even those messages that we have deliberately broadcast, such as the 1975 Arecibo or the 1999 Dutil-Dumas signals, have often been essentially scientific as well (DeVito and Oehrle 1990).[1] Ironically, any intelligence receiving these signals may already have mastered much of the basic science communicated therein. And while both of these messages convey the sheer fact of our existence, as well as scientific data peculiar to terrestrial life, virtually any of our messages would end up doing likewise, including those that we have been sending unintentionally for decades.

There is one realm of human experience, however, about which alien civilizations are likely to be ignorant, and on which many human observers place great value. It is also a realm about which even many decades of radio signals may still fail to enlighten. I refer to religion and spirituality, and it will be my argument that the greatest difficulties of communication with alien life, and possibly the most important ones as well, will come in communicating our religious, spiritual, and ethical understandings to aliens—and in comprehending theirs, should they have any. Such communication still lies far in the future, and even when we do receive a signal, it may be centuries or even millennia before the real conversation about these topics begins. It is nonetheless vitally important: Ideas like good and evil, the soul, and God are taken very seriously by the overwhelming majority of people, yet these are among the most perplexing notions to discuss, even among human beings sharing a common language and cultural background. While I personally count myself among the skeptics, and while I profess no belief in God, it is difficult to see how an adequate picture of human life can be made if religion and spirituality are not somehow a part of the discussion.

The title of this chapter references Arthur C. Clarke's classic science fiction story "The Nine Billion Names of God," which is a tale of how language exerts an unexpected power over the nature of reality itself (Clarke 1967). Language is also central to the story that I wish to tell, although the barriers that I will be discussing are not merely those of translation or of linguistic ignorance at first contact. On the contrary, I will argue here that language encodes values and meanings that constitute at times the very substance of our reality, and that the scant evidence we have thus far suggests that moral and spiritual topics are more prone to this sort of difficulty than others.

A great many educated people assume, I think, that some form of abstract, highly rational spirituality is in some sense universal, at least among the enlightened, and that if we encounter any intelligence in the universe that is not overtly malevolent, it will surely share some spiritual understanding with us. In other words, one might be tempted to argue along the following lines: "Of course, the content of their specific religious systems may be quite different, but we're all after the same thing, right?" This is a dangerous assumption, and I intend to illustrate how badly wrong it can be by using examples drawn from one of the earliest meetings between western civilization and a culture that was almost entirely alien to it.

I refer to the seventeenth-century contact between French Jesuit missionaries and the Native Americans living in what is now eastern Canada. The missionaries recorded these encounters in a voluminous correspondence with their superiors in Europe; the accounts were in turn published. The most recent edition of them runs to seventy-four volumes and covers nearly a century and a half, including those dating from the first half of the seventeenth century, when native beliefs were still relatively uninfluenced by proselytizing or by unconscious cultural mimicry. This chapter will examine passages from some of the earliest records (Thwaites 1896; referenced as JR vol no.: page no.). Later accounts of Native American spirituality from the area show the emergence of syncretic religions, that is, those that were based on borrowings from various indigenous and European sources, as well as entirely new belief systems, while many practices and values found in the earliest texts disappear. These changes are a likely part of any extended contact with previously unknown civilizations, but they are also beyond the scope of this chapter, which is confined to questions of spirituality at or near first contact.

By way of background, it should be noted that the two cultures I am examining—seventeenth-century French Catholicism and the Huron, Iroquois, and Montagnais peoples of the northern Great Lakes region—shared virtually nothing in the way of technology; although both used fire, even the wheel was unknown among the Native Americans of this region. A rudimentary metallurgy, an incomplete pictographic symbol set, and the ability to cure foods using smoke and salt were nearly the sum of their shared technological achievements. Even more importantly for our purposes, geographic isolation had permitted the Native Americans to develop a belief system in almost complete isolation from all Eurasian intellectual traditions. Whereas the Latin, Arabic, Sanskrit, and even Chinese cultural families were never fully isolated from one another, and whereas these traditions at times shared a number of fundamental assumptions owing to borrowings that are beyond the scope of this discussion, it is generally agreed that the Native Americans of New France had developed their ideas about man, nature, and the supernatural in an isolation that had lasted since before the advent of writing. With a few obvious caveats—that is, that the Native Americans nonetheless shared all the basic features of human physiology with their Jesuit interlocutors—they were in most other respects remarkably alien (Billingham et al. 1999). And lastly, although we may prefer to identify more closely with the university-educated Jesuits, who actually understood a great deal of what we now call science, it is a commonplace that in our first brush with an alien intelligence, we may find ourselves in a position more analogous to that of the Huron and the Iroquois—that is to say, the technological inferiors. Yet from whatever perspective we approach the possibility, we should be prepared to be neither the superior nor the inferior, but merely perplexed, as both sides in this encounter most certainly were.

From Science to Religion

Understanding between these two groups was slow to arrive—and almost certainly slower than some of the optimistic scenarios for communication offered in most SETI literature. In *Beyond Contact*, Brian McConnell offers what seems to me a somewhat overly optimistic understanding of how we might begin communicating with alien intelligence. Summarizing Marvin Minsky, Hans Freudenthal, and others, McConnell writes:

> Intelligent species will encounter certain very special ideas, such as the concepts related to mathematics, which are much simpler than other ideas—and [that] interact with each other in very predictable ways. One example is addition. Addition is a universal concept. The equation $2 + 2 = 4$ will always be true, regardless of the perspective of the reader. These special concepts, because they are rare and universal, will form the basis for a common language from which other concepts can be derived. (2001: 194).

This view differs widely from the descriptions that the first Jesuits of New France gave of the Native Americans that they encountered, with whom they found almost no common ground at all. Even many of the concepts that the Jesuits regarded as foundational and universal to all men of sense were entirely absent from both the language and the common understanding of the Montaignais, the Huron, and the Iroquois. As we shall see, just as we regard certain concepts as "special"—abstract mathematics, basic chemistry, and the like—the Jesuits held the same opinion on a number of truths that they regarded as foundational. Their hopes for establishing communication based upon these truths were dashed early on.

Now, the Jesuits approached their task armed with formidable knowledge and training; each had spent many years mastering languages, philosophy, rhetoric, the sciences, and of course theology. Most European philosophical traditions agreed that certain ideas were universal among all humans, or, at any rate, among all people of sufficient intelligence. Chief among these ideas were the notion of the immortal, eternal, indivisible soul, and of a unified God who had designed all things. Contemporary philosopher René Descartes would describe the knowledge of both God and the soul as innate, while Saint Thomas Aquinas, long the most revered intellectual authority on these matters, held that natural reason alone could bring all thinking people to recognize the existence of both God and the soul. Both traditional and contemporary thought agreed, however, that with reason there inevitably came the two ideas of God and the soul.

The Jesuits were shocked, then, when they discovered that neither of these beliefs could be found among the Native Americans they had set out to convert. They sought at every juncture to find such beliefs, for, as missionaries, their success or failure obviously depended upon them. Yet these beliefs were difficult to find, and when they did appear, they diverged so much from the European consensus that it was debatable whether the two groups were even talking about the same things when they conversed.

Note first of all that it is a popular misconception to imagine that all Native American religions invoked some sort of "Great Spirit." The earliest historical records that we have directly contradict this popular wisdom, and most native religions invoking a Great Spirit are either later, syncretic belief systems or the frank forgeries of whites who were pretending to be Native Americans. As some evidence, consider the following passage from one early account of the Montagnais language:

> All words for piety, devotion, virtue; all terms that are used to express the things of the other life; the language of Theologians, Philosophers, Mathematicians, and Physicians, in a word, of all learned men; all words which refer to the regulation and government of a city, Province, or Empire; all that concerns justice, reward and punishment; the names of an infinite number of arts which are in our Europe; of thousands of contrivances, of a thousand beauties and riches, all these things are never found either in the thoughts or upon the lips of the Savages (JR 7: 21).

These were the very ideas that the Jesuits took as the universal starting points for communication with their hoped-for converts. And the most glaring absence of all was the lack of a native word for *God* in any of the major language groups that the Jesuits encountered. The concept behind the word seems likewise to have been absent—an occurrence that contemporaries held was impossible or even inconceivable. To make up for this lack, when the Jesuits composed prayers for the Huron, they simply inserted the French word *Dieu* into all the prayers that they wrote. For example, here is part of a 1636 prayer composed by Jesuit Jean de Brebeuf in the Huron language: "Jesus onandaerari Dieu hoen ondayee achiehetsaron de hiaistan oneké tehainonstas." Brébeuf translated this as, "Jesus, our Lord of God the Son, for this thou wilt exhort thy Father, for he does not refuse thee anything" (JR 10: 69).

Given that "God" was such a new idea to the Huron, the idea that God might have a Son no doubt added to their confusion. In the relation of the following year, a convert is recorded as having made the following prayer: "Thou who art the thought of God, who made thyself man for us, I love thee; help me, keep me, defend me against the Manitou" (JR 11: 169). (*Manitou* denoted a powerful spirit, be it of good or evil; the Jesuits quickly assimilated this to their own concept of the Devil, despite the fact that in some of their earliest encounters, they themselves had been called manitou.) The same convert referred to Jesus as "the thought of God," because, as Jesuit Father Paul Le Jeune writes, "I had explained to him that God was not married, although he had a son, and that his knowledge or his Word was his son. Hence, of his own accord, he called him 'the thought of God'" (JR 11: 169).

The concept of sin is central to Christianity, which views human history as a narrative of sin and redemption. Yet "sin" itself proved to be a difficult concept to grasp. As Le Jeune dryly noted of a convert, "My only trouble was to make her feel sorrow for her sins. The Savages have not this word 'sin' in their language, though they certainly have it in their customs" (JR 6: 137). Elsewhere he bemoaned the way in which the native languages were filled with obscenity: "In the place of saying, as we do very often, through wonder, 'Jesus! what is that? My God! who has done that?' these vile and infamous people pronounce the names of the private parts of man and woman. Their lips are constantly foul with these obscenities; and it is the same with the little children. … The older women go almost naked, the girls and young women are very modestly clad; but, among themselves, their language has the foul odor of the sewers" (JR 6: 253).

As with God and sin, so with the soul. Among the Native Americans that the Jesuits described, there seem to have been many conflicting ideas, none of which can be properly squared with the rest. Consider first the Iroquois, who practiced an elaborate set of burial, exhumation, and reburial rituals, in which corpses were buried individually and then, often many years later, dug up and buried again in a communal grave. So far as we can understand them, these were events of the greatest spiritual significance to the Iroquois, and were collectively known as The Feast of the Kettle. At one of these events, a Jesuit interrogated a man about what this feast meant for the souls of the dead. He recorded the encounter as follows:

> [Returning from the Feast of the Kettle], with a captain who is very intelligent, and who will some day be very influential in the affairs of the Country, I asked him why they called the bones of the dead Atisken. He gave me the best explanation he could, and I gathered from his conversation that many think we have two souls, both of them being divisible and material, and yet both reasonable; the one separates itself from the body at death, yet remains in the Cemetery until the feast of the Dead—after which it changes into a Turtledove, or, according to the most common belief, it goes away at once to the village of souls. The other is, as it were, bound to the body, and informs, so to speak, the corpse; it remains in the ditch of the dead after the feast and never leaves it, unless some one bears it again as a child. He pointed out to me, as a proof of this metempsychosis, the perfect resemblance some have to persons deceased. A fine Philosophy, indeed. Such as it is, it shows why they call the bones of the dead, Atisken, which means "the souls." (JR 11: 287)

The Iroquois did not merely identify the soul with the bones, however. On the contrary, they seemed to believe that each person had several souls, or at any rate they believed that we possess several distinct attributes that the Jesuits would have united in the one concept of the immortal human soul. Said one Jesuit who had lived among them, "they think of the soul as divisible, and you would have all the difficulty in the world to make them believe that our soul is entire in all parts of the body" (JR 10: 141). *Atisken*, closely identified with the bones, seems to have been that part of the soul that lives on after death; meanwhile, the agent that animated the body was *khiondhecwi*; the reasoning agent, *oki andaérandi*; the deliberative or debating agent, *endionrra*; and the emotive agent, *gonennoncwal*. Yet since ancient times, thinkers in the West had held each of these functions to be performed by one unitary thing, the soul.

Early Jesuit reports of Huron beliefs about the soul were likewise puzzling to the Jesuits, but for a different reason. One Huron described the nature of souls as follows: "[Our souls] hunt for the souls of Beavers, Porcupines, Moose, and other animals, using the soul of the snowshoes to walk upon the soul of the snow, which is in yonder country; in short they make use of the souls of all things, as we here use the things themselves" (JR 6: 177). Even while there is a certain likeness to the ideas of Plato in these beliefs, it is far from clear whether the souls in question translate from one realm to the other, as in Christian belief, and it is likewise unclear whether the soul is held accountable for the good and bad it does during its mortal existence: The afterlife here seems purely a recapitulation, not a time of reward or punishment, and it seems open even to things that are not and have never been alive, like snow. While the statement clearly evinces a belief in some sort of soul, it just as clearly is not the Christian soul, and to say the least, it raises more questions than it answers.

So too did the following account of the soul: "They believe," wrote one Jesuit, "in the immortality of souls; and in fact they assure us that after death, they go into Heaven where the souls eat mushrooms and commune with one another" (JR 4: 200).[2] To my knowledge, this reference is unique in New France. The native peoples of the region are only rarely recorded eating mushrooms while on Earth, and that usually in times of famine. Still, one recalls that contemporary Central American peoples ceremonially ate mushrooms with psychedelic properties. Might a secret or eccentric group have done likewise in New France? We do not know whether the heavenly mushrooms mentioned here had any earthly counterpart, nor do we know whether our Jesuit author simply misunderstood his informant, nor can we say with certainty that the informant was not joking or deceiving the Jesuit, as such informants were often recorded to have done. To understand how the spiritual and the material interacted with one another in an alien belief system may be one of the most difficult intellectual challenges of all.

Language and Spirituality

Nor did the difficulties end there, for the Huron language melded words and concepts together in ways quite alien to European understandings. These joinings had profound theological implications; they also present some difficulties for would-be communication with extraterrestrial intelligence (CETI). The following comes from a Jesuit description of one such conundrum:

> A relative noun with them includes always the meaning of one of the three persons of the possessive pronoun, so that they cannot say simply, Father, Son, Master, Valet, but are obliged to say one of the three, my father, thy father. ... On this account, we find ourselves hindered from getting them to say properly in their Language, In the name of the Father, and of the Son, and of the holy Ghost. Would you judge it fitting, while waiting a better expression, to substitute instead, In the name of our Father, and of his Son, and of their holy Ghost? Certainly it seems that the three Persons of the most holy Trinity would be sufficiently expressed in this way, the third being in truth the holy Spirit of the first and of the second; the second being Son of the first; and the first being our Father (JR 10: 117–119).

Compare the Jesuits' expectations above with the confident predictions found in McConnell: "While it may seem outlandish to assume that an alien civilization will use language in the same way we do, the concepts behind nouns, verbs, and modifiers are universally applicable. A noun is simply a placeholder for an object in an expression. A verb is a placeholder for an action or process (change of state over time). A modifier simply provides more information about nouns or verbs in an expression" (2001: 224).

As we have seen, McConnell's assumption about language is problematic, even among the cultures of Earth. While those who used the various indigenous language groups of New France could certainly be made to understand distinct nouns, verbs, adjectives, and the like, this was not at first their prevailing way of thought or speech. If anything, it was the exception.

The Montagnais, for example, had the curious practice of using some verbs upon land while using others to express the exact same idea upon water. For example, "I was wet by the rain" had to be said quite differently depending on just where it had happened; the verb itself conveyed meaningful information about the state of the world in a form that was neither noun, nor verb, nor adjective. And while the Montagnais had nouns for *wind* and *snow* and a verb that meant "to drive," it would have been a gross error to combine the three and say, in effect, "The wind drives the snow." The semi-initated might decide that the proper verb was not the one that meant "to drive," but instead, the one meaning "to drive something noble," because, in the Montagnais estimation, snow was indeed a noble substance. He would then say "The wind [drives something noble] the snow," which would be spoken as *Routin rakhineou couné*, but this, too, would be a mistake. No, the proper expression is simply *Piouan*, which is a single word that expresses the whole idea that we have just been discussing, and which serves in effect as one verb and—at least—two nouns (JR 7: 21–25).

The Montagnais language also had a remarkable tendency to note, through its verbs, various qualities possessed by the nouns that they "took" as direct objects: "They have different Verbs to signify an action toward an animate or toward an inanimate object; and yet they join with animate things a number of things that have no souls, as tobacco, apples, etc." Thus, "I see a man" would be said *Niouapaman iriniou*, but "I see a stone," *niouabate* (JR 7: 21). To denote qualities of an object noun by modifying the root of the verb violated all grammatical categories that the Jesuits had encountered before—and, to add to the confusion, these verbs all possessed moods, tenses, persons, and conjugations, just as European verbs did. This change in verb stems also suggested strongly—though we have little evidence to substantiate this speculation—that the speakers held the objects in question to have different ontological properties. Tobacco, frequently used in offerings to spirits, may well have been considered an "animate" object for grammatical purposes precisely because of its spiritual significance, a nuance that has already taken a paragraph to explain in full, but that would have been obvious to a native speaker in a moment.

Thus concepts and usages that the Jesuits had assumed to be universal were not; ideas they took to be a priori had to be forced into the heads of their charges almost by rote; even the rudiments of grammar functioned differently in the New World. The assumptions that we make about what aliens must think, therefore, seem doubtful to me—for if human beings, with virtually identical biological equipment, can have such large differences in worldview, what is to be said of aliens?

Conclusion

It almost seems ridiculous to end such a speculative chapter with a "conclusion." It may well prove that the example of contact between the seventeenth-century French Jesuits and the Native Americans of New France has little to teach us about communicating spiritual ideas to extraterrestrial intelligences; almost certainly, the specific problem set that they faced will be different from the one that we, or our descendants, may face when communicating with intelligent alien life. Yet there may be some similarities in the overall types of problems presented in both these encounters: I think the most likely parallel will lie in the difficulty experienced in grounding any conversation in foundational ideas shared by both communicating groups. I further think that these foundational difficulties may well come at precisely the points that we now take to be the most unproblematic: Basic concepts of language, ontological categories, supposedly universal knowledge, and the assumed relations among them, may be presented to us in configurations that are presently unknown—and these new configurations may be precisely what give meaning to extraterrestrials' concepts of self, spirituality, and ethics.

From the material I have just presented, it is reasonable to infer that we may initially find the reasoning of alien intelligences to be woefully defective, and that they will conclude the same about ours. It is also reasonable to conclude that this will be a mistaken judgment all around, and that we will not initially grasp the radical differences that separate us intellectually. Will we one day find ourselves repeating incomprehensible alien words in an attempt to grasp ideas that are, to our informants, elementary in any good understanding of the universe? These prospects seem more than likely if past experience is any guide. Seventeenth-century French Jesuit missionaries set out to communicate with their would-be converts based on what they believed were a set of universal understandings, ideas that had to be present among all intelligent people. They instead found themselves frustrated at every turn, and able to discuss the most elementary of ideas only after many years of study and direct personal contact.

Notes

1. For an active SETI message that is not chiefly scientific in nature, consider the Teen Age Message, a signal sent by Russian teenagers in 2001; information is available at http://www.setileague.org/articles/tam.htm. The project transmitted some elementary graphics and audio as well as music performed on a theremin. Insofar as music speaks to humankind's spiritual side, the Vivaldi, Beethoven, and Gershwin of the Teen Age Message may actually represent one of the very few attempts ever made to convey spiritual insights via active SETI.
2. It is unclear which cultural group or subgroup held this belief, although it appears to bear more similarity to the Huron than the Iroquois belief system. The French original runs as follows: *Ils vont au Ciel où elles* [sic., presumably ref. "âmes," souls, in an earlier sentence] *mangent des champignons, & se communiquent les vnes auec les autres.*

Bibliography

Billingham, John, et al. 1999. *Societal Implications of the Detection of an Extraterrestrial Civilization*. Mountain View, CA: SETI Press.

DeVito, Carl L., and Richard Oehrle, 1990. "A Language Based on the Fundamental Facts of Science." *Journal of the British Interplanetary Society* 43: 561–568.

McConnell, Brian. 2001. *Beyond Contact: A Guide to SETI and Communicating with Alien Civilizations*. Sebastopol, CA: O'Reilly & Associates.

Thwaites, Reuben G., ed. 1896. *The Jesuit Relations and Allied Documents*. Cleveland, OH: Burrows Bros. Co. Cited as JR vol: page.

Chapter 13

ET Phone Darwin

What Can an Evolutionary Understanding of
Animal Communication and Art Contribute to Our
Understanding of Methods for Interstellar Communication?

Kathryn Coe, Craig T. Palmer, and Christina Pomianek

"The people who are doing this SETI stuff are not the kind
of people who read Darwin."
                    —Melvin Calvin (quoted in Swift 1990b: 127)

"In the case of extraterrestrial intelligence, let us admit our
ignorance, put aside a priori arguments. … That is, I think,
what Charles Darwin—who was converted from orthodox
religion to evolutionary biology by the weight of observational evidence—would have advocated."
                    —Carl Sagan (1995)

In this chapter we shall examine what an evolutionarily informed approach to social behavior in general, and communication and art in
particular, can contribute to attempts to communicate with unseen and
unknown forms of extraterrestrial life. After a quick overview of evolutionary theory, we take a brief look at the evolution of sociality as we
assume that the specializations necessary for the evolution of complex
and advanced systems of communication will evolve in other places as
they have evolved here on Earth, namely in a social species. Next, we

briefly define and summarize communication in an evolutionary context. Then, we argue that art, within an evolutionary framework, is best seen as a form of communication, involving a message sent by one individual that is aimed at influencing particular social behaviors in others. Finally, we explore how an evolutionary approach to communication, sociality, and the arts might contribute to our knowledge of *how* to send a message to extraterrestrials. This thinking is based on the admittedly uncertain assumption that an understanding of how living things on Earth, which is the extent of the proven biological universe (Dick 2000:18), have evolved to send and receive signals might provide clues to how such signals could be sent to, and received from, extraterrestrial life. Thus we begin with a critical examination of that assumption.

Why Even Consider Evolutionary Theory?

While it is possible that entire extent of life in the universe is found in life on Earth, the reason for even considering the possibility that evolutionary theory might be able to aid attempts to communicate with extraterrestrial life is, at its root, linguistic. Specifically, the meaning of the simple English word *life* frames the question of extraterrestrial communication in a way that makes evolutionary theory potentially relevant. This is because, whatever other attributes it might have, what constitutes the small subset of the universe that we would label "life" is the ability to replicate itself; that is, to reproduce. This fact is important because things that replicate themselves will be subject to selection, with those that replicate themselves more effectively becoming more common than those things that replicate themselves less effectively. If replication sometimes involves errors, or other sources of variability, those traits that promote replication will spread and accumulate over time, and those traits that hinder replication will become less frequent and are likely to disappear. Thus, it is very likely that where and whenever humans find something in the universe that they come to call "life," that thing will be the product of selection. While existing traits may be the product of chance (e.g., random events that occur, such as natural disasters), the theory of evolution by natural selection is the only general scientific theory that explains why living things on Earth are the way they are.

While it is true that the environment influences what life, if any, can develop (Dick 2000: 21), evolutionary theory, theoretically, should apply anywhere to anything that is living. The answer to the question of whether or not this theory can actually help us communicate with extraterrestrial life, if such life has been formed by similar evolutionary principles, is far from Yes. This is because chance factors may play a role in the evolution of any living thing, including the evolution of the big brain and what we call intelligence. As Carl Sagan pointed out, "There is an important sense in which the biologist cannot distinguish the necessary from the contingent, that is, distinguish those aspects of life that any organism anywhere in the universe must have simply in order to be alive, from those aspects of life that are the results of the tortuous evolution by small opportunistic adaptations" (2000: 54). Thus, Sagan observed in regard to the message carried on the Pioneer 10 spacecraft: "The human beings are the most mysterious part of the message" (2000: 20). Yet, despite the often unpredictable and tangled path that evolution here on Earth took to produce complex life, the possibility of selection being both necessary and fundamental to the history of complex life anywhere in the universe means that an evolutionary approach may be of some help.

Behavior in Social Species

Evolution through natural selection refers to differential reproductive success, with the genes of the more-successful reproducers being transmitted to subsequent generations of their kin. While sexual reproduction implies an interaction, it does not imply that the interaction is a social one. The more social species (e.g., mammals and birds) have a number of characteristics, including an often enduring parent-child relationship with the mother often, but not always, at the center (e.g., the jacana). In these species, more kin and more-distant kin are included in the social circle (see discussion in Coe 2003). In other words, sociality is found among those sharing and identifying common descent. Culture, as we shall argue, is a strategy for promoting cooperation among those descendants.

When George Williams (1966: 193) initially wrote about "social adaptations," he focused on "the less common interactions that do seem to be cooperative and benign." The word *social*, as Williams used it, referred not to just any interaction, but to a particular kind of benign or cooperative interaction. While ethologists regularly use the word *social* to refer to *any* interactions between two organisms, we accept William's definition.

As social adaptations, following William's definition, involve sacrifice, in the sense of making oneself vulnerable to others, social living has important disadvantages, not only in increased vulnerability, but in having to confront problems of sanitation and disease spread, as well as increased competition for food, mates, and space. What social living has provided is an opportunity for the development of human intelligence and the accumulation of knowledge, or what we refer to as culture (Alexander 1974). As many human forms of communication are cultural, we turn now to the topic of communication.

Communication

Evolutionary theory has produced considerable knowledge about how forms of communication have evolved on Earth. An understanding of the relevance of this knowledge to the development of potential forms of communication with extraterrestrial life requires definitions of several key terms: *communication, adaptation,* and *by-products.* Communication obviously involves at least the potential of one organism influencing other organisms. Broadly defined, communication includes all interactions between organisms that can transmit information between them. Terry Vaughan (1978: 360) critiques this definition, writing that if we regard all types of stimulus-reception sequences as forms of communication, "then essentially all behavior of one animal that can be perceived by another must be regarded as communication." Most evolutionary theorists focus on much smaller sets of such acts, and follow Daniel Otte (1974: 385) in defining communication signals as "behavioral, physiological, or morphological characteristics fashioned or maintained by natural selection because they convey information to other organisms." This narrower definition focuses on signals and responses that are adaptations, or traits favored by natural selection in the past. The effect of the trait that caused it to be favored by natural selection in the past is known as its function.

At the most general level, an evolutionary approach assumes that communication signals have the function of conveying information from one individual (the signaler) to another (the receiver). If we accept that communication cannot evolve unless it raises the inclusive fitness (or reproductive success) of both signaler and receiver, such messages can evolve initially only if it is advantageous for an animal to produce a stimulus that alters the behavior of a receiver in a specific way. If it is also advantageous for the receiver to change its behavior upon receipt of the signal, then the basis for communicative adaptations has been established. It is under these conditions that "natural selection can cause signal changes to spread through a species only if both signalers and receivers derive net fitness benefits from their participation in the system" (Alcock 2005: 314). The question we confront now is whether knowledge of the communicative adaptations that have evolved here on Earth can help us predict what kind of signals, signalers, and receivers will be successful in extraterrestrial communication.

Channels of communication vary by environment, the ecology of the recipient species, and the cost/benefit ratio of alternative signals. Determining cost/benefit ratios are such things as

1. how effectively the signal reaches the desired receivers;

2. the amount of information encoded in the signal;

3. the cost to the sender of producing and broadcasting the signal;

4. the ease with which the sender can be located by a receiver; and

5. the risk that the signal will be detected by an illegitimate receiver and used against the sender (Alcock 1979: 383).

Each channel of communication has its own general strengths and weaknesses in terms of such variables as range, rate of transmission, flow around barrier, and fadeout time (see table 13.1).

Although an effective method of interstellar communication might be audio, the costs of audio transmission can be high. Visual messages are less expensive and can be sent long distances into space, as for example, on the plaques attached to the Voyager and Pioneer probes.

The obvious challenge to us in attempting to create a system of extraterrestrial communication is that we do not know whether or not our knowledge about how communication works among living things on Earth will lead to the ability to communicate with extraterrestrials, which David Koerner and Simon LeVay appropriately refer to as "life as we don't know it" (2000: 195). There is of course no way of knowing the answer, but there are reasons to conclude there is a chance that not only is extraterrestrial communication possible, but also that it might be accomplished using art. First, researchers interested in and/or hopeful of extraterrestrial communication (see Conway Morris 2003) have supported their view by pointing to the simple fact that visual and auditory communication takes place among very different species, everything from ants (Kuttner 1981) to dolphins (Fleury 1980), and that such species constitute a useful analogy to communicating with extraterrestrials.

Table 13.1. Comparisons among the major channels of communication (adapted from Alcock 1979: 387)

Channel	Ability of signal to reach receiver				Information available		Cost to sender	
	Range	Rate of transmission	Flow around barrier	Night use	Fadeout time	Locatability of sender	Broadcast expense	Risk of exploitation
Auditory	Long	Fast	Yes	Yes	Fast	Fairly easy	High	Medium
Visual	Medium	Fast	No	No*	Fast	Easy	Low to moderate	High

*except bioluminescent signals

Following from these assumptions, as communication on Earth occurs between different species it may offer clues as to how to communicate with extraterrestrials. While it has been hypothesized that predation pressure is the primary cause for mixed species interactions and communication (Noë and Bshary 1997), interspecies communication can occur between prey and predator, predator and prey, or even in a form of cooperation or mutualism. Shorebirds not only use aerial and auditory displays to influence conspecifics, but they use them to warn other bird species away from their territory. Animals also may use warning communication for self-protection, as when an insect mimics the color of a poisonous insect or the pattern of a leaf, or when a non-poisonous snake mimics the color markings of a poisonous snake to deceive a predator. When a member of one species gives a warning call that influences both conspecifics and members of another species that are bothered by the same predator, this is referred to as a form of mutualism (Zuberbühler 2000), an act that has benefit to both species. As these examples of interspecies communication show, communication can occur between different forms of life. Consequently, the fact that extraterrestrial communication obviously involves communication between very different forms of life does not in itself make visual or auditory communication an impossibility.

A final reason for remaining hopeful about the possibility of visual and auditory communication with extraterrestrials is that "ears" and "eyes" are examples of convergent evolution, having evolved in numerous species, many of which are only distantly related. After comparing the mammalian and reptile eye, Thomas Gold states, "In fact, they are so much alike that I would venture to say, while I do not know what some creature on some other planet might look like, that if it is fairly highly evolved and if it is based on the same basic biological mechanisms as we are (it no doubt will have totally different body shape, and so on), there is a high probability that its eyes will look rather similar" (1973: 122). Or, as Simon Conway Morris (2003: xii–xiii) wrote, "the number of evolutionary end points is limited … what is possible has usually been arrived at multiple times, meaning that the emergence of the various biological properties is effectively inevitable." To paraphrase him, it is now time to take the implications of evolutionary theory a little more seriously, and convergence is the norm.

While the eyes may look similar, and sensory organs are of critical importance in a great many species, there will be variability in sensory organs, such as eyes, with some eyes being keener and/or more responsive to light and color; different animals perceive different sections of light energy. Many animals can see things we cannot see, yet, at the same time, many animals lack color vision. While it is true that what an animal can perceive or hear is influenced by the environment in which his/her ancestors lived and the sensory systems they needed to survive and reproduce, it is also true that they do all have sensory organs, and active and fast-moving animals, and in some cases intelligent animals, opt for the camera eye (Conway Morris 2003: 158). We can assume that sensory organs are important in a great many distinct forms of life, not just animals but also in non-animal species such as dinoflagellates, and that to the extent vision is important, an animal will be able to distinguish light from dark, even though they may not see color. The ability to use the senses to classify, distinguish, and recognize patterns is important (Hilbert 1987; Coe 1992). Learning a bird song, as one example, depends on the identification of particular sequences, or patterns, of sounds (Nelson 2000).

We suggest that these observations warrant a consideration of how visual and auditory communication with extraterrestrials might be accomplished. To draw again on the words of Conway Morris (2003), "Just as I speculated that alien astronomers (if there are any) would be searching the skies using camera-eyes, so it would also seem more than likely that inside their eyes the lenses would be packed full of the direct equivalents of the crystalline proteins." We move now from a discussion of biology, to suggest that an understanding of visual art, in particular, may contribute greatly to the answer to the questions posed in this chapter, as it makes it possible to communicate complex concepts using images.

The Arts

In order to understand the role art—in this case music and visual art—might play in extraterrestrial communication, it is important to cut through much of the esoteric rhetoric that has grown up around art since the Renaissance and to focus scientifically, defining art by its necessary and sufficient characteristics. It is also crucial to see art in its original form as a traditional form of communication, instead of how it has been described and reconfigured in modern societies as a form of expression or reflection of esoteric and effete aesthetic values. A focus on aesthetic values, or culture-bound art criticism, is unlikely to be of any use to extraterrestrial contact because, as Robert Kuttner (1981:20) points out "the aesthetic impulse we value so much may be merely a human peculiarity and even if shared it may be insufficient to foster extraterrestrial contact. When we claim art and music to be universal we are really saying we hope it is at least global." When art is viewed as a traditional form of communication it is clearly not only universal among human cultures, but it bears striking similarities to visual communication among many other species. Ethologists often use the metaphor animal "art" when they refer to traits, both permanent and seasonal, observed in a number of species.

Although the term *birdsong* implies similarities between sounds made by birds and music, in most cases, the animal "art" discussed by ethologists is visual. It includes not only the red pouch of the frigate bird, but also the brightly colored feathers of many birds, and the red belly of the stickleback fish (Darwin 1871; Diamond 1991). When elephants in the wild use sticks to make scratch marks on the ground, some writers refer to "art" (Diamond 1991). Observing apes in the wild and in captivity draping themselves with vines and pieces of cloth, Josef Kohler (1897/1925) referred to this behavior as "art." The elaborate nests of bowerbirds, woven in a complex design out of hundreds of sticks and, at times, painted with pigments from crushed leaves or oils, are referred to as "art" (Diamond 1991).

While the frigate bird's pouch seems to be the unlearned product of the developmental process, making and decorating a bowerbird nest involves significant learning. The implicit definition of animal "art" seems to specify neither innateness, nor learning, nor even the expression of a particular emotion. The necessary element of birdsong is patterns of sound that are, in many cases, learned. In the other cases of the animal "art" listed above, it often seems to involve the modification of a body or object through the use of form, line, pattern, or color. This decoration can, but does not necessarily, attract attention to a message, including the message: "look at me or look at this!" Elephants drawing in the sand and primates draping themselves with vines are not performing these activities for an audience. If the behaviors are not noticed, they presumably have no social effect; that is, they do not influence the behavior of an observer. They are neither patterned nor predictable.

These elements common to animal visual "art" are a good guide to creating a working definition of art and are also implicit or explicit in definitions of art used by some of the influential thinkers in aesthetics, including Plato (1977: 14), Leo Tolstoy (1977/1897: 65–66), and Clive Bell (1958, first published in 1914: 389). Thus, the following definition is proposed:

> *Visual Art:* The modification of an object or body through color, line, pattern, and form that is done solely to attract attention to that object or body. Visual art is a mechanism to attract attention to things. As it is used in association with something, it thereby attracts attention to that something. That "something" may be a message to which visual art draws attention. The proximate aim of visual art is to attract attention, perhaps by provoking emotions. To the extent that visual art is an adaptation then its

ultimate function is to influence social behavior in ways that promote success in leaving descendants. (Coe 1992)

Artists, for thousands of years, and often at the encouragement of others, exploit this tendency to respond to color and pattern in order to influence social behavior.

One characteristic of visual art is the replication of a particular design, such that it becomes known as symbolic. In other words, there can be a significant amount of information encoded in the signal. We learn from others what the meaning of a particular symbol is; to outsiders the meaning is generally obscure and undecipherable, although there are some symbols (e.g., a mother tending a child) that are recognized across cultures as they touch on behaviors, emotions, and values that are widely shared in a highly social species. While the message plates on the Pioneer spacecraft, following from the above definition, are examples of art, and they are symbolic to those on Earth, the symbolism would probably mean little or nothing to extraterrestrials. However, one can argue, given the assumption that the extraterrestrials have organs to sense items in their environment, that they will see the art. Furthermore, given the assumption that they have social intelligence, one can argue that they will recognize that the art, as it serves no other function than to attract attention, does communicate something that they might be able to decipher, much as humans were interested in deciphering the Rosetta Stone.

But What Message Do We Want to Send?

The discussion to this point has all been based on the assumption that we want to communicate with extraterrestrials, and that we have already decided (at least generally) what message we want to send. Evolutionary theory cannot tell us what it would be best to communicate, as it cannot provide answers to such value decisions. It can, however, direct us to consider some things in our decision. Evolutionary theory suggests we should carefully consider the decision to attempt to communicate with extraterrestrial life because if we are correct in assuming that anything we would call living has been designed by natural selection, then any life forms we would encounter have been shaped by a fundamentally competitive process. They would have been successful in their competition with other life forms. Obviously it also follows that we, as another life form designed by the competitive process of natural selection, might be seen as a competitor. David Swift sums up the conclusion to this line of reasoning nicely by stating, "It is prudent to remain silent in a jungle" (1990a: 17).

If we want to communicate that we are altruistic, we first have to ask ourselves if this is an honest characterization of our species. If we decide that we are capable of altruism and want others to know this, we must use the known to predict the unknown. If intelligence is a product of natural selection built to facilitate social relationships, and if parents, and mothers in particular, are the foundation of social relationships (Coe 2003), and if we assume, at least for a moment, that we share these traits with other forms of highly intelligent life, then one symbol recognized across human cultures as characterizing altruism is the depiction of the mother-child relationship. What mothering implies that may be crucial to any message of altruism, is that the larger and stronger are responsible for caring for, protecting, and guiding the smaller, weaker, and more vulnerable.

The next question to consider is whether or not we want the extraterrestrial receiver to consider our message to be an honest one. Much of evolutionary signaling theory has attempted to answer the question of why receivers often treat signals as honest when there are such clear competitive advantages to either sending or detecting deceptive signals. The general answer is known as Costly Signaling Theory (CST), which began as an attempt to explain certain biological "handicaps" (Zahavi 1975; Schelling 1960), such as large antlers or tail feathers; an animal that manages to survive despite bearing such costly traits must be truly "fit" (Zahavi 1975: 1). The underlying premise is that signals that are costly are, by virtue of their costliness, harder to fake and therefore more likely to be honest. Thus, if (and this is only hypothetical) we wanted to send the message, "Do not come near or attempt to take our resources because we are powerful enough to make such efforts unsuccessful," it may be more effective to send a message that only a powerful species could send. The problem, however, is that communicative technology that is costly to us, may not seem costly to distinct forms of intelligent life, ones that have followed another path of technological discovery. There may be no way to ensure that our communication is taken as an honest one.

Conclusion

Just as there is no guarantee that extraterrestrial life exists, there is no guarantee that communication with such life will be possible even if such life exists. All we can do is increase the chances of such communication actually occurring by examining forms of communication among living things on Earth. Visual communication is a common form of communication in many species, and humans have highly developed means of communicating visually through art. Given that the essence of art appears to be the use of color, line, pattern, and/or form to attract attention (i.e., be noticed), art is a reasonable tactic to use when attempting to communicate with extraterrestrials. After all, before we can communicate with extraterrestrials we must attract their attention and be noticed. The question we have to address is what message we want to communicate.

Bibliography

Alcock, John. 1979. *Animal Behavior: An Evolutionary Approach*. 2nd ed. Sunderland, MA: Sinauer Associates, Inc.

———. 2005. *Animal Behavior: An Evolutionary Approach*. 8th ed. Sunderland, MA: Sinauer Associates, Inc.

Alexander, Richard D. 1974. "The Evolution of Social Behavior." *Annual Review of Ecological Systems* 5: 325.

Bell, Clive. 1958/1914. *Art*. New York: Capricorn.

Coe, Kathryn. 1992. "Art: The Replicable Unit. An Inquiry into the Origin of Art as a Social Behavior." *Journal of Social and Evolutionary Systems* 1: 217–234.

———. 2003. *The Ancestress Hypothesis*. Newark, NJ: Rutgers University Press.

Conway Morris, Simon. 2003. *Life's Solution: Inevitable Humans in a Lonely Universe*. Cambridge: Cambridge University Press.

Darwin, Charles. 1871. *The Descent of Man and Selection in Relation to Sex*. 2 vols. London: John Murray.

Diamond, Jared. 1991. *The Rise and Fall of the Third Chimpanzee*. London: Radius.

Dick, Steven J. 2000. *Extraterrestrial Life and Our World View at the Turn of the Millennium*. Dibner Library Lecture, Smithsonian Institution Libraries, 2 May. http://www.sil.si.edu/silpublications/dibner-library-lectures/extraterrestrial-life/ETcopy-KR.htm. Accessed on 18 April 2011.

Fleury, Bruce E. 1980. "The Aliens in our Oceans: Dolphins as Analogs." *Cosmic Search* 2, no. 2: 2–5.

Gold, Thomas. 1973. "Discussion." In *Communication with Extraterrestrial Intelligence (CETI)*, ed. Carl Sagan, 112–146. Cambridge, MA: MIT Press.

Hilbert, David R. 1987. *Color and Color Perception*. Palo Alto, CA: Center for the Study of Language and Information, Leland Stanford University.

Koerner, David, and Simon LeVay. 2000. *Here Be Dragons: The Scientific Quest for Extraterrestrial Life*. Oxford University Press: Oxford.

Kohler, Josef. 1897/1925. *On the Prehistory of Marriage*. Chicago, IL: University of Chicago Press.

Kuttner, Robert E. 1981. "The Nature of Extraterrestrial Communication." *Cosmic Search* 3, no. 2: 20–21.

Nelson, Douglas A. 2000. "A Preference for Own-subspecies' Song Guides Vocal Learning in a Song Bird." *Proceedings of the National Academy of Science* 97, no. 24: 13348–13353.

Noë, Ronald, and Redouann Bshary. 1997. "The Formation of Red Colobus Monkey Associations under Predation Pressure from Chimpanzees." *Proceedings of the Royal Society of London* B24, 253–259.

Otte, Daniel. 1974. "Effects and Functions in the Evolution of Signaling Systems." *Annual Review of Ecology and Systematics* 5: 385–417.

Plato. 1977. "Art is Imitation." In *The Republic*. Trans. by Benjamin Jowett (3rd ed. London: Oxford University Press, 1892). In *Aesthetics: A Critical Anthology*, ed. G. Dickie and R. Sciafani. New York: Bobbs Merrill.

Sagan, Carl. 1995. "The SETI Debate: In Defense of the Search for Extraterrestrial Intelligence." Originally appeared in *The Bioastronomy News* no. 7: 4. http://www.hcc .hawaii.edu/~pine/sagan.htm. Accessed on 18 April 2011.

———. 1973/2000. *Carl Sagan's Cosmic Connection: An Extraterrestrial Perspective*, with new contributions by Freeman Dyson, Ann Druyan, and David Morrison. Produced by Jerome Agel. Cambridge: Cambridge University Press.

Schelling, Thomas. 1960. *The Strategy of Conflict*. Cambridge, MA: Harvard University Press.

Swift, David W. 1990a. "From Fringe to Frontier: An Introduction." In *SETI Pioneers: Scientists Talk about Their Search for Extraterrestrial Intelligence*, ed. David W. Swift, 3–18. Tucson, AZ: University of Arizona Press.

———. 1990b. "Interview with Melvin Calvin." In *SETI Pioneers: Scientists Talk about Their Search for Extraterrestrial Intelligence*, ed. David W. Swift, 116–135. Tucson, AZ: University of Arizona Press.

Tolstoy, Count Leo. 1977/1897. "Art as the Communication of Feeling." Trans. by Aylmer Maude (Indianapolis, 1960). In *Aesthetics: A Critical Anthropology*, ed. G. Dickie and R. Sciafani. New York: Bobbs Merrill.

Williams, George C. 1966. *Adaptation and Natural Selection:* Princeton, NY: Princeton University Press.

Vaughan, Terry A. 1978. *Mammalogy*. 2nd ed. Philadelphia, PA: Saunders College Publishing.

Zahavi, Amotz. 1975. "Mate Selection: A Selection for a Handicap." *Journal of Theoretical Biology* 53: 205–214.

Zuberbühler, Klaus. 2000. "Interspecies Semantic Communication in Two Forest Primates." *Proceedings of the Royal Society of London* 267: 713–718.

Chapter 14

A JOURNALISTIC PERSPECTIVE ON SETI-RELATED MESSAGE COMPOSITION

Morris Jones

The planet Earth is awash in mass communications, almost exclusively in the form of humans trying to communicate with other humans. Attempts by the human race to communicate with other civilizations in the universe are extremely rare. But this has not prevented a small and interdisciplinary pool of scholars from planning communication with other worlds.

The design of communications strategies and the messages to be communicated have mostly been addressed by scientists in fields such as mathematics, computer science, physics, and linguistics. This has arisen out of the historical origins and technical challenges of attempting to communicate with extraterrestrials. The Search for Extraterrestrial Intelligence (SETI), and the related attempts at communication, arose from the natural sciences, principally astronomy. It has primarily drawn upon infrastructure, technology, methodology, and personnel from radio astronomy. The slow pace of early SETI research restricted the number of active contributors, as well as their academic scope. But modern SETI research has also recognized the contributions of sociologists, linguists, and anthropologists.

Message construction is an ongoing area of research, and one that is steadily evolving. Clearly, there is more work to be done. But members of the informal community of SETI messaging experts are still largely dominated by scientists (whether physical, biological, or social scientists) and engineers. The inclusion of artists in some SETI forums is a welcome extension of the trend of gradually expanding the scope of inquiry on this topic.

It would also be useful to examine media academics' and journalists' views on content and message construction. The SETI community has never been phobic of journalists and the media, but there is obviously more consultation to be undertaken. Most interaction between journalists and the SETI community has been one-sided. SETI researchers have communicated their activities to the general public through journalism, and the results have generally been successful. General knowledge of SETI programs has become fairly widespread for a scientific topic, and the discipline has attracted relatively little hostility. Changing the direction of communication—"from" journalism "to" SETI—would be a major change in this communication process, but it could be accomplished with the numerous links the SETI community has already built with the media. Recruitment strategies for participants and the staging of communications could take place through journal articles, seminars, and other forums. The strategies used for incorporating other fields of communication, such as the arts, seem to have been successful, and it is probable that this success would be replicated by using similar methodologies.

Origins of News

It is worth considering how journalism and news have evolved. A crude definition of *journalism* suggests that it is the regular supply of information on the state of society and the world. Exactly what makes something "newsworthy," or worthy of inclusion in a news report, is a debate that has never been settled to absolute satisfaction in the media community. It is also a highly subjective question, given the diversity of perceptions and interests. But the word *new* is a subset of this term, implying that some degree of novelty is important. If we already know something, or expect it, then it really isn't news. The arrival of most forms of public transport in your city on or close to their expected timetables is not really news (apart from sardonic remarks about late trains). But the sudden shutdown of most transport due to a strike or breakdown is not an ordinary experience, and is thus newsworthy.

News also deals with fairly concrete, tangible issues. Concepts of aspirations, dreams, and philosophies that are explored by the arts and humanities are traditionally outside the definition of news. The classic questions of who, what, where, when, and why neatly summarize the "hard news" approach to documenting events.

As an aspect of human communication, news and journalism are normally considered to be relatively modern. Regular "newspapers" have been with us for less than four centuries (World Association of Newspapers 2004), and the genuine mass newspaper is a twentieth-century phenomenon. News through electronic media is even more recent. But it could be argued that less-widely disseminated news is as old as human civilization. Discussions around the tribal campfire of what happened on the day's hunt are arguably "narrowcast" news, spread verbally between people within a community. Ancient Rome also had its "Acta Diurna," a daily bulletin of the proceedings of the Roman senate, which was posted in the forum for public consumption. So it is important to observe that news is an ancient tradition, far older than the mass media, or the modern industrialized nation-state that created the mass media.

News as a Biological Imperative

Studies of news and journalism are normally focused within the disciplines of sociology and communications theory. This chapter argues that news and journalism are also heavily tied to some fairly basic tenets of biology and the need for organisms to obtain information about their environment.

Most organisms must react to their surroundings in order to survive. Plants must shed leaves or grow roots to adjust to conditions. Animals must browse, hunt, or flee. Much of journalism is focused on similar criteria. The keyword *orientation* is sometimes used within media papers to discuss this role. Is the highway too jammed to take to work? Should I sell my shares? If I vote my local politician back into power, will I regret it? Basic survival issues are strongly connected to much of what is considered "newsworthy." People are influenced by what happens in the world.

Sociological ties of family, kinship, tribalism, and nationhood are ubiquitous in human society and prevalent within the broader animal kingdom. Their origins are largely centered around activities that allow for the hunting of food, the raising of offspring, and the defense of the group. These ties are also reflected in concepts of proximity in news values. People will have less interest in a major crisis in a distant land than one that takes place in their own vicinity. This will partially be a question of direct personal influence, but people will also be more concerned about events that could affect their own immediate community, with which they have a rapport.

Sensory input is also strongly focused on registering changes in an environment, such as an approaching predator. This too contributes to the fact that news is "new." It would also be redundant to repeat information that is already known to the audience, and the "bandwidth" of communication restricts what can be included. Emotions such as curiosity and the psychological need for orientation also fuel news consumption by reducing fears of isolation and exclusion.

Thus, the desire to receive news, and the structure that news takes, can largely be traced to basic biology. This suggests that extraterrestrials will probably share many of these values and perceptions, if their evolution has not been substantially different from our own. News could be less idiosyncratically human than some may believe.

Are Interstellar Messages News?

In a direct sense, any message transmitted to extraterrestrials is news. It announces information about the existence of a civilization on Earth, which could have been unknown to the recipient. Thus, knowledge of Earth could be a "new" experience.

But the most "newsworthy" aspect of most current messages is likely to be the fact that the message exists. To paraphrase the media scholar Marshall McLuhan (1964), the "medium" (reception of a signal or artefact) is the message. This is understandable from a news values perspective. A signal received on Earth from an extraterrestrial civilization would be highly newsworthy, even if it communicated nothing apart from its artificial origins. Of course, people would want to know what the aliens looked like, but the real story would simply be confirming that they were out there. The newsworthiness of this confirmation will certainly decrease for the second contact made by humanity with another extraterrestrial civilization, as the novelty of the first contact, and knowing that we are not alone in the universe, would not be present.

But how much of the actual encoded content of messages sent from Earth would really be newsworthy to extraterrestrials?

The anthropomorphic principle of message construction is regularly invoked in SETI discussions, suggesting that these projects are more informative to ourselves than to extraterrestrials for what they reveal about human nature. Much of the content of these messages focuses on basic scientific and biological data. The contents of the message plaques carried by the Pioneer 10 and 11 spacecraft include drawings of a human male and female, a diagram of a hydrogen atom, a map of our location in the galaxy with respect to neighboring pulsars, the distance of our sun to the galactic center, and finally, a diagram showing the planets in our solar system. Similar elements are included in other messages beamed into space with radio telescopes or attached to spacecraft such as Voyagers 1 and 2. The general focus has been on pictorial representations of physical phenomena (Vakoch 1998).

But how much of this will be news, or even newsworthy, to extraterrestrials? A consensus seems to be forming within the astrobiological community that any extraterrestrial civilization we can contact will be much older than our own, and therefore more advanced. At the present, human civilization is on the cusp of making some fundamental discoveries about life on other planets. We are detecting worlds circling other stars, we are conducting extensive theoretical studies of the nature of extraterrestrial life, and we are preparing to retrieve potential astrobiological specimens from our own solar system. Soon, advanced telescopes will allow detailed studies of extrasolar planets. A relatively short space of development beyond the current level of our presumably "young" civilization would put extraterrestrial scientists in a much better position to understand life in the universe. The contents of our messages to extraterrestrials would probably contain no novelty, and thus contain essentially no news, apart from displaying our own level of development. Extraterrestrials could already have a catalogue of life in other solar systems and even be able to observe Earth in detail through their own instruments, once cued to our location. So message novelty should arguably be focused on details that cannot be deduced through advanced scientific techniques.

As a further extrapolation of this issue, it is worth reflecting that even our own perceptions of our solar system, thought to be well-understood in the Space Age, have been rocked by scientific discoveries and academic debates in the relatively short time since these messages were launched. We now perceive a solar system that could be more extensive than previously considered, with a multitude of "minor planets" beyond the orbit of Neptune. In 2006, we faced the demotion of Pluto, included as a planet in previous messages, to "minor planet" status by the International Astronomical Union (2006; Soter 2007). The potential inclusion of bodies previously classified as large asteroids as potential "minor planets," or planets in their own right, is also the subject of debate. So our "crib notes" on our own part of space are themselves potentially incompatible with details that extraterrestrials may be able to perceive. How do they distinguish planets from detritus? Will they place us in the wrong neighborhood?

Biologists have also been struck by the ability of molecules less complex than DNA and RNA to convey genetic information, and have engaged in controversies over "prions" and "nanobacteria." Even our biological data are open to revision!

Journalism in an Advocacy Format

The goal of journalism as an industry is to "capture eyeballs" and interest people in consuming news. This usually has commercial goals as an underlying motivation, so advertising revenue can be collected. But some media products strive to attract attention out of a desire for social responsibility (to inform people for their own benefit) or a desire on the part of the publisher to promote or "advocate" a particular viewpoint. The latter style of "advocacy" journalism is sometimes controversial within the media, as it can be biased and ill-informed. But communicators of various flavors, including scholars in communication theory, would maintain that the idea of a totally objective and unbiased form of communication is, by definition, impossible. Semiotics draws much of its scholarly base from addressing this issue.

What, then, are our motivations in trying to communicate with extraterrestrials? To simply say that we want to let the universe know we exist is an incomplete answer. Why do we want to do this? Are we proud of our existence? Do we believe we have a right to be recognized and acknowledged? Do we think civilizations are bound through sociological norms to take part in this sort of activity? Again, anthropomorphism suggests that our own interest in extraterrestrial life would be reciprocated.

Our own motivations may not necessarily be compatible with the interests of extraterrestrials. Other civilizations may or may not be curious, indifferent, or isolationist. They may also be overwhelmed with the chatter of a universe teeming with life, and have no time for Earth. In an effort not only to persuade people to consume news, but to compete against other vendors, news organisations often resort to sensationalist strategies to make their products more appealing. The most vulgar demonstration of this principle is the tabloid media's focus on sex, violence, and other shocking stories to invoke curiosity. It would be unfortunate to produce a "tabloidish" message for extraterrestrials, but message composers may still wish to spice their products with "hooks," designed to attract the attention of extraterrestrials. This could be in the form of interesting art, music, or anything else that is likely to be distinctive. The majority of media content broadcast today is not actually news, but entertainment. Extraterrestrials may find Earth more interesting if "soft" content is communicated rather than prime number sequences.

No Regular News

Most currently envisaged forms of communication with extraterrestrials imagine the speed of light as the fastest way that a message can be communicated. The vast distances expected between inhabited star systems suggests that messages could take centuries, or eons, to arrive at their destination. Some discussion within the SETI community suggests that some civilizations could be extinct by the time we become aware of them. This incredibly slow method of communication points to the singular monologue, or self-contained statement, as the only method of communication used so far: Send a message encompassing the most important aspects of our existence, and send it out as a one-off testimony to the universe. Such a pace of communication will permit news, but is totally incompatible with the traditional concept of journalism. As its name implies, journalism (incorporating the French word *jour*, meaning day) is recurring, regular, and frequent. Electronic media update their bulletins on an hourly basis. The longest frequency for a general news magazine is typically one month, with weekly publication being more common. Clearly, this form of delivery does not fit well into schedules for space launches or free time on radio telescopes. So the approach to composing "news" for interstellar communication will need to dispense with the usual temporal considerations of traditional journalism.

What Should We Communicate?

So what is really newsworthy about humans and life on Earth? Anthropomorphism, again, can make us poor judges of ourselves. The absence of data on any other civilizations gives us no yardsticks for relative measurements. But it's possible that these very barriers to objectivity will unwittingly help us to demonstrate what it is to be human. Our selection of some content, and our omission of other material, will say much about our values.

"Negative content" such as war and crime has been studiously avoided in previous messaging efforts. This is partially due to concern about how such content would be interpreted by extraterrestrials, who may be offended or dissuaded from pursuing further communications with Earth. This reasoning illustrates the fact that SETI communication has generally tried to give a good impression of Earth to the universe, in much the same way that people observe social norms and behavior when they meet each other for the first time. SETI messages are, in some ways, conceived as greeting cards.

Yet negative content represents a substantial portion of all news on Earth. If the goal of journalism is to be generally reflective of the state of human society, these factors cannot be ignored in any detailed narration.

Change over time, producing "news" as new experiences, would be worth exploring. Thus, the news report would be like an almanac or history text.

Other elements would need to be debated by journalists and others involved in message composition.

Ethics and Editorial Control

The production of news on Earth is often highly contested between reporters, editors, and interested groups. Controversy over bias, story selection, and objectivity are ubiquitous. Such problems are likely to multiply in planning the content of any journalism aimed at extraterrestrials. Yvan Dutil and Stéphane Dumas (1999) cite four principal ethical problems in any form of active communications: Who has the right to speak for Earth? Does freedom of speech apply? What are the dangers for us? (For them?) Is there conflict with the SETI detection protocol? These ethical issues, designed for conventional SETI messages (such as pictographs containing scientific data) apply equally to journalistic message composition. While it is true that most active message transmissions have avoided controversial issues, the emphasis on physical data by itself removes much of the potential subjectivity associated with communications. There is no sociological, theological, or political bias in measuring the size of the Earth relative to a given unit of measurement. But any messaging group attempting to incorporate journalism into a more complex message will need to address these issues.

Media-savvy people have grown accustomed to a variety of opinions and editorial approaches in today's oversaturated media environment. Skepticism and careful interpretation allow people to evaluate the media and resist attempts at persuasion. Perhaps an extraterrestrial civilization would also be able to "read between the lines" and interpret bias or subjectivity. Assuming that extraterrestrials would presumably be sophisticated in their own interpretation of messages from Earth is also worth considering for non-journalism messages. For example, excessive emphasis on the positive aspects of life on Earth at the expense of negative issues could arouse suspicions.

The Encoding Challenge

One reason why most actively launched messages have been relatively simple in design is the difficulty of encoding the message. This involves not only cognitive and linguistic barriers but physical limitations. The propagation of electromagnetic waves or small spacecraft across interstellar distances is a challenge for our current technology. The selection of scientific data as message content is mainly a reflection of the importance placed on these concepts by the SETI community. But these concepts also seem easier to encode with current technology.

There is no obvious strategy for "encoding" news onto a communications medium for extraterrestrials. On Earth, the transmission of news requires a rich, sophisticated environment of advanced language skills, sociological preconditions and general knowledge. On our own planet, some general news stories are unintelligible to people with poor knowledge of geography, history, or society. Thus, it must be admitted that encoding news is probably the most complex task ever proposed to the SETI community. Ways of encoding arts such as music and dance have been addressed through fairly sophisticated semiotic approaches that go beyond the pictorial approaches documented by Douglas Vakoch (1998). But even these advanced methods would be useless for news. Thus, news transmission of any sophistication would probably depend on the development of a deep pool of shared knowledge, including language and social issues.

Once such factors are established, a potential response to the encoding of news is simply to use no encoding at all, short of communications strategies already established. A news broadcast to interstellar space could differ little from a local product, apart from translation into a shared common language that could have been developed to enable communication between two disparate civilizations. This suggests that news transmission would probably be the final step in any form of interplanetary dialogue.

Time for Communication

The need to establish "common ground" in communication suggests that some form of two-way exchange would need to be established. It would be necessary to determine that an extraterrestrial civilization existed, was receiving our transmissions, was interested in further communications, and had established common ground for doing so. The time delays involved in carrying out such an exchange would presumably take decades, at best, to reach a level where journalism could be included. Most radio SETI practitioners have now concluded that nearby star systems are devoid of transmitting civilizations, so any discovery is likely to be several tens or hundreds of light-years away. Michael Arbib (1979) states that centuries could pass between exchanges. Milan Ćircović (2004) notes that the age and lifespan of any civilizations we could potentially contact is an unresolved and highly debated issue within astrobiology, depending on factors ranging from sociology to astrophysics. The potential for a civilization to destroy itself is compounded by growing awareness of natural cosmic disasters that could erase life. A long-term message program could realistically find itself disconnected before journalism was introduced.

Conclusion

The transmission of news to extraterrestrials is a challenging task. It will probably not be a major element of any communications efforts with other civilizations for a long time. But it is still useful to consider the issues that would be faced and the techniques that could be used. The very significance of news and journalism as well-developed elements of mass communications on Earth suggests that some insight can be gained by the extraterrestrial messaging community. Journalists could also contribute to the construction of other forms of messages. The potential involvement of journalists and journalism in extraterrestrial communications is largely unexplored in astrobiology circles, and should be further considered.

Bibliography

Arbib, Michael. 1979. "Minds and Millennia: The Psychology of Interstellar Communication." *Cosmic Search* 1, no. 3: 21–24, 47–48.

Ćircović, Milan M. 2004. "The Temporal Aspect of the Drake Equation and SETI." *Astrobiology* 4: 225–231.

Dutil, Yvan, and Stéphane Dumas. 1999. "Active SETI: Target Selection and Message Conception." *AAS Poster presentation*. http://www.obspm.fr/encycl/papers/Dutil-poster.pdf. Accessed on 18 April 2011.

International Astronomical Union. 2006. "IAU 2006 General Assembly: Result of the IAU Resolution Votes." http://www.iau.org/public_press/news/detail/iau0603/. Accessed on 18 April 2011.

McLuhan, Marshall. 1964. *Understanding Media: The Extensions of Man.* London: Routledge.

Soter, Steven. 2007. "What is a Planet?" *Scientific American* 296, no. 1: 20–27.

Vakoch, Douglas A. 1998. "Signs of Life beyond Earth: A Semiotic Analysis of Interstellar Messages." *Leonardo* 31: 313–319.

World Association of Newspapers. 2004. *Newspapers: A Brief History.* http://www.wan-press.org/article.php3?id_article=2821. Accessed on 18 April 2011.

NOTES ON CONTRIBUTORS

William Sims Bainbridge, PhD, is co-director of human-centered computing at the National Science Foundation. He is the author of twelve books in information science, social science of technology, and the sociology of religion, including *The Spaceflight Revolution*; *Goals in Space: American Values and the Future of Technology*; *Nanoconvergence*; *God from the Machine: Artificial Intelligence Models of Religious Cognition*; *The Secular Abyss*; *The Sociology of Religious Movements*; *Religion, Deviance and Social Control*; *Satan's Power*; and *The Endtime Family: Children of God*.

Kathryn Coe, PhD, is professor of public health in the Department of Public Health at Indiana University-Purdue University Indianapolis (IU-PUI). She is the author of many papers on health interventions and cultural tailoring, as well as *The Ancestress Hypothesis: Visual Art as Adaptation*. Her research examines the evolution of social behavior and culture, as well as chronic and infectious diseases. Dr. Coe has over thirty years of experience conducting health research among African Americans, Hispanics/Latinos, and American Indians using a community-based participatory methodology.

Kathryn Denning, PhD, is associate professor in the Department of Anthropology at York University. Her research examines scholarly and popular ideas about Others, their relationships to us, and how we can know them. The Others she studies include the ancient (in archaeology), the animal (in zoos), and the alien (in SETI). In SETI, she studies scientists' reasoning processes, the technology and sites used to search the sky for signals, and ideas about how one might communicate with a radically different intelligence. She is a member of the International Academy of Astronautics' SETI Committee and has research projects with the NASA Astrobiology Institute.

Carl L. DeVito, PhD, is professor emeritus in the Department of Mathematics at the University of Arizona. He has developed one of the most widely cited proposals for interstellar messages, building on plausibly universal scientific concepts, and he has contributed to several edited volumes on interstellar message composition. His books include *Harmonic Analysis: A Gentle Introduction*, *Functional Analysis*, and *Functional Analysis and Linear Operator Theory*.

Albert A. Harrison, PhD, is professor emeritus in the Department of Psychology at the University of California, Davis. In addition to researching the societal dimensions of astrobiology and SETI, he studies human adaptation to spaceflight and spaceflight-analogous environments. His books include *After Contact: The Human Response to Extraterrestrial Life*; *Starstruck: Cosmic Visions in Science, Religion, and Folklore*; *Spacefaring: The Human Dimension*; *Living Aloft: Human Requirements for Extended Spaceflight*; and *From Antarctica to Outer Space: Life in Isolation and Confinement*.

Morris Jones, PhD, is an Australian space analyst and writer, whose work ranges from advanced technical reports on SETI to children's books. He is the author of several books on astrobiology and space exploration, including *Is There Life beyond Earth?*, *Out of This World*, *The Adventure of Mars*, *The New Moon Race*, and *When Men Walked on the Moon*. His articles have been published in *The Bulletin*, *SpaceDaily.com*, and *Novosti Kosmonautikii*.

Jason Kuznicki, PhD, is a research fellow at the Cato Institute and managing editor of *Cato Unbound*, an online forum for discussing critical contemporary issues. He has facilitated many of the Cato Institute's international publishing and educational projects. His ongoing interests include censorship, church-state issues, and civil rights in the context of libertarian political theory. He is an assistant editor of *Encyclopedia of Libertarianism*. Prior to working at the Cato Institute, he served as a production manager at the Congressional Research Service.

Harry Letaw, Jr., PhD, is a physical chemist who serves as principal of Letaw Associates. Following the award of his degree by the University of Florida, his academic positions at other universities included research assistant professor and adjunct associate professor. Early in his career, he published in electrochemistry, spectroscopy, and the physics of solids, and later he managed industrial research companies, most recently as CEO of Essex Optoelectronics. Now retired, Dr. Letaw studies novel means of communicating with extraterrestrial intelligence.

Craig T. Palmer, PhD, is associate professor in the Department of Anthropology at the University of Missouri. His research interests center on incorporating cultural traditions into evolutionary explanations of human behavior such as religion, kinship, and sexuality. He is co-author of *The Supernatural and Natural Selection: Religion and Evolutionary Success; A Natural History of Rape: Biological Bases of Sexual Coercion;* and *When the Fish Are Gone: Ecological Disaster and Fishers in Northwest Newfoundland.*

Alan J. Penny, PhD, is honorary reader and visiting scientist in the School of Physics and Astronomy at the University of St. Andrews, where he researches stellar photometry of bright stars, extrasolar planets, and SETI. He is principal investigator of a team investigating the use of the LOFAR (LOw Frequency ARray) radio telescope for SETI. This project will determine LOFAR's sensitivity and ability to discriminate against terrestrial sources when operating in SETI mode, and if it produces positive results, will proceed to observe nearby stars.

George Pettinico is director of market research at Boehringer Ingelheim Pharmaceuticals, where he leads a department of sixteen professionals, managing about $25 million of research projects. The research he reports in this book was conducted when he was the associate director of the Center for Survey Research and Analysis at the University of Connecticut.

Christina Pomianek is a PhD candidate in the Department of Anthropology at the University of Missouri-Columbia. Most of her research centers on evolutionary and economic explanations of cooperation. Her dissertation research, supported by the Fulbright US Student Program, focuses on participation in cooperative finance in West Kalimantan, Indonesia, and the transition from local informal cooperatives such as "kongsi" and "arisan" to formal banking institutions (e.g., Bank Rakyat Indonesia). Her research examines the economic and social changes associated with increased opportunities for people to get funds outside the community through microfinance institutions.

Seth Shostak, PhD, is the senior astronomer at the SETI Institute and host of the weekly radio program *Are We Alone?* He won the Astronomical Society of the Pacific's Klumpke-Roberts Award in 2004 in recognition of his contributions to the public's understanding and appreciation of astronomy. His books include *Sharing the Universe: Perspectives on Extraterrestrial Life; Cosmic Company: The Search for Life in the Universe;* and *Confessions of an Alien Hunter: A Scientist's Search for Extraterrestrial Intelligence.* He served as chair of the SETI Committee of the International Academy of Astronautics.

Donald E. Tarter holds a PhD in sociology from the University of Tennessee, and he is the author of numerous articles published in scholarly periodicals. Now retired, for years he taught at the University of Alabama in Huntsville, specializing on the social impact of technology. As a longstanding member of the International Academy of Astronautics' SETI Committee, he contributed to discussions about societal responses to the detection of a signal from extraterrestrial intelligence, with a special emphasis on security considerations.

Douglas A. Vakoch, PhD, is director of interstellar message composition at the SETI Institute, as well as professor in the Department of Clinical Psychology at the California Institute of Integral Studies. He serves as chair of both the International Academy of Astronautics (IAA) Study Group on Interstellar Message Construction and the IAA Study Group on Active SETI: Scientific, Technical, Societal, and Legal Dimensions. His books include *Communication with Extraterrestrial Intelligence (CETI); Astrobiology, History, and Society: Life Beyond Earth and the Impact of Discovery; Extraterrestrial Altruism: Evolution and Ethics in the Cosmos;* and *Psychology of Space Exploration: Contemporary Research in Historical Perspective.*

Paul K. Wason, PhD, is director of life sciences at the John Templeton Foundation, where he develops new research initiatives on the fundamental nature and evolution of life and mind, especially as they intersect with meaning and purpose. Prior to joining the Templeton Foundation, he was director of foundations and corporations at Bates College. His book *The Archaeology of Rank* examines social evolution, inequality, and archaeological theory.

INDEX

Q

quantum communication, 99
quantum theology, 11
quasars, 8
Question Factory, The, 194
questionnaires, online, 17, 119, 130, 137,
194
Quneitia, 52

R

Raelians, 125
Reagan, Ronald, 94
reconnaissance, space, 95
religion, 2, 4, 5, 7, 10–11, 16, 22, 44, 45,
46, 88, 90, 102–105, 119, 128, 129, 137,
141, 153, 203–205, 207, 214
    attitudes towards, 102–105, 119,
        128, 129
    coping and, 5
    effects of contact on, 2, 10–11, 90,
        203
    flying saucer or UFO, 10, 128, 129,
        141
    folklore and, 4
    magic, myth, and, 4, 7
    Native American, 22, 203–205, 207
    New Age, 137
    Paleolithic, 44
    science and, 45, 153
    society and, 5
Renaissance, 5, 32, 229
reply from Earth, 7, 17, 92–93, 160–161
Ridpath, Ian, 9
Riner, Reed, 11
Robinett, Warren, 192, 193
Roco, Mihail, 192
Roman Catholics, 5, 10, 105, 107, 205
Roman Empire, 60, 161, 164, 228
Rosetta Stone, 20, 222
    analogy for interstellar
        communication, 20, 171,
        180–182
Roswell, New Mexico, 153
Ruse, Michael, 7
Russell, James, 45

S

Sagan, Carl, 8, 38, 80, 87–89, 90, 93, 109,
147, 148–149, 151–152, 214, 216
samples, survey, 9, 11, 103, 119, 121, 166
Saturn, 1, 12, 34
savages, 207–208
schizophrenia, 67
science 2, 4, 5, 6, 7, 8, 9, 11, 12, 14, 17,
18, 19, 20, 23–24, 39, 41, 57, 61–64,
74–77, 81, 87–88, 93, 95, 103, 119,
120, 122–124, 130, 133, 136, 137–138,
141–147, 149–154, 160, 162–168,
170–171, 173–174, 176, 177, 191–193,
195, 199, 203, 205–206, 226
    Arab, 8
    assumptions of, 146
    behavioral, 142
    biological, 74, 144
    borderland, 143
    about civilizations, 12
    community of, 144
    demarcation of, 143
    education, 152, 153, 195
    fiction, 6, 57, 87, 133, 141, 170,
        192, 204
    folklore and, 4, 5
    Greek, 11
    institutional aspects of, 146, 147,
        148, 149
    as language, 6, 19
    logic of, 162, 163, 164
    modern, 141
    non-science and, 143, 150, 154
    pseudo-, 17, 18, 119, 142, 144, 150,
        153
    public support for, 149
    religion and, 4, 5, 137, 153, 205, 206
    social, 2, 7, 9, 41, 74, 75, 119–120,
        143, 166–167, 170, 173, 227
    technology and, 17, 62, 63, 87, 88,
        110, 123, 124, 130
    understood by Jesuits, 205
    universality of, 19, 23, 160, 162, 163,
        164, 176, 203
Scientific American, 75
scripts, ancient, 175
Search for Extraterrestrial Intelligence
    (SETI), 1–7, 9–11, 13–24, 40–41, 43,
    56–57, 60–63, 71, 74–82, 88, 90, 92–93,
    95–96, 98–99, 123, 142–150, 152–154,
    159–162, 165–167, 171, 174–175, 177,
    180, 191, 199–200, 203, 205, 214,
    226–227, 229, 232–234
    Active, 9
    archaeology and, 13, 56
    assumptions of, 6, 8, 14–15, 90, 99
    astrobiology and, 1, 2, 43
    government support for, 199–200
    human unity and, 14, 90, 99
    journalism and, 227
    motives for, 159
    popularization of, 149
    myths and, 10
    NASA and, 148

CPSIA information can be obtained at www.ICGtesting.com
Printed in the USA
BVOW01s1356150813

328705BV00008B/33/P